Piracy,
Maritime Terrorism
and Securing
the
Malacca Straits

IIAS/ISEAS Series on Maritime Issues and Piracy in Asia

Series Advisory Board

The **IIAS/ISEAS Series on Maritime Issues and Piracy in Asia** is an initiative to catalyse research on the topic of piracy and robbery in the Asian seas. Considerable attention in the popular media has been directed to maritime piracy in recent years reflecting the fact/perception that piracy is again a growing concern for coastal nations of the world. The epicentre of global pirate activity is the congested sea-lanes of Southeast Asia but attacks have been registered in wide-scattered regions of the world.

The **International Institute for Asian Studies** (IIAS) is a post-doctoral research centre based in Leiden and Amsterdam, the Netherlands. IIAS' main objective is to encourage Asian studies in the humanities and social sciences — and their interaction with other sciences — by promoting national and international co-operation in these fields. IIAS publications reflect the broad scope of the Institute's interests.

The **Institute of Southeast Asian Studies** (ISEAS) was established in Singapore as an autonomous organization in 1968. It is a regional centre dedicated to the study of socio-political, security and economic trends and developments in Southeast Asia and its wider geostrategic and economic environment. ISEAS Publishing has issued over 2,000 scholarly books and journals since 1972.

IIAS/ISEAS Series on
Maritime Issues and Piracy in Asia

Piracy, Maritime Terrorism and Securing the Malacca Straits

edited by
Graham Gerard Ong-Webb

International Institute for Asian Studies,
The Netherlands

Institute of Southeast Asian Studies,
Singapore

First published in Singapore in 2006 by
ISEAS Publishing
Institute of Southeast Asian Studies
30 Heng Mui Keng Terrace
Pasir Panjang
Singapore 119614

E-mail: publish@iseas.edu.sg
Website: http://bookshop.iseas.edu.sg

First published in Europe in 2006 by
International Institute for Asian Studies
P.O. Box 9515
2300 RA Leiden
The Netherlands

E-mail: iias@let.leidenuniv.nl
Website: http://iias.leidenuniv.nl

The responsibility for facts and opinions in this publication rests exclusively with the authors and their interpretations do not necessarily reflect the views or the policy of the publishers or their supporters.

ISEAS Library Cataloguing-in-Publication Data

Piracy, maritime terrorism and securing the Malacca Straits / edited by Graham Gerard Ong-Webb.
1.   Navigation—Southeast Asia—Safety measures.
2.   Pirates—Southeast Asia.
3.   Terrorism—Southeast Asia.
4.   Malacca, Strait of—Navigation—Safety measures.
5.   Malacca, Strait of—Strategic aspects.
6.   Southeast Asia—Foreign relations.
I.   Ong-Webb, Graham Gerard, 1975–
VK113 A9P66   2006

ISBN-13: 978-981-230-391-2 (soft cover — 13 digit)
ISBN-10: 981-230-391-X (soft cover — 10 digit)

ISBN-13: 978-981-230-417-9 (hard cover — 13 digit)
ISBN-10: 981-230-417-7 (hard cover — 10 digit)

Cover photo: Courtesy of PIONEER Magazine, PIONEER, Information Department, MINDEF Public Affairs, Singapore.

Typeset by Superskill Graphics Pte Ltd
Printed in Singapore by

Contents

Contributors

Lieutenant Colonel (Ret) Ahmad Ghazali Bin Abu Hassan is Lecturer at Universiti Utara Malaysia.

Jayant Abhyankar is Deputy-Director, ICC International Maritime Bureau, United Kingdom.

Stefan Eklöf Amirell is Research Fellow at the Department of History and lectures at the Centre for Asian Studies at Göteborg University.

Commander Brian Fort serves on the Joint Staff and has served on five surface combatants during his seventeen years of service in the United States Navy, most recently as Executive Officer of the aegis cruiser, *USS Port Royal* (CG 73), deploying in support of Operation Enduring Freedom in October 2001. He was in the Navy Federal Executive Fellow at the George Washington University Elliot School of International Affairs at the time of his contribution.

Eric Frécon is Doctoral Candidate at the Institute of Political Science, Paris, France. He is based at the Centre for International Studies and Research in Paris (www.ceri-sciencespo.com) and benefits from the help of the Institut des Hautes Etudes de Défense Nationale (www.ihedn.fr).

Carolin Liss is Postgraduate Research Student at the School of Asian Studies, Murdoch University, Australia.

J.N. Mak is independent Maritime Policy Analyst in Malaysia. He was recently Visiting Research Fellow at the Institute of Southeast Asian Studies.

Graham Gerard Ong-Webb is Ph.D. candidate and Commonwealth Scholar at the Department of War Studies, King's College London. From 2005 to

2006, he was Associate Research Fellow with the Centre of Excellence for National Security at the Institute of Defence and Strategic Studies based at the Nanyang Technological University, Singapore and was Research Associate at the Institute of Southeast Asian Studies from 2002 to 2005.

Vice Admiral (Ret) Eduardo Ma R. Santos is President of the Maritime Academy of Asia and the Pacific, Kamaya Point, Bataan, the Philippines. During his thirty-three years in the Navy, he commanded combatant ships, a Coast Guard District, the Naval Intelligence and Security Force and Naval Forces Central Philippines, before retiring in 1999 as Flag Officer in Command of the Philippines Navy.

Tamara Renee Shie is Research Associate at the Institute for National Strategic Studies, National Defence University, Washington D.C. Previously, she was a Visiting Fellow with the Pacific Forum Centre for Strategic and International Studies (CSIS).

Jose L. Tongzon is Senior Lecturer in Maritime Business with the Australian Maritime College, Launceston, Tasmania, Australia.

Mark J. Valencia is Maritime Policy Analyst based in Hawaii, USA.

Xu Ke is Research Fellow at the Centre for Maritime Studies, National University of Singapore.

Acronyms

AIDS	Acquired Immuno Deficiency Syndrome
ASEAN	Association of Southeast Asian Nations
ARF	ASEAN Regional Forum
ASC	ASEAN Security Community
ASG	Abu Sayyaf Group
CCNR	Central Commission for the Navigation of the Rhine
DWT	Dead Weight Tonnage
FBI	Federal Bureau of Investigation
GAM	Free Aceh Movement [*Gerakan Aceh Merdeka*]
ICPR	International Commission for the Protection of the Rhine
IMB	International Maritime Bureau
IMB-PRC	IMB Piracy Reporting Centre
IMCO	Inter-Governmental Maritime Consultative Organization
IMO	International Maritime Organization
INS	[Royal] Indian Naval Service
IOC	International Oceanographic Commission
ISPS	International Shipping and Port Security Code
ITPMIS	Integrated Terminal and Port Management Information System
LNG	Liquefied Natural Gas
MALSINDO	Malaysia-Singapore-Indonesia
MILF	Morro Islamic Liberation Front
MNLF	Morro National Liberation Front
MSL	Mean Sea Level
NPA	New People's Army
PAT	Port Authority of Thailand
PCG	Philippine Coast Guard
PMC	Private Military Company
PNG	Petroleum Natural Gas
PNP	Philippine National Police

PSC	Private Security Company
PSI	Proliferation Security Initiative
RMSI	Regional Maritime Security Initiative
SOMTC	Senior Officials Meeting on Transnational Crime
SUA	Suppression of Unlawful Acts Against the Safety of Maritime Navigation
TEU	Twenty-Foot Equivalent Unit
UK	United Kingdom
UN	United Nations
UNCLOS	UN Convention on the Law of the Sea
UNESCO	UN Educational and Scientific Commission
US	United States (of America)
WMD	Weapons of Mass Destruction

INTRODUCTION
Southeast Asian Piracy:
Research and Developments

Graham Gerard Ong-Webb

General Overview

Maritime piracy continues to persist as a phenomenon in itself and as one that both directly and indirectly manifests a range of related social, historical, geo-political, security and economic issues. While piracy has permeated the world's maritime domain throughout history, in contemporary times, the waters of Southeast Asia serves as the dominant region for both the occurrence of this activity and the challenges it poses. Chiefly, developments since the turn of the twenty-first century indicate that contemporary piracy in Southeast Asia has effectively ceased to be a regional issue. Taking into account the inescapable role that the Malacca Straits and other Sea Lines of Communications (SLOCs) cutting across Southeast Asia play in the efficient flow of international trade within the global economy — and the possible impact of piracy in changing this — the economic value and the strategic importance of this waterway has authoritatively transformed the issues of piracy and maritime terrorism into an international concern.[1]

This volume is a second instalment within the Series on Maritime Issues and Piracy in Asia jointly collaborated by the International Institute for Asian Studies (IIAS, based in Leiden University) in The Netherlands, and the Institute of Southeast Asian Studies (ISEAS) in Singapore. The chapters draw mainly from a series of papers presented at an international workshop in September 2004 in Singapore, jointly organized by the IIAS and ISEAS entitled "Maritime Security, Maritime Terrorism and Piracy in Asia: Issues and Perspectives". In a bid to counter both the dearth of newfound scholarship on the topic of piracy and robbery in the Asian seas and the lack of a coherent research programme, the intention of the series is to catalyse research and to foster new and innovative approaches in these areas.

Overview and Contributions of the First Volume

This second instalment follows from the foundational volume, *Piracy in Southeast Asia: Status, Issues, and Responses*, edited by Derek Johnson and Mark Valencia, published in late 2005, and which draws upon a collection of papers presented at an international conference entitled "People and the Sea II", jointly organized by the Centre for Maritime Research (MARE) and the IIAS in September 2003 in Amsterdam, The Netherlands.

The first volume carries out two vital functions. The first function is to provide an overview of the current knowledge and key themes in piracy studies *vis-à-vis* Southeast Asia, in order to provide a reference resource for those working on the topic. These themes cluster around two broad categories:

1. The characteristics of piracy in Southeast Asia — in terms of definitions (including whether or not maritime terrorism fits into the description); the magnitude and nature of the incidences; and the forms of piracy;
2. The measures to suppress this activity (when framed as a security threat) in the region.

Specifically, the operating definition of piracy within the first volume tends towards the International Maritime Bureau's (IMB) view that piracy is "an act of attempting to board a ship with the intent to commit theft or any other crime and with the attempt or capability to use force in furtherance of that act". It is a definition that is viewed as a progressive approach towards framing to piracy in contrast to the definition offered by the International Maritime Organization (IMO), based upon the 1982 United Nations Convention on the Law of the Sea (1982 UNCLOS). The differences between the two definitions are contrasted in Table 1 below.

Regarding the role of "maritime terrorism" (defined for current purposes, as acts of terrorism on vessels or fixed platforms at sea or in port) in its relationship with piracy, the first volume displays among some its authors a tension "between what might be labelled inclusive and particularistic approaches to defining piracy".[2] Mark J. Valencia's chapter, "Piracy and Terrorism in Southeast Asia: Similarities, Differences and their Implications", takes the stance that terrorism (itself a contested term) is distinct from piracy in a straightforward manner. Piracy is a crime motivated by greed, and thus predicated on financial gain. Terrorism is motivated by political goals beyond the immediate act of attacking or hijacking a maritime target. Also, the motivation for action among terrorist groups is usually grounded in religious and political ideology stemming from perceived injustices, both historical and contemporary; something that is absent in maritime piracy. Proponents of this perspective add another distinction: pirates want to sustain their trade while an act of terrorism (which is often suicidal) is often pyrrhic or "one-off". As such, pirates want to avoid attention and will inflict only as much harm and damage as is necessary to accomplish their mission while terrorists want to call attention to their cause and inflict as much harm and damage as possible.

However, Graham Gerard Ong's "Ship's Can Be Dangerous, Too: Coupling Piracy and Terrorism in Southeast Asia's Maritime Security Framework", argues that while such distinctions are highly valid, their

TABLE 1
Contrast between the IMO and IMB Definitions of Piracy[3]

IMO	IMB
Piracy must be committed on the high seas or in a place outside the jurisdiction of any state. A criminal attack with weapons on ships within territorial waters is an act of armed robbery and not piracy.	Distinctions do not exist between attacks on the high seas and in territorial waters.
Piracy necessitates a "two-ship" requirement. Pirates needs to use a ship to attack another ship. This excludes mutiny and privateering from acts of piracy.	A "two-ship" requirement is abolished. Attacks from a raft or even from the quay are acts of piracy.
Piracy is committed for private ends. This excludes acts of terrorism and environmental activism.	Piracy may not only be committed for private ends. Attacks on a ship for political or environmental reasons qualify as piracy.
Because pirate attacks have to be committed by the crew or passengers of privately owned vessels, attacks by naval craft fall outside the bounds of piracy.	The acts of government naval craft can be deemed as piracy in certain circumstances.

rigidity fails to contribute to the demands of new strategies, which require a reconceptualization of the *status quo*.[4] In Southeast Asia, the overlap between piracy and maritime terrorism is greatest not only because of the level of violence involved. It is due to the devastating impact these acts can have upon the safety of people and international maritime navigation especially along the Malacca Straits, the jugular of regional and international maritime trade. Moreover, there has yet to be an internationally agreed set of definitions as to what exactly constitutes piracy or terrorism despite current provisions for such acts in international law and academia. In the end, the terms "terrorists" and "pirates" are — like all social and legal conventions — constructed and determined by governments and societies, not by the perpetrators themselves. In this case, it is all a matter of how we perceive these threats and perceptions can be changed. If we adopt the view that threats to security are socially constructed, then a path can be opened towards demolishing the distinction between terrorism and piracy under the present circumstances. Crucially, it will be found that the distinction between terrorism and piracy is based, to a large degree, upon extraneous assumptions. With some exception to the role of political ideology and financial gain, there is nothing in the letter of the law that distinguishes an act of maritime terrorism from piracy except for the notion of "private ends", a matter of arguable interpretation despite the staunch defence for its exclusivity with regards to piracy. For example, it can be easily argued that terrorism in large part is an act carried out for private ends by a group of individuals; their political ideology is not shared by the majority of the public domain. This rationale finds similar ground with the criticism raised by Czechoslovakia, which objected to the insertion of the "private ends clause" during the drafting of the precursor to UNCLOS II, the 1958 Geneva Convention of the High Seas.[5] In the end, the definition of piracy by the IMB, which has chosen to go against the grain of Article 101 of the 1982 UNCLOS — and that does not *inter alia* require that the act of piracy be committed for private ends — is obviously making an attempt at answering the call for a more inclusive definition of piracy in light of current developments.

In terms of the magnitude of piracy, the editors of the first volume concur that while "it is impossible to determine the precise magnitude of contemporary piracy", there has been a "[net] increase in the number of registered [or reported] piracy attacks" since the mid-1990s. As a socio-economic criminal activity that preys on maritime trade, the rise of piracy over the last two decades has naturally trailed economic globalization especially after the end of the Cold War in 1991. Various chapter authors such as P. Mukundan, the joint authors Johnson, Pladdet and Valencia, as well as Graham Gerard Ong, concur that "the general magnitude of pirate attacks against the world's shipping remains unchanged since the new millennium". They add that this trend is replicated in maritime Southeast Asia (especially in the South China Sea) and in the Malacca Straits, with Indonesian waters accounting for about a quarter of the world's reported attacks.[6] With respect to the forms of piracy, the authors refer to a "wide spectrum of attacks" constituted by opportunistic or "hit and run" attacks, followed by short-term seizures, long-term seizures and hijacking. Cutting across this range in the last few years is the trend towards the declining frequencies of occurrence of attacks on the one hand, but increasing levels of organization, violence and potential risks to security on the other.[7]

Despite acknowledging the efficacy of anti-piracy efforts being shaped by the "international institutional context" and defining strategies for suppression — in terms of defensive technologies, the deepening of internationally coordinated strategies and regional economic development — the first volume steers towards the indexing of Southeast Asian counter-measures mainly in the context of the legal provisions made available by the 1982 UNCLOS and consequently, the generation of other legal initiatives, international treaties and political arrangements to counter piracy within territorial waters, and even maritime terrorism that UNCLOS does not (and cannot) cover. For example, in his chapter, "Combating Piracy: Cooperation Needs, Efforts, and Challenges", Hasjim Djalal frames his discussion of regional approaches — including bilateral arrangements among littoral states, multilateral undertakings by the Association of Southeast Asian Nations (ASEAN) and "Track II" activities such as the South China Sea Workshop process — as efforts serving to enforce maritime legislation either promulgated by UNCLOS or those designed to overcome its shortcomings. The significance of the 1988 Convention for the Suppression of Unlawful Acts Against the Safety of Maritime Navigation (SUA) is also highlighted by Valencia who, citing the words of Ashley J. Roach, describes it as a mechanism designed to

> fill many of the jurisdictional gaps highlighted when the acts endanger the safety of international navigation and occur on board national or foreign flag ships while underway in the territorial sea, international straits or international waters. The convention requires states to criminalize such acts under national law and to co-operate in the investigation and prosecution of their perpetrators.[8]

Greg Chaikin corrects the skew towards analysing counter-piracy measures solely through the lens of UNCLOS in his chapter, "Piracy in

Asia: International Co-operation and Japan's Role", by defining the
issues and challenges as international relations problems where state-
pirate interactions (with pirates considered as non-state or transnational
actors), the ideas and actions of political communities, and the role
of international regimes and regime-building) — through regional
institutions and arrangements such as ASEAN, the ASEAN Regional
Forum (ARF), the Asia-Pacific Economic Cooperation (APEC), and the
Council for Security Cooperation in the Asia-Pacific (CSCAP) — matter
significantly. Chaikin's analysis also acknowledges the possibility —
given that piracy continues to rise on a general scale that goes unabated
— that Grotian ideas towards achieving global welfare and the
environmental order are anachronistic and even dangerous.[9]

The second function of the initial volume is a multi-functional one
consisting of three epistemological components: (1) as a platform to bridge
existing efforts within piracy studies; (2) as a means of establishing both
the agenda and the "building blocks" or key research questions for research
that will underpin the rest of the series; and (3) as a way of "indicat[ing],
in a preliminary manner, important new avenues for research, including
those as yet untraveled".[10] With these functions in mind, Johnson and
Valencia map out twenty-five research questions clustered around the
geo-politics of piracy, the conflation between piracy and terrorism, the
criminology of piracy, the economics of piracy, and the transformation of
the meaning of piracy over time, which are found in Table 2.[11]

Overview and Contributions of the Second Volume

The aim of the IIAS-ISEAS joint workshop in 2004, and by extension,
the second volume, is to sustain the momentum of the research
collaboration, and to build upon the twin functions of the first volume.
In regard to the function of gathering and clarifying knowledge
surrounding the characteristics of piracy and maritime terrorism in
Southeast Asia and the measures to suppress these activities as security
threats, the second volume seeks to supplement the previous volume
with the latest statistics on reported piracy attacks and recent
developments in maritime policy. It also attempts to fill out some of the
geographical gaps in the coverage of piracy and armed robbery (and
also maritime terrorism) in Southeast Asia by looking at the
phenomenon in the waters of the Philippines — an archipelagic state
with a deep stake in the regional maritime realm — on the "supply"
side of the discussion, and to place greater emphasis and clarity on

TABLE 2
Building Blocks in Piracy Research — 25 Research Questions

A. *Geopolitics of Piracy*
1. Why it is so difficult to forge cooperation in suppressing piracy?
2. How does piracy affect international relations and how do international relations affect responses to piracy?
3. Which, if any, nation's leadership in an anti-piracy effort might be acceptable in the region?
4. What is politically acceptable for the United States? What is the appropriate role of other Asian countries like China, Japan, and India?
5. How can the geo-political issues be circumvented or downplayed in order to get governments to respond to piracy more effectively? Specifically, how can Southeast Asian countries best be encouraged to cooperate to suppress piracy without allowing sovereignty issues to intervene?
6. What are the appropriate short-term responses and long-term strategies? What are their respective costs and benefits?

B. *Conflation between Piracy and Terrorism*
7. Is there an evolving relationship between piracy and terrorism?
8. Is this real, imagined, possible, or probable?
9. What are the advantages and disadvantages of conflating piracy and terrorism in terms of stimulating political co-operation, and in terms of legal and physical responses?

C. *Criminology of Piracy*
1. What are the context and causes of piracy?
2. Who are the pirates?
3. What are their motives?
4. What are the socio-cultural and economic environments within which they are operating?
5. Are some "high end" pirates linked to other illegal activities such as smuggling, kidnapping, black marketeering, or poaching?
6. What is the role of corruption both in enforcement and perpetration?
7. Are some pirates simply unemployed fishermen and, if so, why are they unemployed?
8. How do pirates react to attempts to control their activities?
9. What specific kinds of regional developments are required and what are their costs and benefits? Are there stakeholder groups like ship owners who might be willing to fund such initiatives?

D. *Economics of Piracy*
1. What is the impact of piracy on shipping and trade?
2. What are the actual costs of piracy, both measurable and intangible?
3. What are the costs of alternative counter-piracy measures?
4. Are the costs of responses justified by the costs of piracy?
5. Are the "costs" of policing the oceans a major problem, or is piracy more a problem of international relations than of actual costs?

E. *Transformation of the Meaning of Piracy*
1. How is piracy and piracy suppression represented in official and media documents?
2. What interests predominate and which are absent from such representations?

counter-measures in "demand" for securing the Malacca Straits, which is often considered the "jugular" of the maritime Southeast Asia.

On servicing the second function of building an epistemology for piracy studies and establishing a research agenda, the second volume conducts two tasks. In terms of the first task, it attempts to answer the research challenges put forth by Johnson and Valencia by investigating some of the key research questions raised in the first volume, but with specific illuminations borne out of the context of the Malacca Straits with implications for the study of other regions. The geo-political, strategic and security implications that obtain from the relationship between piracy and the Malacca Straits frames the parameters of the second volume, which tips towards the fields of security (defined simply as the methods towards understanding and reducing threats against and the vulnerabilities of socio-political actors or units such individuals, groups and states) and criminology (the study of behavourial phenomenon often judged by societies to be deviant and socially or legally unacceptable). While the IIAS-ISEAS series intends to analyse the topic of piracy in a value-neutral manner expected of a multi-disciplinary approach, the overly stark perception of piracy as a threat by the regional media, policy-makers and commercial shippers — as opposed to a more impartial view of piracy as a socio-historical phenomenon underpinned in part by marginalized communities within the maritime realm — becomes too overwhelming to ignore in the case of the Malacca Straits for present purposes of analysis.

The main roots of the security discourse on piracy and maritime piracy in the waters within and surrounding the Malacca Straits stem chiefly from state-level concerns about the economy (disruptions to the efficient flow of trade), the environment (the fall-out from an inter-ship collision), national security (threats to territorial integrity) and human security (threats to the safety and welfare of a vessels crew and passengers). Shipping, the main fodder for piracy, is the heart of global trade. Eighty per cent of world trade is currently conducted by sea, supported by a massive maritime trade network of 46,000 commercial vessels and 1.25 million seafarers calling at 4,000 ports. With the containerization of trade since the 1970s, 90 per cent of general cargo is now transported in containers. The Straits, as a whole, is the vital sea lane that bridges the Indian and Pacific oceans and which serves as the shortest route between three of the world's most populous countries — India, China, and Indonesia. By virtue of its geographical make-up, the Straits serve as a natural bottleneck creating the potential for an inter-ship collision or grounding of a large vessel, risking closure. The waterway is known to carry an annual volume of commercial traffic of more than 50,000 ships; making it the world's busiest. In addition, more than a third of global trade and two-thirds of the world's liquefied natural gas (LNG) trade also passes through the Straits. Mega-hubs like Singapore — which is the second busiest in the world and with the rankings of ports in Malaysia, Thailand, and China following closely behind — have become key container ports with connectivity in a "hub-and-spoke system" to regions worldwide such as Southeast Asia, Northeast Asia, the Middle East, the United States, Europe, and Africa. In addition, they form the backbone of the global integrated supply chain that also involves the economies of non-maritime continental states. With increasing globalization, maritime trade and interactions across the maritime realm continue to intensify.

In terms of the second task, this volume further explores the debate surrounding the apparent "nexus" between piracy and maritime terrorism and its impact on how the issues are framed and dealt with. The overall consensus is that an inclusive definition of piracy that includes maritime terrorism as a related function of this maritime activity may not be useful. The authors imply that there is greater detrimental impact from excessively conflating the two phenomena when the current body of scholarship and analysis demands greater categorical rigour in breaking through uninformed assumptions and myths.

Chapter Contributions

Within the backdrop described above, the opening chapter, "Piracy, Armed Robbery and Terrorism at Sea: A Global and Regional Outlook", by Jayant Abhyankar, Deputy-Director of the IMB, provides a compendium of trends and developments in piracy and the available counter-measures by late 2004 which supplements Mukundan's chapter in the first volume. He also articulates the bureau's position on maritime terrorism as a discrete phenomenon by affirming that there is no evidence to show that there is a current nexus between pirate groups and terrorist organizations, as two entities colluding and working together to achieve common or separate goals. He also concludes that despite the international community demonstrating a proactive approach in tackling piracy worldwide, they will continue to be on the defensive simply because pirates continue to have all the tactical advantages over law enforcement agencies and the military. Abhyankar's chapter attends to Research Questions A.1, A.6, B.7, B.8, C.1, C.2, C.3, C.4, C.5, C.6, and C.9.

Eduardo Ma R. Santos's chapter on "Piracy and Armed Robbery against Ships in the Philippines", and Stefan Eklöf Amirell's chapter, "Political Piracy and Maritime Terrorism: A Comparison between the Straits of Malacca and the Philippines", both play the role of filling in the afore-mentioned research gap on developments in Filipino waters. Santos posits that, in light of the fact that a total of 1,329 piracy cases — often involving significant levels of violence — were committed in the country's vast waters and ports between 1993 and 2004, piracy against vessels will remain a major security concern for the Philippines in the coming years. The problem is expected to worsen as the country is still on the verge of an economic crisis that will force a portion of the population to look to alternative means of livelihood, particularly those in the Southern Philippines. Continuing insurgency and separatism in the country is likely to contribute to the prevalence of piracy as rebels will increasingly look to alternative activities to supplement their finances. Also, as the national campaign against land-based terrorism begins to pay off, terrorists operating in the Philippines may look towards the maritime theatre to accomplish their political agenda. Overall, though piracy will be a primary concern of the Philippine Government, the inadequacies of the country's military and police forces will mean that the threat will continue to prevail. Eklöf Amirell adds that while there is currently no evidence to suggest that GAM members — who seem to be involved in some of the piracy attacks and kidnappings in the northern parts of the Straits of Malacca — are linked to international terrorist organizations, the opposite appears to be true in the case of the MILF and the ASG in the Southern Philippines. There are indications that these latter groups have some links with the JI and the al-Qaeda. He warns that although both groups have so far confined their activities to the Philippines in principle, their international and ideological connections with the JI and al-Qaeda should raise concerns of a maritime terrorist attack in other adjacent Southeast Asian waters, especially when some of these groups are found to have a maritime background. Both Santos' and Eklöf Amirell's chapters make the attempt to illuminate upon Research Questions A.1, A.6, B.7, B.8, C.1, C.3, C.4, C.5, C.6 and C.9.

Eric Frécon's chapter, "Piracy and Armed Robbery at Sea along the Malacca Straits: Initial Impressions from Fieldwork in the Riau Islands", makes the daring attempt at describing his fieldwork on pirates and their activities along the lines of what Ger Teitler calls piracy's "public appearance":

> [F]acts about their organisations, international ramifications, culture, management style, financial style, financial support structure, patterns of expenditure, forms of recruitment and relations to receivers and officials in legal, police or harbour circles.[12]

Frécon attempts to address Research Questions B.7, C.1, C.2, C.3, C.4, C.5, C.6, C.7 and C.8. His preliminary field investigation confirms that the mainstay of piracy continues to be committed by small groups that are not necessarily linked to large organizations or triads. Today, regional pirates tend to be young in age against the traditional or legendary stereotype. To be sure, "veteran" pirates continue to exist within the trade though they seem to be disappearing from the scene due to imprisonment, retirement, old age and death. They also tend to come from a disenfranchised economic background, in which corruption and collusion on the part of local police officials in allowing piracy to remain an activity that is relatively unchecked. Frécon also confirms that non-existence of a "nexus" between pirates and terrorists. For example a village community in Batam island known as *Kampung Hitam* (Black Village), which has a well established pirate fraternity, does not even have a *pesantren* (Koranic school) like those found in Ngruki on the Indonesian island of Solo. Staying alive, evading capture and sustaining their trade are important imperatives for the average pirate and it exceeds the trappings of the JI's programme of action steeped in an austere religious and political ideology. He also finds the pirates he interviewed to be of a less educated profile than the members of al-Qaeda or the JI.

Brian Fort's chapter, "Transnational Threats and the Maritime Domain", steers the volume back towards the international relations agenda mapped out by Valencia and Chaikin in the first volume. He also injects the security framework of analysis by framing piracy, maritime terrorism and international crime in the context of transnational threats in the maritime domain. He argues that while all international crime does not always lead to piracy and (maritime) terrorism, following the trails of international crime can provide related leads to these activities because of the financial motive that is a common characteristic cutting across most criminal operations in either generating capital, to consume it, or both. Fort tackles Research Questions A.1, A.2, A.3, A.4, A.6, B.7, B.8, B.9, C.1, C.3, C.4, C.5, C.6, and C.9.

In his chapter, "The Politics of Anti-Piracy and Anti-Terrorism: Responses in Southeast Asia", Valencia develops the key ideas expounded in his previous two chapters in the first volume. Expounding on the key argument that the objectives of piracy and maritime and land-based terrorism are often different, the move towards conflating the two phenomena may either enhance cooperation of indigenous states in prevention efforts or undermine such cooperation, depending on whether threat perspectives diverge and the issues of territorial sovereignty and jurisdiction come to the fore. He also questions the efficacy of naval patrols — regionally or externally led — on the grounds that the arresting authority of regional and foreign naval vessels exercising rights of transit through waterways such as the Malacca Straits is unclear. The sheer size of the vessels used in patrols inhibit their effectiveness in pursuing pirates and would-be terrorists using smaller craft; which, by extension, would infer that security patrols would be better suited to the police rather than the military. However, short-term counter-measures intelligence sharing and coordination, as well as ship defence will be useful for staving off piracy and maritime and land-based terrorism to some degree. Still, long-term solutions aimed at eliminating the root causes of piracy and terrorism may have to be fitted to the particular problem. To attack the problem of piracy at its root, there should be more concerted efforts at assisting both state economic development and maritime enforcement capacity building in Southeast Asia, since piracy is fuelled by poor economic conditions. Likewise, addressing the threat of maritime and land-based terrorism and involves tackling more complicated and sensitive questions of religion, ideology, sovereignty and foreign policy. Ultimately, to combat the threat of piracy and maritime terrorism, both indigenous countries and external maritime powers should focus on what has created the threat and its symptoms. Valencia expounds upon Research Questions C.1, C.2, C.3, C.4, C.5, C.6, C.7, C.8, C.9, D.3, D.4, D.5, E.1, and E.2.

Like Fort and Valencia, Carolin Liss pursues an international relations approach to the discussion of counter-measures, this time focusing on the rise of Private Military Companies (PMCs) and Private Security Companies (PSCs) as non-state actors employed by the maritime private sector against piracy threats to their vessels, in "Piracy in Southeast Asia: Private Responses — Companies in the Fight Against Piracy". In describing their general internal structure, information policies and the nature of their operations, Liss looks at the conditions in the maritime world that hinder or facilitate the anti-piracy services offered by PMCs/PSCs. She concludes by suggesting that, while their advertisements, services and work practices should be regarded with some scepticism, PMCs/PSCs are likely play a significant role in maritime security in general and in the fight against piracy in particular. Her chapter provides an insight into Research Questions A.6, D.3 and D.4.

"Unilateralism and Regionalism: Working Together and Alone in the Malacca Straits," by J.N. Mak. Mak upsets the train of present scholarship and analyses by operating on the assumption that non-traditional maritime security issues are central ones in the region, especially among the littoral states. He contends that maritime issues tend to be accorded a low priority in Southeast Asia, reduced to the realm of functional cooperation and "low politics". If anything, the paltry record of maritime cooperation in the past in the ASEAN region has been marked by contention, dissension and contestation. Mak argues that this is evident in the Malacca Straits, which has witnessed intense contestation between littoral states and user states especially from 1965 to 1982 over the nature of transit passage and the regulation of maritime traffic. He believes that the Straits are currently witnessing a third "battle" over approaches to safeguarding the waterway against pirates and terrorists. Mak traces the root of the problem in maritime cooperation in terms of a clash of interests between "coastal states" (Malaysia and Indonesia) with relatively insular interests, and "maritime nations" (Singapore) tending to have global interests, identities which produce introverted and extroverted views towards cooperation at the regional and international levels. Mak addresses Research Questions A.1, A.2, A.3, A.4, A.5, A.6, B.7, B.8, B.9, D.1, D.2, D.5, E.1, and E.2.

In her chapter, "Maritime Piracy in Southeast Asia: The Evolution and Progress of Intra-ASEAN Cooperation", Tamara Renee Shie focuses her analysis on the role of ASEAN in fighting piracy and other non-traditional maritime criminal activities. She stresses the need to acknowledge the significance of the organization within regional efforts instead of writing off ASEAN, which she believes only serves to relieve Southeast Asian nations from their collective responsibilities in addressing the problem. Ignoring the role of ASEAN also diminishes the leading role Southeast Asian nations should undertake in regional anti-piracy measures as such measures are likely to fail in the absence of their support. Neglecting ASEAN's attempts — both successful and unsuccessful — in the policy calculus also overlooks the value in studying the factors steering regional responses to piracy and the structural contexts of the international system since 1967 when the organization was formed. In particular, the shift from a bipolar to a multipolar international system, coupled with the forces of globalization and increased economic and political inter-dependence, have had the effect of driving states towards working together on common security issues. By extension, the ASEAN region — which Shie carves into the three phases of an "early ASEAN", "ASEAN expansion", and "ASEAN in the new millennium" — has witnessed successive regional attempts towards countering piracy as it intensified. Shie's chapter explores Research Questions A.1, A.2, A.3, A.4, A.6, E.1 and E.2 in the context of ASEAN.

Turning towards a normative discussion of future cooperation and security in the in the Malacca Straits, Ahmad Ghazali Bin Abu Hassan's chapter, "The Rhine Navigation Regime: A Model for the Straits of Malacca?" investigates the possibility of the navigation and management regimes that regulate the usage of the Rhine River — flowing through one of the most densely populated and industrialized parts of Europe before entering the North Sea — as possible models for application in the Straits of Malacca, which share certain geographical and economic similarities. Ghazali's work provides certain normative clues and obliquely addresses the issues posed by Research Questions A.1, A.2, A.3, A.4, A.5 and A.6. In particular, Ghazali considers the Central Commission for the Navigation of the Rhine (CCNR) established by the Congress of Vienna in 1815, and the International Commission for the Protection of the Rhine against Pollution (ICPR) derived from the Mannheim Convention concluded in 1868 as relevant examples of maritime cooperation over a shared commercial waterway. Despite the model value of these commissions, Ghazali envisages the reluctance of the littoral states to participate in any progressive regional efforts towards such mechanisms would stem from the prevailing concerns over territorial sovereign rights. In the final analysis, in order to address such concerns, Ghazali recommends that the establishment of a commission for the comprehensive management of the Straits of Malacca should come under the principles of reciprocity and voluntary participation. The willingness of the littoral states to submit some of their rights to a common establishment should also be matched by equally substantial concessions by other participating user states.

The normative flavour of the second volume is couched in geo-economic terms through the chapter "Whither the Malacca Straits? The Rise of new Hub Ports in Asia", by Jose L. Tongzon, which deals with Research Questions A.2, A.4, A.5, A.6, D.1, D.3 and D.4. He raises the uncomfortable (and often overlooked) question of whether the Malacca Straits will continue to be a vital SLOC for maritime commerce. Ultimately, while the geography of the Straits is fixed, dynamic factors such as technology, the economic competitiveness of the littoral states and their national ports, and the employment of creative economic strategies to bypass geographical constraints, can serve to strengthen or wither its importance. Tongzon surmises that, on the one hand, certain developments that seem to work in favour of the Straits. The growing demand for oil by China, the intensification of trade links between Europe and Asia, and growing Asian economic integration, would result in the use of the Malacca Straits for supporting these related economic developments. On the other hand, there are also developments that seem to work against the Straits and these include the rise new ports and pipelines in the Asia-Pacific region — such as the Shanghai Port Container Terminals and Laem Chabang, and the building of China's pipeline and Thailand's plans for a strategic land bridge. These developments could lead to the diminishing importance of the Straits and thus the littoral ports of Singapore and Malaysia. Whether positive factors would prevail over negative ones would largely hinge on the success or failure of securing the Malacca Straits, prudent government economic strategies and the determination of future trends in international shipping shaped by the global market. Their implications are overwhelming since the relationship between shipping and piracy would mean that a drastic plunge in shipping volumes would probably lead in turn to a drop in levels of piracy. Carried to its hypothetical extreme, if there was a total absence of vessels of any kind in the Straits, there would be a total absence of piracy in effect.

The final contributing chapter "Piracy, Seaborne Trade and the Rivalries of Foreign Sea Powers in Southeast Asia, 1511 to 1839: A Chinese Perspective", by Xu Ke argues that the diverse perception and policies among Chinese Empire and colonial powers (who were also maritime powers) resulted in the reconfiguration of the balance of maritime power in pre-modern Southeast Asia. Xu asserts that before the advent of the European colonizers in the early sixteenth century, the relation between piracy and seaborne trade was quite simple: The pirates were the predators and the merchant ships were their prey. As such, the pirates robbed merchant ships on the trade routes and captured goods and people as their booty. He observes that the Portuguese conquest of Malacca in 1511 marked the entrance of European colonial sea power penetration in Southeast Asia. Subsequently, the other European colonizers — including the Spaniards, the Dutch and the British — seized the region's main entrepôts in rapid succession and plundered the wealth of indigenous and Chinese traders as they set up their colonial domains in Southeast Asia. The link between piracy and seaborne trade relations became complex, since piracy was used by European colonizers as means to control seaborne trade and to expand their influence and domains. The colonial powers also attempted to establish trade relations with China. Consequently, the Chinese Empire banned overseas trade in order to stave off foreign influences. However, illegal private traders also known as "merchant pirates" intensified their trading activities first with Nanyang and then with the colonial powers. Xu brings the rest of the volume, which focuses on piracy in its more immediate currency, back into the meta-narratives of general history, conveying the message that the unfolding of events and phenomenon related to modern piracy in the Malacca Straits, Southeast Asia and the wider region will also become part of the region's history as we move forward. The question is whether the future is contingent upon unforeseen events or whether history repeats itself in the grand march of time. Xu's discussion provides some insight into the gaps in the phenomena as it had existed in the past and to some degree relates to Research Questions A.1, A.2, A.3, A.4, C.1, C.2, C.3, C.4, C.8 and E.1.

The volume closes with a final chapter, "Conclusion: Towards a Research Programme", based on the findings of the post-workshop roundtable discussion in late 2004 where paper presenters discussed how the initial research agenda mapped out through the IIAS-ISEAS research collaboration and Johnson and Valencia's volume, could further evolve into a mature research programme.

Contemporary Piracy and Anti-Piracy Measures in 2005: Post-Volume Developments

The various chapter contributions in the second volume — on piracy, maritime terrorism in Southeast Asia, and the developments and prospects for international cooperation specific counter-measures — end their analysis of events towards the closing of 2004. In academic scholarship, the strength of a theory or argument is constantly tested by the course of events as they unfold. Events either reinforce their weight or weaken them, prompting, in turn, the search for alternative perspectives and fresh questions. The research questions and analyses under investigation in this volume pertain to those of an enduring nature, and the resulting inferences can provide lasting academic value to the general understanding of the issues and challenges that have arisen in the past, both near and far. Nevertheless, the remainder of this introductory chapter provides a *précis* of the trends in piracy and maritime terrorism, as well as developments in counter-measures and regional cooperation after 2004 until early 2006 in order to facilitate the analytical leap readers would have to make between the recent past and the currency of events.[13]

Piracy

In the broad history of the late twentieth century, the trend in piracy, in terms of the volume of attacks, has not changed. According to the annual piracy reports provided by the International Maritime Bureau (IMB), the number of piracy attacks, on a global scale, has seen a net rise over the last fifteen years. Certainly, the total number of worldwide reported attacks dropped by 27 per cent from 445 incidents in 2003 to 325 incidents in 2004 and a subsequent 15 per cent drop to 276 attacks in 2005 over 2004.[14] However, in 1991, the number of worldwide pirate attacks stood at 107. At the end of 2004, there were 325 reported attacks or an increase of 200 per cent. Year on year, Southeast Asia continues to maintain around a quarter share of the world's attacks in the last half-decade, with the majority of attacks occurring in the Malacca Straits and the waters of Indonesia.

In terms of the imminence of a maritime and economic catastrophe borne out by a piracy attack in the Malacca Straits, leading to the closure of the narrow and congested waterway by way of an inter-ship collision, critics may argue for some perspective. In 2004, there were a total of thirty-eight attacks in the Straits. When placed against the grain of 50,000 ships transiting the Straits, the probability of an attack is 0.07 per cent. Even if the figures are doubled to take into account the 40 to 60 per cent of all attacks, which the IMB says goes unreported, produces a probability of 0.1 per cent. The 2005 tally of twelve reported attacks in the Straits would generate a probability range of 0.02 to 0.04 per cent. Yet, regional policy-makers would argue that the consequences of such an outcome are simply too devastating to ignore. In addition, these low statistical probabilities hide the manner in which piracy victimizes and brutalizes a vessel's crew and its shipping company, by way of kidnapping for ransom activities increasingly undertaken by pirates. It has been reported that about US$1 million in ransom was paid out by ship owners in the region in 2004, with an average ransom fee negotiated at an estimated range between US$50,000 to US$100,000. In that year, forty sailors were kidnapped in about twenty incidents. Four seafarers were killed because of botched negotiations. By the end of June 2005, there were five confirmed ransom-driven kidnappings in the Straits.[15] The end of 2005 saw the final tally of kidnappings at ten reported incidents.[16]

Maritime Terrorism

As this volume went to press, there has been no "maritime spectacular" prophesized by various analysts on the threat of maritime terrorism. It is true that al-Qaeda's devastating assault on the USS Cole at a port in Yemen in October 2000 and the Bali terrorist attacks in October 2002 — which indicated a shift towards maritime-related economic targets in Southeast Asia — exposed the vulnerability of the global and regional maritime realm. Also, the masterminds of the USS Cole actually planned another attack on a U.S. ship visiting a Malaysian port in 2000. In 2001, the Malaysian Special Branch disrupted a plan by the Kumpulan Mujahidin Malaysia (KMM) to ambush a visiting U.S. vessel. In early 2002, Singapore intelligence also disrupted an al-Qaeda plot to attack a U.S. ship docked in the country. Senior al-Qaeda operative, Omar al-Faruq, who is now in U.S. custody, also told officials of plans to attack an American naval ship in Surabaya, Indonesia's second largest port, during his interrogation. In 2002, the Abu Sayyaf Group (ASG) based in the Philippines claimed responsibility for an explosion of a large ferry in the country killing around a hundred of its citizens.

It is quite possible that current efforts at securing vital sea lanes and major ports that run along the Straits are finally generating a deterrence dividend against maritime terrorism, judging from the fact that no such attack has occurred since the foiled attempts mentioned earlier. It is also equally likely that terrorist organizations may be ruling out an attack in the maritime theatre because current state awareness and responses have removed the element of shock and surprise which terrorists prize highly in their operations. However, the decline of this threat is better explained by two other factors. First, in line with Fort's treatment of the link between finance and transnational threats to the state, the fight against global terrorism has led to the general attrition in the leadership, manpower, resources and the financing of al-Qaeda to the point where it has now concentrated its limited resources to its campaign in the Middle East, specifically in U.S.-occupied Iraq. The al-Qaeda linked attacks in the Spanish city of Madrid in March 2004 and the London bombings on 7 July 2005 may weaken this claim but it strengthens the assertion that terrorist organizations prefer to hedge their bets on land-based targets which are tried and tested in their success, against maritime-based ones. Still, as national and regional cooperative endeavours indicate, policy-makers do not appear to be taking their chances on the "strategic surprise" brought out by a possible act of maritime terrorism.

Securing the Malacca Straits

In June 2005, Malaysia's Deputy Prime Minister Najib Razak made the
effort to break the existing impasse in littoral cooperation against piracy
by articulating what is tantamount to a regional maritime security doctrine
at a key Asian security conference in Singapore:

1. Maritime security is an area of enforcement within regional security
    in which the need to cooperate is greatest and where consensus
    building and a united position are key. Given the narrow nature of
    the Straits, it is easy for criminals to escape across national
    boundaries into another jurisdiction. Datuk Seri Najib suggests
    that including the Royal Thai Navy into current coordinated patrols
    by Malaysia, Indonesia and Singapore (established in July 2004)
    may further enhance security along the approaches to the Straits.
2. Technology will play a decisive role in empowering the littoral
    states to achieve more effective coordination and enforcement. For
    example, surveillance through maritime patrol aircraft, coastal radar
    linked to satellites and radio tracking technology in providing
    real-time information for enforcement operations could be carried
    out.
3. The littoral states must be in the driver's seat in maintaining
    regional maritime security and they retain primary responsibility
    for implementation of any measures designed to strengthen safe
    passage. While the need for greater cooperation extends to states
    using the Straits, good intentions are best translated in terms of
    financial support, intelligence sharing, training and provision or
    loaning of equipment such as ships and aircraft.
4. Stronger enforcement, regional cooperation and a better use of
    technology is best directed towards the effort in detaining pirates
    at source rather than in the high seas. In this case, it means attacking
    the bases from which pirates operate and cutting off the resources
    and manpower they depend on. It is also a proposition for the
    littoral states to develop their law enforcement capacities and
    promulgate harsher laws in dealing with pirates and other
    criminals.
5. Any form of preventive measures and operational arrangements
    to secure the Straits must not impinge on the territorial integrity
    and sovereignty of the littoral states, in tandem with international
    law. Consequently, the region must counter-propose the idea of

foreign vessels being escorted by their naval or coast guard ships passaging through the Straits. In addition, while private armed escort services on commercial vessels plying the Straits should not be denied transit passage, they must cease operations when in the territorial waters of the littoral states. As an alternative, the littoral states could provide their own law enforcement personnel on vessels travelling through the Straits.

6. Additional mechanisms that can act as effective deterrents must constantly be explored. Against the longstanding grain of criticisms by security analysts and observers regarding the fanatical obsession of the littoral states over their individual territorial sovereignty, Datuk Seri Najib made a path-breaking suggestion that, while it was important to take current measures at a comfortable pace, an "open mind" should be kept in evolving coordinated naval patrols into a regional "joint" patrol (which will allow for inter-territorial hot pursuit) at some point in the future.

The spirit of these principles and proposals appears to have set a decisive course in the region's maritime security agenda while allowing for latitude within the residual differences in threat perception of the littoral states. For example, Malaysia maintains that there is no credible evidence to suggest a "nexus" between piracy and terrorism, while Singapore has chosen to factor in the possibility that terrorists might collaborate with pirates to seize a ship and sail it into a harbour to set off a massive explosion. In the end, the array of precautions cast by Malaysia and Singapore serves as a security dragnet that will apprehend and deter terrorists, smugglers, and criminals on top of pirates, hence satisfying all their separate maritime concerns.[17]

In the wake of Deputy Prime Minister Najib's enunciation, the littoral states of Indonesia, Malaysia and Singapore launched a joint maritime air-patrol called the "Eyes in the Sky" (EiS) initiative, on 13 September 2005, a mere three months since it was first proposed in the June speech, and also launched just over a year after the three countries established round-the-lock coordinated MALSINDO (Malaysia-Singapore-Indonesia) naval patrols along the Straits (formalized into the Malacca Strait Sea Patrol [MSSP] in late April 2006), which is discussed by some of the contributors of this book. Operationally, the littoral states (plus Thailand) have each contributed two maritime patrol aircraft (MPA) while the triad will conduct up to two patrols per week along designated sectors of the area of operation under the international and national airspace over the Straits of Malacca and Singapore. The MPAs would be allowed to fly above the waters of the states in question no less than three nautical miles from land; a flight path roughly hovering over the stream of commercial maritime traffic. Each aircraft will also have a Combined Maritime Patrol Team (CMPT) on board, comprising a military officer from each participating state. As a collective, the CMPT is to establish a comprehensive surface picture over the designated area by broadcasting any suspicious contacts on designated radio frequencies to ground-based agencies — called Monitoring and Action Agencies (MAAs) — in each of the participating countries; depending on where a piracy or maritime terrorist incident is taking place along the Straits. Subsequently, the MAAs will coordinate amongst themselves to undertake any follow-on responses within their own territorial waters. There will also be EiS Operations Centres (EOCs) established in each of the participating states, which will coordinate the flight schedule of the patrolling aircraft taking off from their respective airbases.[18]

The EiS itself is still in its delicate operational infancy. Both the MAAs and EOS had yet to be set up at the inception of the EiS in late 2005. It is not clear if they have become operational at the time this book went to press. However, it is clear that the focus of the EiS in its infancy is to get the spirit of endeavour right at the various levels, before turning to matters of form. At the ministerial, diplomatic, and defence levels, the debut flights are meant to translate talk into action and therefore, to foster the political capital and fortitude needed for the subsequent follow-through. The act of putting the cart before the horse also contributes to greater operational efficiency and effectiveness of the EiS in the medium to long term, though it stands to be sacrificed in the short run. The purpose of the flights, as they currently stand, appears to be more about ironing out the operating procedures on aerial surveillance by the CMPT. This is crucial since if the littoral states cannot get things right in the air, the overall effectiveness of the endeavour becomes moot, whether or not the MAA and EOCs are implemented. As a joint endeavour, its success may generate the dividend of inspiring the evolution towards joint naval patrols from its current "coordinated" arrangement in the near to medium term. Already, the three littoral states also signed an agreement in late April 2006 to form a Joint Coordinating Committee (JCC), an umbrella organization tasked with overseeing the EiS and MALSINDO patrols. While there are no new changes to either of the patrols, the agreement will establish the JCC and empower it as a channel of communication, intelligence exchange and coordination for all operational security measures relating to the Straits.

In truth, the EiS suffers from several inherent limitations in its response and effectiveness against piracy and other associated threats relating to the factors of (1) the MPA's operational and surveillance limitations and (2) the large area of operations constituting the Malacca Straits. As a case in point, the Republic of Singapore Armed Forces Fokker 50 MPA has a top search speed of 200 knots and a flight endurance of eight hours. The fastest time that the aircraft can survey the entire 960-kilometre Straits is about two-and-a-half hours at best (the same time it takes to fly from Singapore to Bangkok). Malaysia's Hercules C130 may fare slightly better in the traversion at roughly 380 knots and a flight endurance of up to fourteen hours. However, sophisticated radar technology notwithstanding, real-time gaps will prevail in the intelligence picture the CMPT hopes to create at anyone time simply because they cannot survey the colossal waterway in one fell swoop. Second, depending on the prevailing radar and detection technology possessed by the littoral states, it is unclear whether the rather inconspicuous (and often wooden) motorboats that pirates tend to use, will be easy to spot and identify. Such craft generate relatively small heat signatures and physical profiles that can easily fall under the threshold of military radar and infra-red systems. The majority of pirate attacks also tend to occur in the dead of night. The cover of darkness further screens pirate activities from the MALSINDO and EiS patrols. Third, the operational limitation of keeping to the three nautical mile limit from shore also restricts the scope that the MPAs can play in early detection. Today's pirates use the surrounding islands, islets and coves as bases and staging areas before conducting rapid strikes at their targets along the Straits before retreating inland. Over time, the littoral states will have to mitigate and negotiate the concerns over national security and sovereignty if they are to broaden efforts at countering piracy and other threats at sea.

Ultimately, the EiS, while serving as a form of deliberate window-dressing aimed at allying the concerns of the international community, glosses over the outstanding problems of sovereignty, jurisdiction, political will (the lack of it) and the deficit of equipment that are really needed to reduce the threat of piracy to a level that is acceptable to the littoral states.

Likewise, it is not entirely clear whether the MSSP or MALSINDO patrols have done much to reduce the scale of piracy attacks along the Malacca Straits since it was established in the third quarter of 2004. As indicated in Table 3 below, no coherent trend emerges from the comparison between the two quarters prior to the patrols, the two remaining quarters for 2004, the four quarters of 2005 and the first quarter of 2006. If anything,

TABLE 3
Quarterly Breakdown of Reported Incidents of Piracy/Armed Robbery At Sea
in the Malacca and Singapore Straits, 2004-2006[19]

	2004				2005				2006	
	1st Quarter	2nd Quarter	3rd Quarter	4th Quarter	1st Quarter	2nd Quarter	3rd Quarter	4th Quarter	1st Quarter
Malacca Straits	2	3	3	5	2	6	No reports	No reports	2
Singapore Straits	5	1	No reports	No reports	2	4	1	No reports	Not available
Total	7	4	3	5	4	10	1	No reports	2

the first quarter of 2004, 2005 and 2006 opened with two reported attacks in the Malacca Straits. While there were no reports of attacks in the Singapore Straits in the third and fourth quarters of 2004, the first two quarters of 2005 saw a rise in reported incidents. Lastly, it is difficult to specify what constitutes a "rise" or "fall" with any accuracy in the context of single-digit aggregates of reported incidents against an average volume of 50,000 ships passing through the Straits annually or 12,500 vessels per quarter, unless one assigns a "zero tolerance" approach as a benchmark. Ultimately, it may be prudent to suspend judgment about the effectiveness of such patrols until a few more years worth of reporting data become available. Meanwhile, Malaysia's assessment in April 2006 that "[p]irates have largely been run out of the Malacca Strait less than two years" because of the patrols and that "the [current] situation is very stable, very benign", may be hasty.[20]

The notion of hastiness may be a sentiment shared by the Joint War Committee (JWC) of Lloyd's Market Association, which declared the Malacca Straits a war risk area since July 2005 — the month of the first anniversary of the MSSP patrols, along with twenty other locales worldwide, in jeopardy of conflict, strikes, terrorism, and other related dangers. This puts the Malacca Straits, as well as other areas within Indonesian waters such as the ports of Dumai and Belawan, in notorious company, like war-torn Somalia, insurgency-stricken Iraq and a politically unhinged Lebanon. More importantly, it means that shipping firms that use the waterway stand to pay higher premiums. The middle of 2005 also saw a series of criticisms by the governments of the littoral states over the issue of private armed escort services offered by PMCs/PSCs to shipping companies since 2004 but which only came to the fore after catching the attention of the media.[21] Overall, such responses from the private sector seem to indicate that the littoral states are not doing a satisfactory job in providing for the security of the Straits.

In April 2005, Singapore, Japan, Laos and Cambodia were the first countries to sign the Regional Cooperation Agreement on Combating Piracy and Armed Robbery against Ships in Asia, or ReCAAP. A legal framework initiated by Japanese Prime Minister Junichiro Koizumi in 2001, supported by sixteen Asian countries from Southeast Asia, China, India, Sri Lanka, Bangladesh, the Republic of Korea and Japan. Among other things, the agreement involves the setting up of an Information Sharing Centre (ISC) in Singapore, aimed at facilitating communication and information exchanges between the member countries through the shared collection, analysis and distribution of on reported attacks in their respective waters.[22] The plan for a twenty-four-hour ISC was formalized in April 2006 and it will become operational in December 2006.

While an information gathering and processing can be vital towards a better understanding of the trends in piracy in the bid to pre-empt further attacks, it remains to be seen if the ISC will be able to collect information exceeding the standards of the IMB Reporting Centre in Kuala Lumpur, Malaysia. The IMB has an established rapport with commercial shippers — in face of the natural tendency by seafarers and shipping companies from reporting attacks — and a set of reporting procedures that have been evolving since 1992. It is also not entirely clear if the ISC will be able to create a more sophisticated methodology for the quantitative analysis of reported incidents, which would require currently unobtainable (or even unquantifiable) knowledge about the causal factors behind piracy. Next, it remains to be seen whether commercial shippers and regional anti-piracy patrols will receive information from the ISC that is timely and useful in avoiding risk-prone areas and to subduing attacks respectively. Lastly, while eleven countries have signed the ReCAAP agreement, Indonesia and Malaysia are among the five remain signatories that have yet to do so, reflecting the outstanding challenges in forging closer cooperation among the three littoral states — a sentiment conveyed by some of the contributors to this volume — which is ultimately essential if the tide against piracy is ever to be lastingly turned.

In the end, it is clear that the suggestion by some analysts and policy-makers that stronger enforcement, regional cooperation and a better use of technology is best directed towards the effort in detaining pirates at source rather than in the high seas may be the most astute one if the regional fight against piracy is to be won decisively. This second instalment within the Series on Maritime Issues and Piracy in Asia endeavours towards making a small contribution towards the need for sustained thinking about piracy, maritime terrorism and the security of both the Malacca Straits and Southeast Asia at large. These are challenges that will continue to figure significantly within the region's geo-political, economic and socio-cultural landscape long after their consideration by the media wanes, when patient erudition is the deserving response.

Notes

1   In this volume, the term "Malacca Straits" will be used — instead of the singular noun "Malacca Strait" employed by other scholars and analysts — as a geographical shorthand to refer to the Malacca and Singapore Straits unless

stated otherwise. The 805-kilometre long Strait of Malacca opens westward to the Indian Ocean and separates Malaya from the Indonesian island of Sumatra. At its southeastern end, the Strait of Malacca joins the 105-kilometre long Singapore Strait, which connects to the South China Sea and Pacific Ocean. Together, the two waterways form a seamless entity in which the Malacca Strait dominates its more modest counterpart. Also, the Malacca Strait spills obtusely over the territorial waters of Malaysia, Indonesia and Singapore. Lastly, shippers and pirates cannot tell where one strait exactly ends and the other begins. The Malacca Straits is a label that essentializes these factors.

2   Derek Johnson and Mark J. Valencia, "Conclusion: Towards an Agenda for Piracy Research", in Johnson and Valencia, eds., *Piracy in Southeast Asia*, p. 161.

3   Derek Johnson, Erika Pladdet and Mark J. Valencia, "Introduction: Research on Southeast Asian Piracy", in *Piracy in Southeast Asia: Status, Issues and Responses*, edited by Derek Johnson and Mark J. Valencia (Singapore: International Institute for Asian Studies, The Netherlands [IIAS], and the Institute of Southeast Asian Studies [ISEAS], 2005), pp. xi–xii.

4   Graham Gerard Ong, "Ships Can Be Dangerous, Too: Coupling Piracy and Terrorism in Southeast Asia's Maritime Security Framework", in Johnson and Valencia, eds., ibid., pp. 45–76.

5   The Czech Government affirmed that the International Law Commission committed a grave omission since it did not mention acts of piracy for political ends or what some scholars classify as "politically motivated piracy" or "political piracy" which includes the attacks and seizures that are labelled as "maritime terrorism". Instead, the clause was maintained and has come to find itself within Article 101 of the 1982 LOS Convention.

6   P. Mukundan, "The Scourge of Piracy in Southeast Asia: Can Any Improvements be Expected in the Near Future?" in Johnson and Valencia, eds., op. cit., p. 36; Derek Johnson, Erika Pladdet and Mark J. Valencia, "Introduction: Research on Southeast Asian Piracy", in Johnson and Valencia, eds., ibid., pp. xii–xiv; Graham Gerard Ong, "Ships Can Be Dangerous, Too: Coupling Piracy and Terrorism in Southeast Asia's Maritime Security Framework", in Johnson and Valencia, eds., ibid., pp. 47–49.

7   Johnson, Pladdet and Valencia, op. cit., pp. xiv–xvi; P. Mukundan, op. cit., pp. 35–36; and Mark J. Valencia, "Piracy and Terrorism in Southeast Asia: Similarities, Differences and their Implications", in Johnson and Valencia, eds., op. cit., pp. 79–82.

8   Mark J. Valencia, op. cit., p. 86.

9   Greg Chaikin, "Piracy in Asia: International Cooperation and Japan's Role", in Johnson and Valencia, eds., op. cit., p. 124.

10   Derek Johnson, Erika Pladdet and Mark J. Valencia, op. cit., pp. ix; Derek Johnson and Mark J. Valencia, op. cit., pp. 162–63.

11   Johnson and Valencia, op. cit., pp. 163–65.

12   Ger Teitler, "Piracy in Southeast Asia: A Historical Comparison", *Maritime Studies* 1, no. 1 (2002): 68, <http://www.marecentre.nl/mast/documents/ GerTeitler.pdf>.

13   This section draws heavily from Graham Gerard Ong, "The Threat of Piracy and Maritime Terrorism", in *Regional Outlook 2005–2006* (Singapore: Institute of Southeast Asian Studies, 2005).

14   *Piracy and Armed Robbery against Ships: Annual Report, 1st January – 30th December 2004* (Kuala Lumpur: IMB Regional Piracy Centre, 7 February 2005), p. 16; *Piracy and Armed Robbery against Ships: Annual Report, 1st January – 30th December 2005* (Kuala Lumpur: IMB Regional Piracy Centre, 31 January 2006), p. 16.

15   Graham Gerard Ong, "The Threat of Piracy and Maritime Terrorism", in *Regional Outlook: Southeast Asia, 2005–2006* (Singapore: Institute of Southeast Asian Studies, 2005), pp. 12–15.

16   *Piracy and Armed Robbery against Ships: Annual Report, 1st January – 30th December 2005* (Kuala Lumpur: IMB Regional Piracy Centre, 31 January 2006), p. 15.

17   Graham Gerard Ong, "Charting a Unified Course for Safer Seas", *Straits Times*, 25 June 2005.

18   Graham Gerard Ong and Joshua Ho, "Maritime Air Patrols: The New Weapon Against Piracy in the Malacca Straits", *Institute of Defence and Strategic Studies Commentary*, 13 October 2005 (70/2005).

19   The quarterly figures are tabulated by counting the number of reported cases within each quarter of the year from the annual narration of actual attacks found at the end of the following IMB reports: "Narration of Attacks, 1 January – 31 December 2005: Actual Attacks, Southeast Asia", in *Piracy and Armed Robbery against Ships: Annual Report, 1st January – 30th December 2005* (Kuala Lumpur: IMB Regional Piracy Centre, 31 January 2006), pp. 33–43; "Narration of Attacks, 1 January – 31 December 2004: Actual Attacks, Southeast Asia", in *Piracy and Armed Robbery against Ships: Report for the Period, 1st April – 31st December 2004* (Kuala Lumpur: IMB Regional Piracy Centre, 7 February 2005), pp. 29–43. It serves to note that there exist certain errors in the reporting and tabulation of piracy attacks in the Malacca Straits region by the IMB. When the summary statistics of reported actual attacks for the first two quarters of 2005 — derived from the IMB's quarterly reports — and the statistics created from the narration of attacks used to create Table 2 are compared, deviations were found for the following (the summary statistic are in brackets): Indonesia — 14 (16); the Malacca Straits 2 (6); and the Southeast Asian region 26 (35). For the two quarterly reports, see "Narration of Attacks, 1 January – 31 March 2005: Actual Attacks, Southeast Asia", in *Piracy and Armed Robbery against Ships: Report for the Period, 1st January – 31st March 2005* (Kuala Lumpur: IMB Regional Piracy Centre, April 2005), pp. 19–22; and "Narration of Attacks, 1 January – 31 June 2005: Actual Attacks, Southeast Asia", in *Piracy and Armed Robbery against Ships: Report for the*

Period, 1st April – 31st June 2005 (Kuala Lumpur: IMB Regional Piracy Centre, July 2005), pp. 24–29.

[20] "Malaysia Claims Pirates now Scarce due to Joint Sea Patrols in Malacca Strait", *Jakarta Post*, 25 April 2006.

[21] Graham Gerard Ong, "A Case for Armed Guards on Ships", *Straits Times*, 26 May 2005.

[22] K.C. Vijayan, "24-hour Sea Piracy Info[rmation] Centre Soon", *Straits Times*, 21 April 2006.

1

Piracy, Armed Robbery and Terrorism at Sea: A Global and Regional Outlook

Jayant Abhyankar

Introduction

Piracy has always been romanticized by writers and film-makers and many people often harbour visions of bearded renegades sailing seas of endless blue, something akin to a maritime "Robin Hood" of sorts. In truth, modern day piracy (in whatever form) is a violent, bloody, and ruthless practice. Pirates steal, maim and even kill. In addition, it is made even more fearsome by the knowledge on the part of the victims that they are on their own and defenceless and that no help is waiting just round the corner. Pirates endanger navigation by leaving vessels underway, including fully laden tankers, without command. This creates the potential for grounding or collision leading to an environmental disaster. What makes the situation worse is that some countries, instead of being proactive about the difficulties, tend to be recessive and put forward copious arguments to deny the problem exists or to state they cannot do anything about it. So the practice flourishes and unless some action is taken, we are on course for a dramatic increase in this crime.

Purists might say, and they would be legally correct in so doing, that the magnitude of piracy *per se* in the world today is relatively insignificant. Under the United Nations (UN) Convention on Law of the Sea of 1982 (UNCLOS II), piratical acts are committed on the high seas or in a place outside the jurisdiction of any state, though most of the present day acts take place within the territorial waters of a sovereign state. While this may be legally correct, such a distinction is irrelevant in the eyes of the victim. It is for this reason — and for *statistical purposes* — that the International Chamber of Commerce's (ICC) International Maritime Bureau (IMB) has adopted the following definition:

> An act of boarding or attempting to board any ship anywhere with the apparent intent to commit theft or any other crime and with the apparent intent or capability to use force in the furtherance of that act.

In its *Annual Piracy and Armed Robbery Against Ships Report* for 2003, the IMB reported a total of 445 attacks on ships either at sea, at anchor or in port. The use of violence in pirate attacks continues with 21 seafarers killed, 71 missing, 359 taken hostage in that year, with 20 ships fired upon. Ships were boarded in 332 instances and a total of 19 ships were hijacked.[1] The purpose of this chapter is to analyse developments up to the time of writing and to identify possibilities for future action towards minimizing the impact of piracy. For a start, the last decade has seen four specific "types" of piracy. More often than not, they vary according to the region. However, there are also regions that share similar characteristics in certain kinds of attacks.

Regional Variations in Maritime Piracy

Ship Boarding and Theft Involving the Minimum Use of Force

The first form of piracy involves the minimum use of force in ship boarding and the theft of cash and valuables from the ship's safe and the crew. The notable feature of this type of attack is the degree of skill that is used to board the ship, coupled with the fact that violence is not normally used unless resistance is offered. The intruders usually come alongside a ship underway, often during the night, and take possession of whatever cash and negotiable valuables come easily to hand after boarding it. These attacks are also not on the high seas as all the waters in the area are within the territory of the various countries, which border them. It is these behavioural and geographical profiles that characterize the bulk of "Asian" piracy. A well-known target area used to be the Philip Channel between Indonesia and Singapore but the emphasis has now shifted to the Malacca Straits and the Indonesian waters in the last few years. It is also this comparative "non-violent" approach, except in Indonesian waters, that oddly enough makes the problem more difficult to combat.

Ship Boarding and Theft Predisposed Towards the Use of Force

The second type of piracy involves the boarding of a ship and the theft of its cargo and crew's personal valuables that is more disposed towards violence than Asian piracy. This kind of piracy is the main feature of "South American" and "West African" piracy and the characteristics of both of these kinds of attacks include:

- The high degree of violence by heavily armed criminals after boarding a ship;
- The target items include money, negotiable goods and items of cargo and ship's equipment;
- The total value of goods stolen per attack tends to be higher than in the Asian piratical attack and there is a degree of pre-planning;
- There is a demonstrated lack of competence or willingness to respond on the part of law enforcement; and
- Some of the target ships are at anchor.

The only similarity between Asian piracy and the South American and West African variants is that these pirates come alongside in small craft and mount high-sided ships with remarkable agility. From that point onwards no other similarity exists, as the South American and West African attackers often offer gratuitous violence and will steal anything that is unsecured. If the ships' equipment is stolen, the safety of the ship — in terms of its ability to steer and navigate safely and effectively — can be placed at great risk.

Political Piracy

Third, some types of maritime attacks appear to exhibit a certain military or political feature. Notable among these was the attack by terrorists on the cruise ship *Achille Lauro* on 7 October 1985, in the eastern Mediterranean. This attack was instrumental in the creation of the 1988

SUA Convention by the International Maritime Organization (IMO). The year 1993, in particular, saw a new trend with regard to piracy off the waters of China where crafts manned by persons dressed in military uniforms intercepted and fired on passing ships. However, these attacks have diminished over the years possibly due to the publicity given to them in the international press.

Hijacking in Piracy: The Case of the Alondra Rainbow

Finally, against the grain of non-violent attacks that tend to characterize Asian piracy, a violent form of piracy tends to exist in Southeast Asia involving the hijacking of ships underway, overpowering the crew in question and stealing the vessel's entire cargo. In some cases, the pirates actually return the ship in the hands of the crew. In more extreme cases, the crew are either thrown overboard or even killed. As two prominent examples in the shipping community, the unfortunate MV *Cheung Son* with 23 Chinese crew was hijacked by pirates in late 1998 and the crew were murdered in cold blood. MV *Tenyu* was hijacked in September 1998 and her 15 crew consisting of two Koreans and 13 Chinese are still missing. In recent years, the waters off the province of Aceh in Northern Sumatra have also become a high-risk area for hijacking of ships and crew.

However, the *Alondra Rainbow* incident remains as the classic example of a piracy attack involving hijacking in Southeast Asia and it illustrates how the industry and the authorities can work together to defeat the pirates. On 22 October 1999, the *Alondra Rainbow* loaded a cargo of 7,000 metric tonnes of aluminium ingots and sailed from Kuala Tanjung in Indonesia for Miike in Japan. Shortly after her departure, a gang of pirates armed with swords and guns hijacked the ship. The 17 crew members were threatened with death and transferred to the MV *Sanho*, which came alongside at sea. They were held captive for a week and eventually set adrift in a life raft on 29 October 1999. They were rescued by a Thai fishing boat ten days later on 8 November 1999, off the North East coast of Sumatra. On 28 October 1999, the IMB Piracy Reporting Centre commenced broadcasting a message to ships at sea *via* the safetyNET service of Inmarsat-C satellite with a request to report any ship, which matched the description of the *Alondra Rainbow*. The excellent response from various masters at sea helped locate the missing ship. On 14 November 1999, the master of a Kuwaiti tanker reported sighting a ship matching the profile of the *Alondra Rainbow* heading into the Arabian Sea. The IMB Piracy Reporting Centre passed this information along with a photograph of the *Alondra Rainbow* to the Indian Coast Guard and requested their assistance.

The response of the Indian authorities was swift. The Coast Guard immediately despatched a patrol aircraft to search the area. Upon sighting the suspect ship, the Coast Guard advised that her profile matched the photograph of the *Alondra Rainbow*. However, the suspect ship had a name *Mega Rama* and was flying the Belize flag. Quick checks by the IMB Piracy Reporting Centre revealed that no such ship was registered in Belize. The patrol aircraft then attempted radio contact with the ship but she maintained radio silence. Thereafter a coast guard patrol vessel was sent to intercept the ship, 70 miles West of Ponnani. Despite warning shots fired across her bow, the ship increased speed and continued her path. It was only when a missile-carrying corvette, the INS *Prahar*, was called into action that the high seas chase was brought to an end. The naval ship deployed a graduated use of force to bring about the suspect ship's capture on the 16 November 1999; approximately 300 miles south west of Mumbai. The fifteen Indonesians found on board allegedly attempted to destroy the evidence by setting fire to and scuttling the ship. The naval boarding party put out the fire, brought the flooding under control and towed the ship to Mumbai. Investigations showed that Mr Burham Nanda, chief engineer along with Mr Christinous Mintando, the ship master, met an employment agent at a coffee shop in Batam, Indonesia on 4 October 1999. They finalized the plans to hijack *Alondra Rainbow* and boarded *MV Sanho* which was anchored in Jakarta. The *Sanho* sailed with about thirty-five persons on board. A dozen of its crew were armed with weapons, with the ringleader colloquially referred to as "boss". The *Sanho*'s first port of call was the island of Batam where she took bunkers, water and provisions. On 17 October 1999, she left for Kuala Tanjung, Indonesia arriving there on 22 October 1999. One member of the gang had already boarded the *Alondra Rainbow* while she was loading her cargo. In the late evening of 22 October 1999, about ten to twelve persons armed with pistols and lethal weapons were transferred from the *Sanho* onto a speedboat. When the *Alondra Rainbow* was sighted, the speedboat reached behind her stern. The member of the gang who had hidden on board the *Alondra Rainbow*, lowered ropes for his accomplices to climb on board. The crew of the *Alondra Rainbow* were captured and their hands were tied. At this stage, the *Sanho* came alongside and Mintando and fourteen other individuals posing as conventional crew climbed aboard and took charge of the *Alondra Rainbow*. The original crew of the *Alondra Rainbow* were transferred to the *Sanho*.

On 23 October 1999, Mintando and the fourteen crew changed the name of the *Alondra Rainbow* to the *Global Venture* and proceeded to Miri in East Malaysia, arriving there on 26 October 1999. Black paint was supplied at Miri and her hull was repainted over its original blue. On 27 October 1999, about 3,000 metric tonnes of aluminium ingots were transhipped on to another ship called *Bonsoon II*, which came alongside. After this, the employment agent instructed Mintando to sail toward Karachi in Pakistan. At some stage the name of the *Alondra Rainbow*, alias *Global Venture* was changed again to *Mega Rama*. In the meantime, the *Bonsoon II* proceeded to the Philippines and discharged the stolen 3,000 metric tonnes of cargo there. The *Mega Rama* was finally captured after nearly three weeks and taken to Mumbai as described earlier. At least two of the fifteen Indonesians on board had featured in the hijacking of the *Tenyu* in September 1998, which suggests that they are part of an organized syndicate.

While India is a signatory to UNCLOS II, this convention had not been incorporated in to the national legislation. The Indian Penal Code does not address the offence of piracy or hijacking of ships. Further, at the time of arresting the alleged pirates, India was not a signatory to the Convention for the Suppression of Unlawful Acts against the Safety of Maritime Navigation (SUA). However, Indian law enforcement could have prosecuted the pirates under *Piracy Jure Gentium*, an offence against all nations. The offender is said to be punishable by his captors (in this case the Republic of India), wherever he may be found, to whatever nationality he may belong, and in whatever court having jurisdiction. Similarly, the pirates could be tried under the British Admiralty Laws, as theses existed at the time of independence in 1947. In the end, the Mumbai police successfully established jurisdiction and charged the alleged pirates with eleven counts under provisions of the Indian penal code. Initially, the alleged pirates of the *MV Alondra Rainbow* were produced before the metropolitan magistrate in Mumbai after their capture and later brought before the highest sessions court. The hearing commenced on 14 March 2001. In March 2003, the accused were sentenced to seven years of hard labour.[2]

Piracy: The Statistics

Drawing upon the IMB *Piracy and Armed Robbery Against Ships Annual Report* for 2003, the total number of incidents reported worldwide increased to 445 in 2003 compared to 370 in 2002. The IMB also recorded the second highest number of attacks in 2003 since the IMB Piracy Reporting Centre commenced compiling statistics in 1991. The 2003 figures also show an increase in the number and violence of the attacks. However, they also show that some kinds of attacks and attacks in certain areas have dramatically reduced. This proves once again that when law enforcement agencies take these attacks seriously, there will be a corresponding reduction in the attacks.

Violence Continues to Rise

The report for 2003 also shows that the violence used in the attacks continued to rise, with 21 seafarers killed, 40 assaulted and 88 injured; an increase over the 10 killed, 9 assaulted and 38 injured in the previous year. There were 71 crew or passengers missing in 2003 and this should be considered along with the 21 confirmed killed. The number of attacks using guns rose to 100 from 68 and the number of hostages taken nearly doubled to 359 seafarers. Ships were boarded in 311 instances and a total of 19 ships were hijacked.

Indonesia, Bangladesh and Nigeria Top the Rankings

Indonesia continued to record the highest number of attacks with 121 reported incidents in 2003. Bangladesh ranked second highest with 58 attacks and Nigeria ranked third with 39 attacks. Attacks in Nigeria almost tripled compared with 2002 and it is regarded as the most dangerous area in Africa for piracy and armed robbery. The report also identified Chittagong (Bangladesh), Lagos (Nigeria), Chennai (India), Dakar (Senegal), Cochin (India), Balikpapan (Indonesia) and Ho Chi Minh City (Vietnam) having 7 or more attacks in the year. In fact, Chittagong topped the list with 40 recorded incidents in 2003.

The Malacca Straits and Indonesia

The Malacca Straits, one of the busiest shipping lanes, experienced a welcome drop in the number of piracy attacks in 2002 with 16 incidents as compared to 75 in 2000. The 2003 figures, however, show a rise to 28 incidents. This means that the Indonesian Authorities must increase their anti-piracy efforts. A reduction in the attacks in Indonesia can dramatically change the situation in Southeast Asia.

Some Positive Regional Developments

However, there are some positive developments to speak of in Southeast Asia, the African continent and South America. The number of attacks in Thailand, the Singapore Straits, Malaysia, the Ivory Coast, Gabon Cameroon, Guyana and Ecuador actually dropped. In fact, attacks in Malaysia reduced to 5 in 2003 from 14 in 2002.

Incidents of Hijackings are Going Down

The number of ships hijacked for the theft of the ship and cargo dramatically reduced in 2003. The type of hijackings now taking place involve more vulnerable targets such as tugs and barges. Ships are also hijacked in order to abduct the crew for ransom. These kidnappings are believed to be largely the work of militia groups in politically vulnerable areas. In 23 per cent of the attacks, tankers were the targets. It remains a matter of concern that these ships tend to carry dangerous cargo and could be temporarily under the control of unauthorized individuals such as pirates.

Assessing the Potential Environmental Impact of Piracy Attacks: Danger in the Philip Channel

For a variety of reasons, short-term seizures have caught the imagination of the maritime industry, the press and the public. Much is made of the unacceptability of the situation but it is necessary to view the problem in perspective. While theft by violence is inexcusable, the frequency of these attacks and the sums stolen compared with the frequency and size of similar shore-based crimes is relatively small against the grain of the total volume of shipping and other vessels plying out waters worldwide. Therefore, in spite of pressures put upon law enforcement, these attacks will not necessarily loom large in their order of priorities.

What is continuously present but often accorded little attention or interest — if even acknowledged — is the potential for an environmentally related disaster to occur. In the early 1990s, most of the attacks in Southeast Asia took place in a 32-kilometre long stretch of the Philip Channel, the southern half of the waterway between Singapore Island and Indonesia. In this area, which is the West-East seaway, ships of all types were attacked including conventional cargo ships, container ships and tankers. Tankers proceeding eastbound are generally laden and come from Persian Gulf ports. The statistics relating to ships using this area show that the greatest

TABLE 1.1
Locations of ACTUAL and ATTEMPTED attacks, Jan to Dec 1992–2003

Region	Locations	1992	1993	1994	1995	1996	1997	1998	1999	2000	2001	2002	2003
S E ASIA	Cambodia		1	1	1	1	1						1
	Indonesia	49	10	22	33	57	47	60	115	119	91	103	121
	Malacca Straits	7	5	3	2	3		1	2	75	17	16	28
	Malaysia	2		4	5	5	4	10	18	21	19	14	5
	Myanmar (Burma)					1	2		1		3		
	Philippines	5		5	24	39	16	15	6	5	8	10	12
	Singapore Straits			3	2	2	5	1	14	9	7	5	2
	Thailand				4	16	17	2	5	5	8	5	2
FAR EAST	China/ HKong/Macau	1	1	6	31	9	5	2		8			
	East China Sea		10	6		1	1			2	2	1	1
	Hong Kong/Luzon/ Hainan (HLH) Area		27	12	7	4	1	3		1			
	Papua New Guinea					1	1		1	–	1	1	
	Solomon islands												
	South China Sea	6	31	6	3	2	6	5	3	9	4	2	2
	Taiwan				2						2	1	1
	Vietnam				4		4		2	6	8	12	15
INDIAN	Bangladesh	5		2	2	4	9	9	25	55	25	32	58
	India		1	2	8	11	15	12	14	35	27	18	27
SUB CONTINENT	Sri Lanka		2	1	6	9	13	1	6	3	1	2	2

continued on next page

TABLE 1.1 – cont'd

Locations	1992	1993	1994	1995	1996	1997	1998	1999	2000	2001	2002	2003
AMERICAS												
Brazil		4	7	17	16	15	10	8	8	3	6	7
Caribbean			1									4
Colombia		1		1	3		4	4	1	1	7	10
Costa Rica											1	
Cuba												4
Dominican Republic					1	3	4	2	4	5	7	6
Ecuador			3		3	10	10	2	13	8	12	2
Guatemala									1			
Guyana		1			2						12	6
Haiti							2	1	1	1	1	1
Honduras									1			1
Jamaica					1	3	2	2			2	5
Martinique												1
Mexico								1		1		
Nicaragua				1	1							
Panama				1	1	1	1					
Peru				1	2	1		2	1	1	2	2
Salvador					1				4		6	7
Trinidad & Tobago										1		
Uruguay												
USA						1	1		1			
Venezuela					1	3	1				1	2
AFRICA												
Algeria						1	1		3	1		1
Angola		3	1					6	3	1	8	13
Benin								1		1		3

Cameroon	2	5	7	2	3	5	3				
Congo			1	1	1	2				1	
Egypt		5	2	1							
Equatorial Guinea				1							
Gabon	2	7	3	2	3	2			1		
Gambia		1									
Ghana	3	5	5	2	2	4	2	2			
Guinea	4	2	3	6	6	2	3	2	1	1	
Guinea Bissau		2	1		1				1	1	
Ivory Coast	2	5	9	5	5	1	4	4			
Kenya	1	2		5		7					
Liberia	1										
Mauritania			1	1							
Madagascar			1		1		1				
Morocco		3		1		3					
Mozambique	1			2		2			1		2
Nigeria	39	14	19	9	12	9	9	4			
Oman		1									
Red Sea/Gulf of Aden	18	11	11	13	1	3					
Senegal	8	3	1				6	2			
Sierra Leone		1	3				3	3			
Somalia/Djibouti	3	6	8	9	14		5	4	14	1	2
South Africa	1	3	1	1	3		4	3	2	2	
Tanzania	5	1	7	2			5	1		1	
Togo	1	5	1	1	2						
Yemen				1							
Zaire											

continued on next page

TABLE 1.1 – *cont'd*

Locations	1992	1993	1994	1995	1996	1997	1998	1999	2000	2001	2002	2003
REST OF WORLD												
Albania						5	1					
Arabian Sea									2			1
Arabian Gulf									1			1
Australia											1	
Bulgaria												
Denmark				1		1					1	
France							1					
Georgia												
Greece					1	2				1		
Indian Ocean									1	1		
Iran				8	2	3	1	3	1	1		2
Iraq										2		
Italy				1	2		1	2			1	
Malta						1						
Netherlands						1						
Portugal						1						
Russia				1		1						
Turkey				1	1	2						
UAE									1			
United Kingdom												
Location Not Available	31	2		1			1			1	2	
Total for the year	106	103	90	188	228	247	202	300	469	335	370	445

Chart A

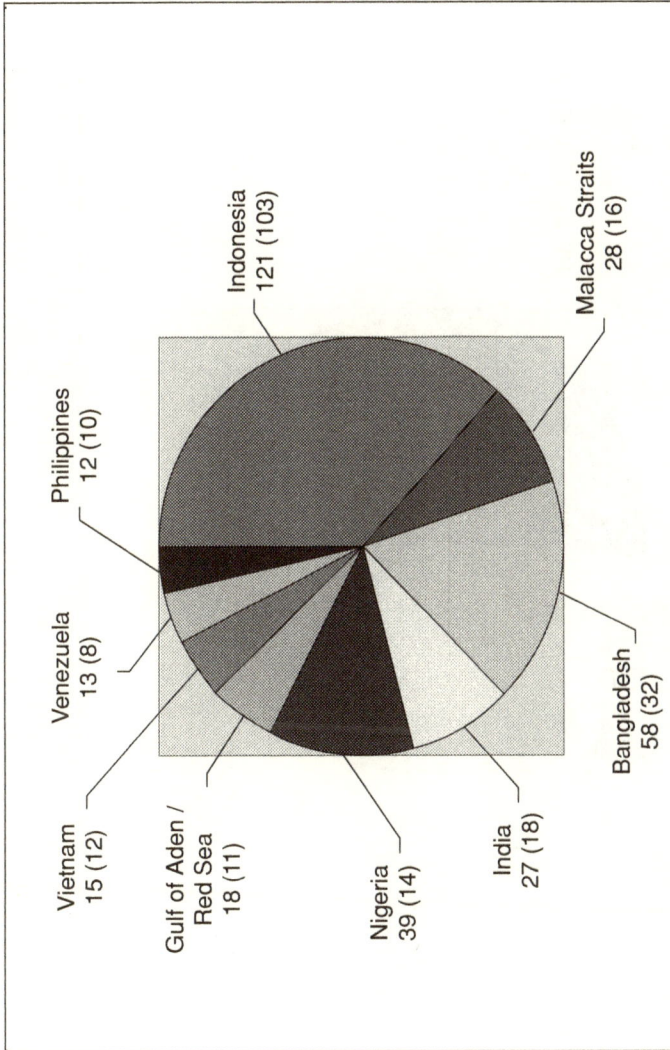

Indonesia 121 (103)

Malacca Straits 28 (16)

Philippines 12 (10)

Venezuela 13 (8)

Bangladesh 58 (32)

Vietnam 15 (12)

Gulf of Aden / Red Sea 18 (11)

Nigeria 39 (14)

India 27 (18)

Note: The following nine locations shared three-quarters of the total reported incidents, that is, 331 from a total of 445 reported attacks in 2003. Numbers (in brackets) are for 2002.

Chart B

Rest of World
5 (4)

SE Asia/Far East
189 (170)

Americas
72 (65)

Indian Sub
Continent
87 (52)

Africa/Red Sea
93 (78)

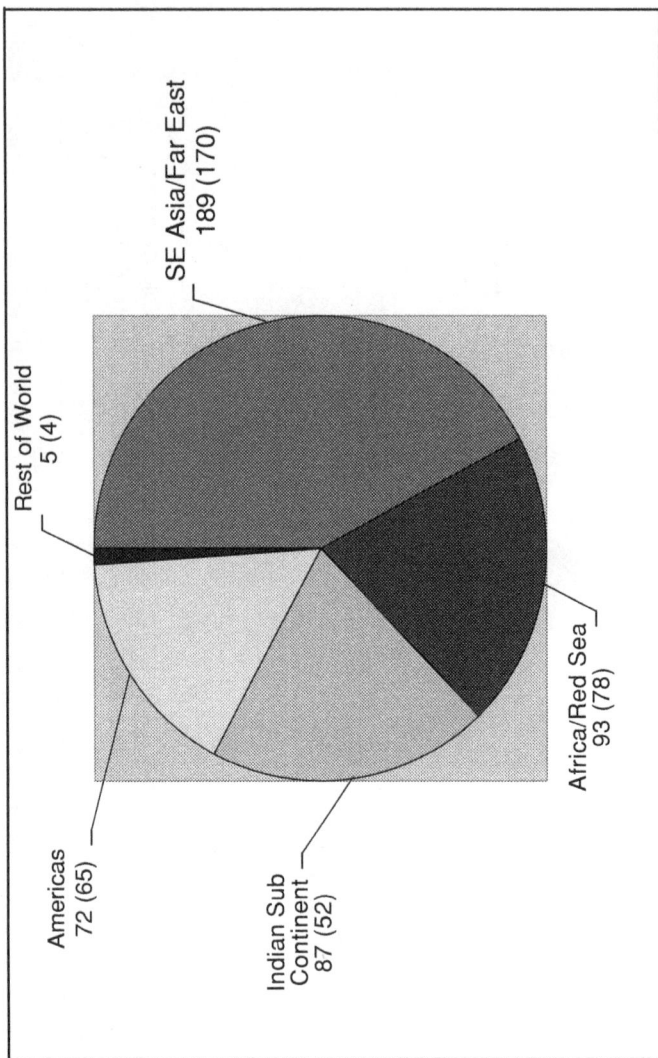

Note: Regional breakdown of total 445 reported incidents in 2003.
Numbers (in brackets) are for 2002.

TABLE 1.2
Ports and Anchorages with Three or more Reported Incidents for 2001–03

Location	Country	2001	2002	2003
Chittagong	Bangladesh	14	25	40
Lagos	Nigeria	18	12	21
Chennai	India	11	7	10
Dakar	Senegal		3	8
Cochin	India	4		7
Balikpapan	Indonesia	8	21	7
Ho Chi Minh/Vung Tau	Vietnam	7	9	7
Georgetown	Guyana		9	6
Callao	Peru		5	6
Manila	Philippines			6
Samarinda	Indonesia		11	5
Jakarta-Tg. Priok	Indonesia	18	11	5
Rio Haina	Dominican Republic	4	7	5
Buenaventura	Columbia		3	5
Dar Es Salaam	Tanzania	7		4
Puerto Cabello	Venezuela			4
Haiphong	Vietnam			4
Guanta	Venezuela		3	3
Luanda	Angola			3
Lawi Lawi	Indonesia			3
Haldia	India	3		3
Adang Bay	Indonesia			3
Belem	Brazil			3
Dumai	Indonesia			3
Kingston	Jamaica			3
Pulau Laut	Indonesia			3
Warri	Nigeria			3
Abidjan	Ivory Coast	9	5	
Tema	Ghana	5	4	
Owendo	Gabon		4	
Hoogly	India		4	
Bontang	Indonesia		4	
Kosichang	Thailand		4	
Tarahan	Indonesia		3	
Santan	Indonesia		3	
Panjang	Indonesia	3	3	
Kakinada	India	4	3	
Barranquil	Colombia		3	
Sub Total		161	198	180

possible time interval between ships proceeding in any one direction is about twenty minutes and the lateral clearance between two ships going in opposite directions is sometimes no more than a mile (1.6 kilometres). The hazards of the area are such that the master of a large tanker will point out the fact that the maintenance of lookouts and other navigational responsibilities while transiting the narrow and crowded waterway means that no extra personnel are easily available for an anti-piracy watch.

The potential consequences of a tanker having her bridge unmanned and, therefore, and without control during a pirate attack are quite clear. In one recorded incident, due to the fact that when the attackers left a ship, the crew could not immediately free themselves, the bridge was unmanned for a period of seventy minutes. Had this incident taken place in the Philip Channel, a disaster would have been almost inevitable. In the first nine months of 1999, there were thirteen reported piracy attacks in the Indonesian part of Singapore Straits. On 16 January 1999, *MT Chaumont*, a fully loaded Very Large Crude Carrier (VLCC) was attacked by pirates while navigating in narrow waters of the Philip Channel. The pirates threatened the chief officer with a machete to his neck and tied his hands.

Learning From the Exxon Valdez Disaster

In March 1989, the world was appalled at the ecological and environmental carnage caused by the *Exxon Valdez* disaster. For reasons unconnected to piracy, the ship's holds were breached and some 50 million litres of oil were released. A conservative figure states that cleansing operations were necessary along 3,500 kilometres of coastline. Hence, the world has seen that a spillage of this magnitude can occur. The international community has also seen the consequences of such a catastrophe through direct experience. Disastrous though the consequences of the *Exxon Valdex* incident were, in one respect, Alaska was probably the best place it could have happened as the area is sparsely populated. Transpose the circumstances to a similar incident in the Philip Channel and the resultant oil pollution would be disastrous. Apart from the pollution, every possibility exists that the seaway would have to be closed to shipping and the fishing in the area would be ruined for many years.

Unfortunately, it does turn out that many people tend not to acknowledge potential problems until they actually occur. The IMB is convinced that, because there will be no second chance with an oil-spill, a proactive attitude to the possibility is essential and it would be foolhardy to the point of irresponsibility not to take all possible measures to prevent the first one.

Practical Aspects of Piracy Prevention

Much has been written concerning the preventive measures and many guidelines for mariners have been published. On the one hand some measures are to be taken by the ship owners and crew themselves, and some other measures are to be taken by governments. These measures are more complex, especially when national borders are crossed in the interdiction of pirates.

Obviously, the most effective way to tackle the problem squarely is to prevent the pirates boarding the ship in the first instance. The knowledge and experience of so many ship masters, their officers and crew is of great use here and the following points are a distillation of "tried and tested" techniques made available in further detail by the IMO:

- Keeping a lookout and radio watch
- Exhibiting a readiness to respond
- Not resisting boarders
- Conduct during an attack
- Pre-planning and post-incident response.[3]

Efforts by the IMB

The maritime industry is also doing what it possibly can. For example, through the support of seventeen organizations such as protection and indemnity (P&I) clubs, ship owners and insurers, the IMB Piracy Reporting Centre in Kuala Lumpur was set up in 1992.[4] The centre is now recognized throughout the maritime industry for its valuable contribution in quantifying the problem of world piracy and providing assistance, free of charge to ships that have been attacked. The IMB now broadcasts its Piracy Situation Reports daily to all ships in world piracy hotspots including Asia, the coasts of Africa and South America through Inmarsat-C satellite's safetyNET service. As a result, ships receive up-to-date intelligence on pirate activity in these areas. The IMB also promptly passes reports of attacks to the law enforcement. Average time taken by the IMB to onward transmit the message is ten minutes. The IMB also posts the weekly updates of attacks on its Internet website.[5] The report is compiled from the Piracy Reporting Centre's daily status bulletins. Thus the ship owners and authorities ashore as well as ships at sea can access the weekly updates.

The Role of Technology

As it has been pointed by the IMB in the past, technology can play an important role in the battle against piracy.[6] For example, the IMB is quite supportive of two technological products called Secure-Ship — a preventive and deterrence system to deter boarding attempts — via a non-lethal, 9,000 volt pulse electrifying fence surrounding the ship — and ShipLoc — an inexpensive satellite tracking system designed to locate ships at sea or in port via tiny transmitter concealed onboard ships and monitored through any personal computer with Internet access.[7] Fitted together, ShipLoc and Secure-Ship may be a possible answer to combating piracy more effectively by most vessels (except tankers and gas carriers to which Secure-Ship cannot currently be fitted).

Maritime Terrorism

The attacks on the World Trade Centre in New York on 11 September 2001 generated a great deal of discussion at the IMO and elsewhere on the vulnerability of shipping to terrorism. Verifying the contents of containers, ensuring the security of containers in transit, the identity of crew members on board vessels, the transport of biological and chemical weapons, attacks against vessels and their use as weapons became the subject of intense debate and resulted in the creation of International Ship and Port Facility Security (ISPS) code.

Many stakeholders in the shipping community had hoped that while it was necessary to prepare for all eventualities, the industry would probably escape the attention of the terrorists. After all, attacking a merchant vessel carrying cargo is unlikely to fuel the publicity sought by terrorists. However, on Sunday, 13 October 2002, the Limburg, a 299,000-tonne tanker, suffered an explosion as it was approaching the pilot station at Mina Al-Dabah in Yemen. One crew member died and 90,000 barrels of crude spilled into the sea. Investigations confirmed that a boat filled with explosives had rammed the vessel.

The kind of attack launched on the Limburg is difficult to prevent. No shipboard action can protect the ship in these circumstances. These are slow vessels and their manoeuvrability restricted. It is therefore impossible for the vessel to avoid a fast moving boat intent on a beam-on collision.

The answer must therefore lie with the coastal state to ensure that the approaches to their ports are made secure. Port authorities should specify approach channels for tankers and other vulnerable vessels. These channels and the areas on each side of them should be monitored by coast guard or police vessels to ensure that no small craft, leisure, fishing or unauthorized vessel enters this restricted zone. If they do, the vessel must be immediately approached and investigated. The idea is to have a "clearway" through which authorized vessels can navigate without the fear that a small vessel close to the fairway will suddenly project itself towards it at high speed.

In the final analysis, the risk of terrorist attack can perhaps never be eliminated, but sensible steps can be taken to reduce the risk. The issue is how seriously do the governments take the threat of maritime terrorism. Post-*Limburg*, we cannot continue to hope for the best, and ignore vital past lessons.

Conclusion: A Way Forward

The following incident is typical of some of the recent violent attacks: On 5 January 2004, while underway, an Indonesian product tanker *MT Cherry 201* was attacked and hijacked by armed pirates in the Malacca Strait. The pirates armed with guns boarded the ship and took thirteen crew members hostage. They later released the master so that he could convey their demand for ransom. After one month of negotiations with the pirates, the pirates shot dead four crew members. The remaining eight crew members jumped overboard and escaped.

In view of the increasing ferocity and numbers of piratical attacks such as this cited case, one could be excused for asking "why?" and "what will happen now?" The answer to the first question is simple: The pirates have all the advantages. They have the knowledge of what is being carried by specific ships and, perhaps the most relevant point, they have all the sea room in which to operate. This and the fact that modern radar will enable them to watch to see if they themselves are being followed means that they can wait and commit their crime with impunity knowing that they will have time to escape at the first suggestion that any intervention force is on its way.

The difficulties are enormous. Not only is there an enormous maritime space to be covered but there also currently exists an impediment towards effective action by way of the strained financial circumstances of certain governments involved in the fight against piracy. To create a response capability able to catch and match the pirates would require the expenditure of considerable resources and some countries just do not have the necessary financial budget. When one adds to these difficulties the political problems which arise when pirates are acting in waters which are the territory of two neighbouring states and move quickly from one jurisdiction to another, it is little wonder that so much remains to be done.

The answer to the second question is not so simple. In the wake of the *Achille Lauro* incident in the autumn of 1985, the IMO responded with the creation of recommendations for "the implementation of measures to prevent unlawful acts against passengers and crews on board ships". The IMO both retained the initiative and maintained the impetus for this by conducting several regional missions and seminars on piracy and ship security matters as well as discussing the issue in its Maritime Safety Committee. The recently introduced ISPS Code will hopefully result in enhanced maritime security and reducing the number of incidents of maritime violence.

The IMO's SUA Convention is meant to ensure that states take appropriate action against any person committing offences such as seizure of ships by force, acts of violence against persons on board ships and the placing of devices on board a ship which are likely to destroy or damage it. While this convention was primarily designed for terrorism, it can be applied to most incidents involving piracy and armed robbery against ships.[8]

While any initiative is highly welcomed, in reality, it is doubtful if the hardened criminals described above will be affected by such measures. Because the main problem is to be able to catch the pirates, and not so much as what to do with them once caught. It has already been shown that some coastal states lack the resources to react at sea and this is understood and has to be accepted but what is lacking is coordinated response on-shore. It has to be accepted that pirates operate at sea only for the purposes of committing their crime. Finally they must come ashore, somewhere to dispose of their gains and this is where they would be vulnerable and law enforcement would be more efficient. This can only come to pass if there is collective action by national law enforcement. Until recently piracy was not a major issue for the law enforcement of individual countries as it did not affect their own population but literally was a problem of "those that pass in the night". It is a welcome relief to note that most countries are now demonstrating a proactive approach in tackling piracy. It is hoped that this state of affairs continues and countries cooperate to rid their seas of this menace.

Notes

1   *Piracy and Armed Robbery against Ships: Annual Report, 1 January – 31 December 2003.* ICC International Maritime Bureau (Released in January 2004).

2   Judge Vachha cited in *The State versus Christianus Mintando and Others (2003), Sessions Case 197 of 2000*, The Court of Sessions for Greater Mumbai, India.

3   International Maritime Organization. MSC/Circ.622/Rev.1, "Piracy and Armed Robbery Against Ships: Recommendations to Governments for preventing and suppressing piracy and armed robbery against ships"; MSC/Circ.623/Rev.3, "Piracy and Armed Robbery Against Ships: Guidance to ship owners and ship operators, ship masters and crews on preventing and suppressing acts of piracy and armed robbery against ships". Both documents are available on the Internet at <http://www.imo.org>.

4   The Piracy Reporting Centre can be reached at +603-2031-0014 (telephone), +603-2078-5769 (facsimile), +MA-31880-IMBPCI (telex) and through e-mail at imbkl@icc-ccs.org.uk.

5   <http://www.icc-ccs.org>.

6   See P. Mukundan, "The Scourge of Piracy in Southeast Asia — Can Any Improvements be Expected in the Near Future?" in *Piracy in Southeast Asia: Status Issues and Responses*, edited by Derek Johnson and Mark Valencia (Singapore: Institute of Southeast Asian Studies, 2005), especially pp. 40–41.

7   Developed by Secure Marine in the Netherlands, an intruder coming in contact with the fence will receive an unpleasant non-lethal shock that will result in the intruder abandoning the attempted boarding. If the fence is tampered with, an alarm will go off, activating floodlights and a very loud siren. The fence is collapsible, enabling quick folding against the railing when required. Special, quick release gates are used in case a pilot wants to board, lowering a gangway or launching a life raft. The fence can be dismantled or re-installed by the crew as required. When a ship approaches a piracy prone area the crew can re-install the fence, which takes a few hours. When the ship leaves this area, the master can decide to leave the fence collapsed against the railing or dismantle it if bad weather is due. A smart remote control system enables complete control cover the systems functions without requiring wires to be pulled through the ship. The fence has also been tested in various sea conditions including Force 7 seas, with salt-water waves splashing over it. Further information is available at <http://www.secure-ship.com>. In the case of ShipLoc, the IMB has been working together with CLS, a world leading satellite tracking system operator on this device which has already been installed on a number of ships. For their own safety, the crew of the ship need not be informed of the existence or location of the transmitter. In addition to tracking ships that have come under a piracy attack and/or a hijacking, ShipLoc can also be used as a management tool to monitor progress of a voyage around the

world. ShipLoc monthly rental is well affordable and gives the owners up to fifteen positions for the ship a day. The IMB piracy Reporting Centre will also monitor a ShipLoc-fitted ship that is hijacked, and liaise with law enforcement agencies until the ship is recovered. In addition to an anti-hijacking role, ShipLoc facilitates independent and precise location of ships at regular intervals. Further details can be obtained at <http://www.shiploc.com>.

[8]   The Convention for the Suppression of Unlawful Acts Against the Safety of Maritime Navigation, Rome, 10 March 1988.

2

Transnational Threats and the Maritime Domain[1]

Brian Fort

Introduction

On the night of 22 July 2004, a United States Navy aircraft carrier, the *USS Kennedy*, collided with a wooden *dhow* while conducting operations in the Arabian Gulf.[2] The wooden dhow was no match for the 82,000-tonne aircraft carrier. Search and rescue teams found no survivors and only a small area of debris.[3] Whether this was a tragic maritime accident, a failed terrorism attempt, or perhaps even a terrorist practice run may never be truly known. I do not want to sound alarmist nor like a conspiracy theorist, and I have no evidence that the collision was anything more than a maritime tragedy, but in the eyes of terrorist operations planners, I would pose the question — does it really matter? The collision revealed a definitive vulnerability to such a maritime terrorism tactic in a relatively broad swath of littoral water. Although an official report has yet to be released, the security implications are already substantial. Whether as a result of inaction, inappropriate action, or action determined by the bridge crew and/or commanding officer to maintain their course and speed until it was too late to manoeuvre and avoid collision, the end result was that the carrier collided with the dhow. If the dhow had been laded with explosives, might it then have proven to be a match for the carrier? Would it have made the headlines as the most terrible act of maritime terrorism to date in the new century?

The author was the executive officer of a U.S. Navy cruiser operating in the Arabian Gulf in the months following the terrorist attacks of 11 September 2001. While some scoffed at us, we took the threat of dhows to the aircraft carrier we provided defence for very seriously. On several occasions we sprinted away from the carrier to encircle a nearby dhow and attempt to determine its intentions. While we may have never really believed those intentions were anything other than fishing or recreation, we took their potential threat at face value. With that in mind it is not too hard to understand, that my own personal first reaction when I learned of the collision was that of terrorists attempting to learn how to exploit any vulnerability in naval force protection at sea.

In comparison, the very nature, quantity, quality, and brutality of pirate attacks in Southeast Asian waters in recent years has demonstrated and continues to demonstrate significant vulnerabilities for terrorists to exploit in maritime security. The surge in piracy, particularly in Southeast Asia, is only matched by the surge in its reporting by numerous global media outlets. With global security lagging the global economy I believe the links between piracy and maritime terrorism are more blurred than ever and must be recognized. The same avenues that have led to global economic successes have also paved the way for the emergence of numerous transnational threats. The aim of this chapter is to review the world of transnational threats, provide a prelude to later discussions on the nexus between piracy and maritime terrorism, and discuss countering these threats in the maritime domain by drawing parallels from the author's experience at sea.

Transnational threats are activities perpetrated by non-state actors that not only transcend national borders but also have regional or global impact.[4] Yet, at least prior to the 9/11 attacks, they seemed easy to overlook because they are so varied in nature and scope. Further, their effects are obscured by the fact that many are somewhat insidious with gradual and long-term consequences rather than immediate ones. With the exception of global terrorism, most transnational threats clearly have a lower overall profile in global security considerations than do big-power geo-politics, regional wars, and the proliferation of weapons of mass destruction (WMD). But while some transnational threats are not direct threats to state security, they can be threats to a state's economy and the quality of life of its citizens, and therefore threaten national interests. The combined effect of transnational threats such as terrorism, drug and human trafficking, weapons proliferation, and piracy — along with their critical enablers, corruption and money laundering — cannot be overlooked for their damaging long-term consequences for global political and economic stability, and thus for global security.

The Globalization of Transnational Threats

All transnational threats are not the result of contemporary globalization. Indeed, most of the underlying activities — such as smuggling, corruption, uncontrolled migrations, and piracy in Southeast Asia — have occurred throughout history. Many have been enduring concerns for national governments. But globalization has increased both the range and effects of these activities by providing the physical means to transcend even the most surveyed borders and to move across ever-increasing distances. At the same time, the increasing globalization of national economies now means that the effects of these threats on any one country (based on the level of integration with the global economy) can have devastating effects on all.

The global war on terrorism has exposed a number of critical weaknesses and vulnerabilities in terms of how global security is viewed. What has been found is that there are a number of gaps in firstly, how enemies to global security are defined, and secondly, how states are organized to deal with these threats.

Currently, the effort to combat transnational threats is based on a rather myopic view of terrorism that often overlooks its connection to international criminal activity, in particular the use of funds from these activities to finance terrorism. Yet, it is precisely the fluid and often overlapping nature of both types of transnational actors that is frequently misunderstood. Indeed, what is required is "new security packaging" that would allow the global community, regions, allies, and states to formulate an effective long-term strategy rather than stay mired in a reactive posture.

Whereas the Cold War period produced a tightly bipolar structure with identifiable peer rivals, the 1990s heralded a looser global array, coupled with a complexity and mystery that often caught analysts and policy-makers off guard, unable to describe what they were facing, much less proactively address coming predicaments. As cliché as it sounds, the 9/11 attacks served as a "wake up call" for global security. As it mentioned earlier, more than anything we are confronted with a number of transnational threats that are normally thought of as being simply in the domain of organized criminal activity. The fact of the matter is that terrorists are also involved in international criminal activity. So one of the major gaps that confront us is the one that stove piped international organized crime and terrorism into two separate and mutually exclusive categories. It is now known that al-Qaeda, for instance, is involved in drugs, particularly heroin in Southeast Asia for weapons deals, as well as in money laundering and the sale of illegal or "blood" diamonds from Africa.[5]

The second gap flows directly from the first. Because organized criminal activity has for so long been considered a police matter, potential aggressors were considered strictly in the military domain. In other words, what has been found after 9/11 is that stove-piping this way has been a mistake. Global security needs to be viewed as a "security continuum" where lines are blurred and organized criminal activity may not solely be the domain of law enforcement anymore, nor may matters that deal with situations that involve states be thought of as purely military matters. In Afghanistan for example, after the military campaign, U.S. forces found themselves mainly involved in a manhunt to track down members of al-Qaeda and their supporters in the Taliban. However, as military personnel will argue, they are trained as war fighters, not investigating agents to track down and arrest people. On the other hand, the U.S. Federal Bureau of Investigation (FBI) does not have the necessary transportation and equipment, notwithstanding the ability to secure an area, in order to be able to conduct a manhunt in what essentially can be considered a war zone.

Finally, there has been a gap in our general understanding of what factors have enabled groups such as al-Qaeda and other terrorist organizations to grow with almost near impunity. The answer lies in money. The reliance on the corruptibility of officials and the ability to launder the proceeds of their criminal activity are the two things that they need, and they are therefore their vulnerabilities. After all, terrorists must live somewhere physically in the world, so, what has happened is that both terrorists and organized criminal groups have looked for and have found weak states that they have then exploited for their systemic weaknesses such as having a history of corruption. In fact, in some situations, they have duped and suborned individuals in governments into virtually selling their sovereignty so as to create "states of convenience" for themselves. Corruption is no longer simply the greasing of the wheels of commerce, the paying off of government officials to expedite matters, or the rigging of elections. It is has become much more insidious and dangerous when mixed with terrorism. Secondly, terrorists need to be able to move their money in a clandestine and efficient manner in order to conduct their operations.

Corruption certainly facilitates entry into financial sectors and at the end of the day, some countries' financial systems may be as dependent on the steady influx of large amounts of dirty money as is its hierarchy on regular criminal kickbacks and bribes. The role of money laundering is to lower the risk of being connected with the crimes from which the money derived and further, allows the integration of operations in the legitimate business world. According to a report by the Federal Bureau of Investigations (FBI), the International Monetary Fund estimates that somewhere between 2 and 5 per cent of the world's gross domestic product (US$600 billion to US$1.5 trillion) is laundered annually.[6] This indicates that organized crime and terrorists are exploiting significant weaknesses in international financial systems.

The question is that when illicit capital can be moved through several different countries in one day in order to disguise its origins and to confuse authorities, is it a police matter or is it a threat to our global security? It could be argued to be both, because it depends on what the money does to a state; whether it finances terrorist operations or destroys banking systems. By the time these things are tracked down, the criminals have absconded with millions, because the volume and complexity of such transactions often requires extensive investigation of up to a year to expose what might have averaged only minutes or hours to complete *via* electronic wire transfers. It can be inferred that criminals and terrorists manipulate money in somewhat different ways. Organized criminal activity is motivated by simple profit — the amassing of staggering sums either legally or illegally. For terrorist groups, on the other hand, the money (however amassed) is a means to other ends.

Criminal activity such as drug trafficking operations, for example, is so immense that drug traffickers are known to weigh money, rather than count it. The retail transactions of drugs are mostly in smaller denominations such that some distributors accumulate 500 to 1,500 kilogrammes of bills on a monthly basis meaning that it must be carried in suitcases, on the persons of mules, or shipped in maritime cargo containers. The money is often therefore a liability as it necessitates a near-constant search for a safe place for it to be stored, discreet bankers to help invest it legitimately, and any number of schemes to obscure its origins. This contingency leaves international criminals vulnerable to having their operations severely disrupted by law enforcement and other officials.

Conversely, terrorists are interested in sustaining an interlocking global cell structure and finding ways to discretely distribute money. Logistically, the biggest obstacle they face is banking reporting requirements. Groups such as al-Qaeda must find ways to disaggregate and distribute significant amounts of money into smaller denominations in order to sustain or expand a network of comparatively small cells of typically three to four operatives that do the recruitment and conduct operations. Additionally, if the money is derived from criminal activity such as narcotics trafficking, then it must first be amassed, laundered, and then re-distributed. Again, the more transactions that occur, the more vulnerable these groups are to detection of their activities.

Maritime Piracy as a Transnational Threat

Piracy overlays seamlessly onto this template of transnational threats with the maritime domain providing an environment ripe for exploitation. By blurring the lines between international crime and terrorism earlier, this section aims to set the stage for a similar conflation with respect to piracy and maritime terrorism. And, while all international crime does not always lead to terrorism, following the trails of international crime can lead to the terrorists themselves, because the bottom line is that terrorism costs money. With money as the critical enabler, the links then between piracy and terrorism may become clearer in some respects, and for purposes of analysis, the terms maritime terrorists and pirates will be used interchangeably, in which the latter refers to "high-end" piracy associated with crime syndicates and not to the more petty activities associated with maritime muggings.

Piracy of the organized kind — through exploitation of maritime laws and secrecy regarding flags of convenience — has often resulted in the theft of millions of dollars of cargo, kidnappings or worse murder, and the creation of "phantom" ships used for other transnational crimes such as drug and human trafficking. Without the link to terrorism, piracy could be viewed as just another international crime — a high profit, low risk venture. However, much like drug trafficking which eventually overtook other forms of less lucrative smuggling, piracy may be a venture which global terrorist organizations may not continue to leave to amateur pirates any longer. Ultimately, I believe this kind of piracy if left unchecked may result in the doomsday scenario of a weapon of mass destruction delivery.

Therefore, if piracy remains in the realm of just another transnational security threat, then it will continue to get the same limited attention that so many other terrible transnational crimes get until an igniting event occurs. Eric Ellen's words still ring true today when he lamented that not even "shoot-'em-up" television news shows seem interested in piracy: "An aircraft seized by hijackers is big news, but when a ship is taken, no one could care less."[7] The world cannot afford another 9/11, and we can certainly not afford the global nightmare of a terrorist use of WMD — both scenarios of which global maritime security is currently vulnerable. By associating piracy with terrorism, the aim is to continue to draw piracy's attention to the world stage in a call for continued and further action against this transnational security threat, which has the potential for consequences of a terrible and ultimate nature.

Maritime Terrorism as a Transnational Threat

And yet even with all that has been addressed in the written media in the since 9/11, I believe that for the most part, piracy is still the "weak sister" to global aviation security concerns because it has not been clearly linked to terrorism. For instance, in the past four years, only two significant maritime terrorist attacks have been listed on the U.S. State Department's "Chronology of Significant International Terrorist Incidents"; the October 2000 attack on the U.S. Navy destroyer, *USS Cole*, in the port of Aden and the attack on the French oil tanker *Limburg*, in 2002, off the coast of Yemen.[8] The question is, how is it that a makeshift incendiary device exploding at an automatic teller machine at a worldwide bank with no one claiming responsibility makes the list of international terrorist incidents, and yet the attack on a fully laden oil tanker by pirates wearing military-style fatigues with automatic weapons does not? Among other things, it is possible that the political agenda of an unnamed bomber against a teller machine outweighs an incident of international crime in the eyes of the media. One thing is certain, with respect to maritime terrorism and the attacks on the *Cole* and the *Limburg*, these attacks were television events and the political statements of the terrorists were clear — *we can penetrate your force protection, and we can affect world commerce*. The holes in the sides of each ship were clear indicators of defeated force protection requirements, and the residual economic effects of the *Limburg* attack made clear the effects on the economy of Yemen. In the months that followed the tanker attack, Yemen's shipping industry was dealt a very serious blow. Insurance underwriters imposed a 300 per cent increase in premiums on all vessels coming into Yemeni ports, forcing many vessels to re-route to competitors' ports. Port activity dropped nearly 50 per cent, ultimately resulting in Yemen losing nearly US$4 million dollars per month.[9] And yet, this attack does not even come close to the devastation that would befall the maritime industry, much less world economies following a doomsday explosion involving WMD in a major world port or the shutdown of the Malacca or Singapore Straits due to a horrific maritime calamity. There are enough warning signs that point to the linkage between piracy and maritime terrorism to require action now. If the link is discounted and policies are not enacted to set the stage for broader regional and global collaboration, the arena of the maritime domain will continue to be exploited.

As the adage goes, hindsight is always "20/20". The fallout from the various investigations and reports following the 9/11 attacks seal that obvious statement. The now famous "Phoenix memo" from the summer of 2001 before the attacks alerted the FBI that "an inordinate number of individuals of investigative interest" were attending or had flight schools in the state of Arizona.[10] The parallel between that memo and the often-referenced *Aegis Defence Services Maritime Terrorism Report* detailing the pirate attack on the *Dewi Madrim* are alarmingly clear. Only the pirates in that attack could tell us whether they were learning how to manipulate the controls of the large chemical tanker for some more devious purpose or whether they were "joy riding" as part of their piracy.

Numerous initiatives all focusing on various aspects of maritime security, such as the Proliferation Security Initiative, the Container Security Initiative, and the International Ship and Port Facility Security Code, have been established to address security weaknesses in the maritime domain. I believe they are all steps in the right direction, but they may not be enough. Short-term corrective actions are designed to be austere or "painful" (such as the closing of U.S. ports following the 9/11 attacks) because they must remain in place until long-term solutions take root. It is difficult to accept that globally, these short-term actions were painful enough as it were and therefore, not enough in the interim. As recent as 25 August 2004, in testimony to the U.S. House of Representatives Sub-committee on Coast Guard and Maritime Transportation, maritime transportation is still considered one of the America's "most serious vulnerabilities".[11]

Coping with Piracy and Maritime Terrorism: A Security and Naval Perspective

To cope effectively with complex and dangerous transnational threats, there are six significant challenges in general that must be tackled:

- Understanding the true nature of the problem;
- Resolving bureaucratic inefficiencies;
- Dealing more effectively with root causes;
- Improving intelligence sharing;
- Closing the security gap between military and law enforcement authorities in situations where their competencies overlap; and
- Engaging in a more comprehensive threat assessment.[12]

Specific to coping with piracy however, the author draws his experience at sea — particularly in maritime interdiction operations targeting smugglers, to derive parallels for ways to counter piracy threats — while attempting to strike a balance between a political and security perspective on the one hand and a naval one on the other. This is because once maritime terrorists have control of a vessel and a decision is made to take back that vessel — which is a naval task — the endgame is much more challenging and risky with the odds for disaster much more likely. Thus, one of the main strategic challenges facing the global community is to *pre-empt* this threat rather than to *react* to it. This will require suitable coordination and adequate resources to maintain a long-term effort.

First, and anti-piracy actions notwithstanding, the key to any success against piracy starts with the intelligence process, both fundamental and actionable. By fundamental intelligence, this means referring to the basic five "Ws": Who, what, where, when, and why. States and organizations require more fidelity and granular awareness of the maritime domain similar to the commercial airline industry. This awareness in the maritime domain does not exist in whole today, and yet the technology has already existed for some time and is in use by many commercial shippers. Directly from the Internet in fact, many of the very basics of real-time vessel tracking, including webcam bow shots for example, are readily available. The International Maritime Organization (IMO) is helping to improve the maritime awareness picture by mandating the fit of Automatic Information Systems on certain classes of vessels, encouraging states to implement long-range identification and tracking initiatives, and promoting new developments such as the Marine Electronic Highway project for the Malacca and Singapore Straits.[13]

Beyond the global development of a more transparent maritime domain picture, it will be actionable intelligence and the sharing of that intelligence that determines a potential security threat and may ultimately dictate a set of response actions to that threat. Considering the events of 9/11, the aviation industry already had the fundamental intelligence picture.

However, bureaucratic and inter-agency inefficiencies contributed to the lack of action based on such actionable intelligence. Once the events of 9/11 were set into motion and the security threat was ultimately realized, it was too late to evoke any set of corrective action protocols. There can be no excuse for not learning from these lessons. The same analogy applies in the maritime domain. Once terrorists have sailed over the horizon, it is all too often too late to do much to stop them.

Knowing that states possess both fundamental and actionable intelligence capability may deter some maritime terrorists, but as the aviation industry also knows it will not stop them altogether. Actionable intelligence must lead to a timely maritime response to a security threat. Seafarers know all too well just how fast threatening situations involving vessels at sea can develop. Suppose for instance, pirates took over the bridge of a ship making 20 knots in autopilot. If the pirates made no notice of navigation required, particularly in the sea lanes of Southeast Asia, the pirated vessel would transit 10 nautical miles in just thirty minutes. In a narrow and congested sea lane, that is a dangerous and volatile situation that happens extremely fast. And although not as dynamic as a high speed air or car chase, if a nation makes a decision to intercept a vessel in its territorial waters, that decision requires time and dynamic planning to put forces into place and then maintain a constant vigilance on the maritime picture to force an interception, in what will probably be a very narrow swath of water.

The issue surrounding the territorial waters of a state brings up the obvious impact of sovereignty which is an extremely relevant and potentially show-stopping discussion whenever discussing maritime responses to security threats. Throughout history secure waterways have been key to fostering the global economy through maritime trade. It is obvious that maritime terrorists not only have no respect for sovereignty, they thrive and exist on the very argument. They fundamentally require it because it gives them safe harbour from the high seas. Stopping maritime terrorists requires collaboration. To quote from the IMO's 2004 World Maritime Day Background Paper with respect to finding the right balance for strategic sea lanes, "to work with interested parties to find ways in which they might collaborate — while always observing the sovereign rights of the coastal states concerned".[14]

Collaborative efforts must also be internal to the state. As already pointed out, maritime security concerns overlap between military and law enforcement operations. However, the process should not end there as inter-agency cooperation and judicial finality is absolutely essential in attaining complete victory against this threat. Currently, a comparison of the numbers of pirate attacks to the number of pirates held accountable for their actions demonstrates the difficulties inherent in the entire process from determination, to action and capture, to judgment.

Finally, when the endgame results in maritime interdiction, it must be recognized that this is an increasingly dangerous undertaking. For example, two U.S. Navy sailors and one U.S. Coast guardsman were killed while intercepting an unidentified dhow in the vicinity of the Khawr Al Amaya Oil Terminal in the North Arabian Gulf on 24 April 2004. Maritime terrorists onboard the dhow blew themselves up as the sailors approached in their rigid hull inflatable boat.[15] Maritime interdiction also requires the ability to defeat the same type of anti-piracy defences put in place to stop pirates in the first place. It means attempting to gain access to bridges that may be sealed or welded shut, and it means possibly defeating heavy weapons such as rocket-propelled grenades, shoulder-fired missiles, and high-powered automatic weapons. In Southeast Asia, all of this must be done in narrow, crowded waterways. Reviewing the weapons capability and number of acclaimed ex-special forces soldiers from worldwide militaries that private defence and protective services currently employ to counter maritime terrorism certainly demonstrates their expectations of what they are possibly up against in such an encounter. And to complicate maritime interdiction even further, when such action results in a compliant boarding where military or law enforcement forces have to make a determination of legitimacy, it is often not uncommon to find that pirates and smugglers not only know the international laws and rules, they actually follow them (albeit with stolen cargo or a stolen vessel).

Dangerous Waters in the Malacca Straits?

In the U.S. Navy, the following narration would be called a sea story; in the Royal Navy, it would be referred to as "spinning a dit". Nonetheless, it is a tragic story of loss of life at sea which occurred in the Malacca Straits nearly twelve years ago to the time of writing. Similar to the collision incident involving the *USS Kennedy* and the dhow, this collision could be simply viewed as another maritime tragedy or it could be something much more sinister, involving piracy and/or other transnational threats — probably before the term was ever used — such as arms smuggling, human trafficking, with potential impacts on the maritime environment.

Drawing upon the book, *Dangerous Waters*, by John Burnett, the incident is described as follows. On the calm, clear night of 19 September 1992, the 100,000-tonne crude carrier, *Nagasaki Spirit*, collided with the 27,000-tonne container vessel, *Ocean Blessing*. The collision occurred just before midnight at the northern entrance of the Malacca Straits. It was a classic "T-bone" collision in which the *Ocean Blessing* was believed to have been making 21 knots based on the engine room log repeater found in the aftermath and the V-shaped ripping in the side of the *Nagasaki Spirit*. A massive fire ensued and at least 12,000 tonnes of crude oil spilled out into the Straits. Forty-four sailors did not survive to tell the tale of what occurred prior to the collision. The final message of the captain of the *Nagasaki Spirit* leaves little doubt, however:

> Have been fired upon and now have fire in Nos. 5 and 6 and central tanks. Abandoning vessel immediately and into two 16-man life rafts and will activate EPIRB in Lat 04 33N, Long 98 43E, at 1623 GMT Sept 19. No time to report further as abandoning vessel.

No lifeboats were ever found, onboard the *Ocean Blessing* investigators found only small piles of ashes — the remnants of human remains, and no remains were found onboard the *Nagasaki Spirit*.[16]

Speculation has it that the *Nagasaki Spirit* was taken by pirates and the *Ocean Blessing* had also been pirated or was trying to avoid the same as she was observed by another ship to move "in an erratic manner — changing speeds from 10 to 20 knots, from side to side, as though the deck watch officer was trying to employ evasive maneuvers to avoid being boarded by pirates". The fire that burned for three weeks onboard the *Ocean Blessing* was a result of weapons and other untouchable "diplomatic" cargo being smuggled in some of the 1,500 containers carried onboard. And what of the crew of the *Nagasaki Spirit*? Four months after the collision, ten bodies were discovered in a reefer onboard the vessel, *Hai Sin*, a vessel being dismantled for scrap. The bodies had no identification and had clearly been doused with gasoline and burned. Secondary to the investigation it was determined that the *Hai Sin* was actually the *Erria Inge*, an Australian flagged bulk carrier which had coincidently enough been pirated in the prior year and as yet unaccounted for. It was finally determined that the bodies were not the crew of the *Erria Inge*. Were they the bodies of some of the crew of the *Nagasaki Spirit*, part of a human trafficking scheme gone wrong or not related at all? One thing is certain in the world of transnational threats and in particular to the grim reality of piracy and the maritime domain, *post factum*, "Dead men tell no tales."

Notes

1   The opinions expressed in this paper are the author's own and not the expressed opinions of the United States Navy or George Washington University Elliot School of International Affairs.

2   Prevalent throughout the region, dhows are traditional Arabian boats used for, among other things, fishing, trade, and smuggling.

3   From Coalition Forces Maritime Component Commander/Commander, U.S. Naval Forces Central Command/Commander, U.S. 5th Fleet Public Affairs, 23 July 2004.

4   Kimberley Thachuk, "Transnational Threats: Falling Through the Cracks?", *Low Intensity Conflict and Law Enforcement* 10, no. 1 (Spring 2003): 47–67.

5   *Washington Post*, 2 November 2001 and 18 February 2002.

6   <http://www2.fbi.gov/publications/leb/2001/may01leb.pdf>.

7   Ken Cottrill, "Modern Marauders: Today's Pirates Terrorize the High Seas with an Arsenal of High-tech Weapons", *Popular Mechanics*, 1 December 1997, <http://www.popularmechanics.com/science/law_enforcement/1280886.html>.

8   U.S. Department of State, Patterns of Terrorism 2000 and 2002.

9   "Yemen: The Economic Cost of Terrorism", Fact Sheet, Office of Counter-terrorism, 8 November 2002, U.S. Department of State, <http://www.state.gov/s/ct/rls/fs/2002/15028.htm>.

10 Cited from the now famous memo written by FBI agent Kenneth Williams who sent the memo to the Bureau's top echelons in Washington and New York warning that a cadre of Osama bin Laden disciples may be conducting training activities in American flight schools in preparation for future "terror activity against civil aviation targets". Williams suggested a nationwide FBI review to determine whether such a "coordinated effort" could be seen in other localities. The Williams memo was roundly ignored, of course, until after the World Trade Center was levelled. A copy of the memo is available at <http://www.thesmokinggun.com/archive/0412042phoenix1.html>.

11 "Written Testimony before the Subcommittee on Coast Guard and Maritime Transportation", Committee on Transportation and Infrastructure, United States House of Representatives, Washington D.C., 25 August 2004.

12 The author thanks Kimberly Thachuk, Senior Fellow in the Institute for National Strategic Studies at the National Defence University for these points. See also Kimberly L. Thachuk and Sam J. Tangredi, "Transnational Threats and Maritime Responses", in *Globalisation and Maritime Power*, edited by Sam J. Tangredi (Washington D.C.: National Defence University Press, 2002), pp. 57–78.

13 *IMO 2004: Focus on Security*, World Maritime Day 2004 Background Paper, <http://www.imo.org/includes/blastDataOnly.asp/data_id%3D9886/Englishbackground.pdf>.

14   Ibid.
15   "Two Sailors Killed in Arabian Gulf Oil Terminal Attacks" (Story Number: NNS040424-01), Navy Newsstand, 24 April 2004 <http://www.news.navy.mil/search/display.asp?story_id=12977>.
16   Ibid.

3

Piracy and Armed Robbery against Ships in the Philippines

Eduardo Ma R. Santos

Introduction

Southeast Asia, with its complex littoral regions where the mixture of overlapping jurisdictions, thousands of miles of coastlines, and a challenging environment, has provided a fertile area for the growth of transnational threats like terrorism, human and drug trafficking, and piracy. The Philippines is not spared from these threats to the maritime security of the region. In fact, the country's situation is compounded even more by the unresolved disputes in the South China Sea.

This chapter will focus on piracy and armed robbery against ships in the Philippines, which for the past twelve years have victimized approximately 4,000 persons and 1,500 vessels and have seized hundreds of million pesos in properties. As such, the International Maritime Bureau (IMB) continues to list the Philippines as an area prone to piracy and armed robbery against ships. The IMB definition of piracy and armed robbery as "an act of boarding or attempting to board any ship with the apparent intent to commit theft or any other crime and with the apparent intent or capability to use force in the furtherance of that act" is adopted in this chapter. This definition thus covers actual attacks whether the ship is berthed, at anchor or at sea. Petty thefts are excluded unless the thieves are armed. As it will be shown, piracy significantly affects the Philippines' maritime shipping and fishing industries, considered to be significant sectors of the country's economy. The Philippines, being an archipelagic country, depends on its sea routes as the primary economic links within and without the country and the maritime shipping industry plays a vital role as the country's primary conduit for trade and commerce. Rampant piracy could pose a disruption along these links, which could have severe economic repercussions for the country or and further exacerbate the already critical national economic situation.

Factors and Trends, 1993–2004

Factors

The country's problem of piracy and armed robbery is more complex since they are motivated by a number of factors. These factors, whether taken separately or in combination, contribute significantly to their prevalence, especially of piracy. Among these are the following:

1. Historically, piracy has long been practised along the country's southern waters as a legitimate means of livelihood. It has its roots from ancient times when traditional rulers resorted to piracy as an instrument of warfare. Piracy has been endemic in the Philippines for so many years. In fact, piracy was once a favoured vocation at the time of the Spanish effort to colonize Mindanao and Sulu. Piracy was Sulu's weapon against Spanish aggression. Even worse, there are local communities where piracy is viewed as the only means of survival. These underlying economic conditions that have existed for generations helped spawn a culture of piracy.

2. The inherent littoral configuration of the country. The country is characterized by waters dotted with many small islands, coves and islets and narrow channels, which are ideal hideouts for pirates with swift motorboats. Moreover, the country's rich fishing grounds host a number of fishing fleets that are attractive targets for pirates.

3. The current socio-economic instability that will certainly bring more economic uncertainties which in turn could force more people to resort to this relatively simple criminal activity with the prospect of high financial returns.

4. The insurgency and separatist problems has presented piracy as a viable means of raising funds for the rebels. Piracy has been

especially attractive to Southern Philippine secessionist and terrorist groups like the Moro Islamic Liberation Front (MILF) and Abu Sayyaf Group (ASG) due to their ethnic affinity with seafaring and access to weapons. Moreover, the general sense of lawlessness spawned by insurgency and separatism contributes to the prevalence of piracy, particularly in the waters of the Southern Philippines.

5. In the current security milieu, there is a growing concern that terrorists may merge with pirates to carry out seaborne terrorism. Given the propensity of the MILF and the ASG to engage in piracy and their inter-relations with regional terrorist networks like the Jemaah Islamiyah (JI), the threat of piracy assumes a new dimension.

6. The inadequate capability of maritime law enforcement agencies to address the problem due largely to lack of resources. Moreover, naval and law enforcement assets are often re-deployed to address internal security operations that includes insurgency, separatism and terrorism whenever necessary.

Trends

A total of 1,329 piracy cases were committed in the country's vast waters and ports in the past twelve years. The yearly breakdown of piracy incidents in the Philippines is shown in Chart 3.1. The highest recorded occurrence of piracy was in 2003 (155 incidents) while the lowest was in 1999 (83 incidents). Ninety-six piracy cases have been recorded since January 2004. Economic difficulties as well the government's limitation in conducting anti-piracy and armed robberies against vessels contributed largely to the current surge of incidents.

For the past twelve years, a total of 3,916 persons and 1,574 vessels have been victimized by pirate groups throughout the country. Of the victimized persons, 431 were killed while 189 were wounded. Some 426 persons are still missing and believed to have been taken hostage or killed. Of the victimized vessels, 193 were stolen outright, while 679 were robbed of their engines and other equipment. Losses for a ten-year period are placed at 407.81 million Philippine pesos (P). The most affected areas of piracy in the country are the rich fishing areas in Southern Philippines specifically the waters, coastal areas and ports of the Sulu, Basilan, Tawi-Tawi and Zamboanga provinces and the major ports particularly those in Manila, Northern Luzon and some ports in the Visayas. Bustling with maritime activity as indicated by the heavy vessel, passenger, cargo and

CHART 3.1
Trend of Piracy and Armed Robbery Against Vessels, 1993 to July 2004

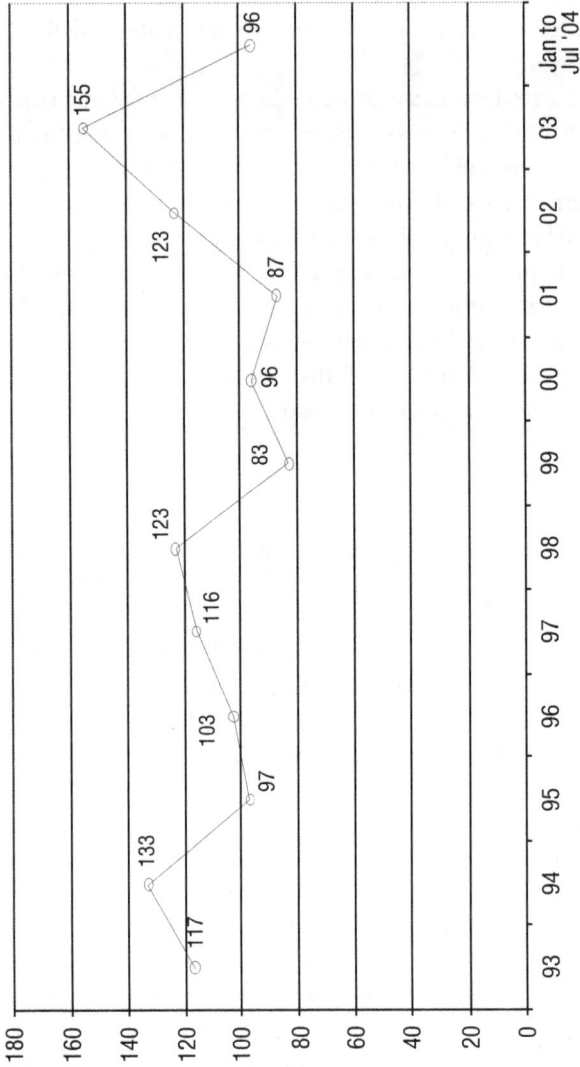

container traffic in the area, the Port of Manila has long been the target of sea marauders.

The types of piracy prevalent in the country are attacks on small fishing boats and *motorbancas* and boarding of commercial vessels in major ports. With robbery as the primary motive, short-term seizure is committed mainly against fishing boats, passenger/ferry boats and motor vessels, which are usually intercepted in the high seas. Violence was characterized by some of these incidents. Long-term seizure is occasionally perpetrated in Southwestern Mindanao and in the country's border waters with Malaysia, where barter trade vessels, ferry boats and motor vessels are commandeered and subsequently abandoned after being stripped of their equipment and other valuables, the crew held hostage and ransom money demanded for their release. Harbour boarding is committed against motor vessels, barges and tankers while anchored at Manila Bay, particularly the Manila container terminal.

Heavily-armed and organized pirate groups use double-engined watercraft to attain high speed during evasion from patrols and disengagement after robbery and attack. These groups operate with four to twenty members utilizing between one to three vessels. Other *modus operandi* are assessed to be as follows:

- Using the disguise of government law enforcement elements;
- Applying force, notably surprise attacks aided by machine-gun fire to intimidate potential victims;
- Tailing potential targets up to an area where attacks can then be made;
- Using the pretence of having developed engine trouble to entice targets to render assistance, after which a surprise attack can be conducted;
- Using unmarked and unregistered vessels to avoid being identified by law enforcement officials and pirate victims;
- Killing of victims at sea or throwing them overboard;
- Intercepting and harassing fishermen and compelling them to jump overboard before taking away their engines and fishing equipment;
- Intercepting fishing boats and taking away their entire catch for later disposal in public markets;
- Conducting routine patrols in areas frequented and transited by fishing passenger boats, flagging down the victims to collect monthly "protection fees";

- Attacking and/or firing upon commercial watercraft in order to force the latter to abandon ship; and
- The carrying out of engine theft of watercraft beached on the shorelines, which are later put on sale to contact buyers in other provinces.

Pirate groups operating in the country can be generally be categorized into two groups: (a) Loosely-organized petty thieves and small-time criminal elements; and (b) organized and heavily armed groups. The latter group, especially those operating in Southern Philippines, are equipped with powerful VHF (Very High Frequency) radios and other sophisticated communication equipment and armed with handguns like revolvers and pistols to high-powered weapons such as AK47 assault rifles, M16s, F1 FAL, M1 Garand, and Carbines. They have at their disposal bigger and faster watercraft capable of entering narrow coves and islets and outmanoeuvring pursuing naval patrols. In the wider expanse of Southern Mindanao and Moro Gulf, pirates use outrigger-type *motorbancas* and sturdier boats equipped with either single or twin engines that can run at maximum speeds of 25 to 35 knots.

Members of insurgent and bandits groups are also engaged in limited seaborne raids and piracy for income. The ASG is notoriously known for raiding three tourist resorts in Palawan, Philippines and Sabah, Malaysia in April and September 2000 and May 2001, taking with them several foreign and local hostages for ransom. This group continues to engage in this activity to generate much needed funds. Likewise, some elements of the insurgent groups like New People's Army (NPA) — the military wing of the Communist Party of the Philippines — are also known to engage in seaborne extortion activities for income generation purposes. Some segments of the secessionist movement MILF and the Moro National Liberation Front (MNLF) are constantly involved in armed robberies at sea in Southern and Southeastern Mindanao and extortion as their regular sources of funds and income.

In terms of the situation in 2003, a total of 155 cases of actual attacks and attempted attacks against ships and other vessels were noted during this year. This represents a 26 per cent increase as compared to 123 incidents noted in 2002. These consisted of four piracy incidents (cases that took place in the high seas), 134 armed robberies against vessels, and 17 hijacking incidents (where the vessels and not goods were taken). Of the 155 incidents noted, 16 incidents were assessed to be perpetrated by the MILF elements as shown in Table 3.1.

The boundary between Malaysia and the Philippines was the site of three of four piracy attempts in 2003. Three vessels successfully eluded the attempt by increasing their speed, lighting the ship's deck and area around the ship, and sounding the alarms. The fourth piracy attempt occurred along the northern boundaries in the vicinity of Cagayan where a small boat pursued the foreign vessel, *MV Berg Kobe*, prompting crewmen to activate the alarm and illuminate the area with searchlights. A motorlaunch with one Malaysian and three Filipinos on board was hijacked in Kudat, Malaysia and was then recovered on 21 October 2003 in Bgy. Calagapan, Balabac, Palawan without the crew, engine and equipment. However, in terms of location, Zamboanga del Sur, similar to 2002, had the most number of armed robberies against ships with 47 incidents, followed by

TABLE 3.1
Attacks or Attempted Attacks Against Ships (2003)[1]

Provinces	Piracy	Armed Robbery	Hijacking	Casualties		
				Killed	Wounded	Missing
Zamboanga del Sur		47		1	2	1
Sarangani		20		1	1	2
Palawan	1	12		4		
Negros Occidental		12				
Davao Sur		10			1	
Davao Oriental		3	7		1	
NCR		8			2	
Sultan Kudarat		6	2			
Western Samar		5				
Iloilo			4			
Tawi Tawi	2	1				
Cavite		2				
Guimaras		2				
Lanao del Sur		1				
Maguindanao			1	1		
Surigao		1				
Masbate		1		1	1	
Cebu		1				
Panay			1			
Batangas		1				
Sorsogon		1				
Cagayan	1					
TOTAL	4	134	17	8	8	3

Sarangani with 20 cases; Palawan with 13 cases; Negros Occidental with 12 cases; Davao del Sur and Davao Oriental with 10 cases each; and also National Capital Region and Sultan Kudarat with eight cases each. There were also some isolated incidents of piracy/sea armed robbery in other parts of the country. In all cases, inadequate patrols in these areas have benefited both pirates and armed robbers.

Consequently, the Port of Manila in the National Capital Region was included in the IMB's list of sites with recorded number of pirate attacks in 2003. Armed robbers were reported to have victimized 3 barges, 2 container ships, a cargo ship, and a bulk carrier last year. Seventeen pirate groups were also noted active in robberies and piracy during this period. Of these, 2 were active in Luzon, 3 in the Visayas, 11 in Mindanao, and 1 in the water boundaries of Palawan and Malaysia. Six of the pirate groups have either links or are actual members of the MILF in Mindanao. Loosely organized groups are also known to operate in other parts of the country notably in city ports. Sites of more violent incidents include Zamboanga del Sur, Palawan, Sarangani, Maguindanao, Davao del Sur, Davao Oriental, Masbate and the National Capital Region. In sum, a total of 158 vessels have fallen prey to piracy and sea-armed robbery in 2003. The most number of victims were fishing boats and motorbancas with a total of 137. Other victims were barges, motor vessels speedboats, general and container vessels, an LNG carrier, a tanker and a tug. On violence inflicted, 8 persons were killed, 8 were wounded, and 3 were missing as a result of pirate attacks and armed robberies conducted. In the previous year, 20 persons were killed, 14 were wounded and 44 were missing. Losses as a result of piracy and armed robbery against vessels for 2003 is estimated at P8.67 million that included the cost of seven watercraft lost and about 58 boat engines seized by pirates.

For 2004, the Philippines remains confronted with the problem not of piracy alone but more cases of sea armed robbery against vessels as well as hijacking. The number of cases noted as of July 2004 is placed at 96. This is already 60 per cent higher than the figures for the same period last year, an indication that the situation remains alarming. Twelve of the incidents noted this year involved elements of the MILF. (See Table 3.2)

The sea robberies in Southern Mindanao are being perpetrated by the Ambak Pare group and the members of the MILF. The MILF is also behind the sea marauding incidents in Southwestern and Northern Mindanao. Among the notorious MILF leaders who are engaged in piracy and extortion activities are Nurhan Amil (also known as commander Ramsy of Zamboanga del Sur), Mosanip Maquib (also known as commander Marish

TABLE 3.2
Attacks or Attempted Attacks Against Ships (January to July 2004)

Provinces	Piracy	Armed Robbery	Hijacking	Killed	Wounded	Missing
Sarangani		23		11		9
Masbate		17				
Zamboanga del Sur		16		1		
Davao del Sur		11				
Zamboanga Sibugay		3	3	6	2	2
Negros Occidental		3				
Antique			4		4	
Palawan		2				
Sultan Kudarat			2			5
Zamboanga Norte		2				
Lanao del Norte		2				
NCR		2				
Bataan		1				
Iloilo		1				1
Sorsogon		1				
South Cotabato		1		2		4
Sulu		1				
North Cotabato		1		3		
TOTAL	0	87	9	22	6	21

of Zamboanga del Norte) and commander Samal Masgal of Cotabato. The latter, together with his twenty fully armed men, admitted killing three fishermen on board a small fishing craft in Midsayap, North Cotabato in the last week of July 2004. In Masbate and in other parts of the country, different pirate groups are operating independently, among them the notorious Villamor, Alinso-ot and Sumayan groups based in Biliran, Western Samar, Masbate, Iloilo and Aklan. The Sumayan group may have been partially neutralized with the arrest of its leader and three members, but it is still being blamed for some of the piracy incidents in the area. It is more focused in Southeastern Mindanao particularly in the waters of Sarangani and Davao del Sur, and Southwestern Mindanao, particularly in the waters of Zamboanga del Sur, and in Masbate. Attacks have become more violent resulting in the death of 22 persons, wounding of 6 persons and the loss of 21 persons who were presumed dead. Some 54 vessels also fell prey to pirate attacks Losses this year is placed at P2.83 million. These included 14 watercrafts and 30 engines lost to pirates.

The Political and Socio-Economic Impact of Piracy and Sea Armed Robbery in the Philippines

In the Philippines, piracy has become a more complex problem because of the socio-economic and political factors. The prevailing economic difficulties have forced many Filipinos to resort to piracy and other criminal activities as an easy source of money. The involvement of the MILF and the ASG and to a lesser extent, even the NPA, has given a political dimension to what is basically an economically motivated activity. These groups use piracy, seaborne robberies and extortion as resource-generating activities and even as a political tool. Since 2001, thirty-seven piracy cases have been attributed to secessionist rebels. However, it is possible that they may be involved in other pirate attacks in Mindanao where they are very active. Secessionist rebels are also suspected to be providing firearms and protection to some pirate groups in Mindanao.

In economic terms, the actual losses that the local shipping industry has incurred as a result of attacks is difficult to estimate since pirates prey more on marginal fishermen rather than on the tankers, barges, container ships and other vessels engaged in commercial shipping. However, the high cost of enhancing security facing most international shipping firms and companies could have impact on the more than 200,000 Filipino seafarers working for international fleets. Filipino seafarers could be further affected if some shipping firms will be forced to lay off workers due to rising security costs on top of the intense competition of the maritime industry itself. This, in turn could have an impact on the dollar remittances of Filipino seafarers to the Philippines. According to the Philippine Overseas Employment Agency, dollar remittances coming from Filipino seamen amount to an average of US$400 million (P120 billion) annually. This is highly significant when the fact that the dollar remittance of overseas Filipino workers is one of the biggest sources of the country's foreign exchange, is taken into account.

It is also difficult to assess the specific losses that the fishing industry in the region has incurred due to piracy despite the fact that there is an obvious impact upon this sector. While Southeast Asian pirates are not usually after the fish catch of their victims, they continue to prey on big fishing boats and trawlers being operated by the multinational fishing firms. They usually rob these vessels of their engines, boat equipment, cash and other valuables. In the Philippines, the fishing sector is the most affected by piracy activities. It includes large, multinational joint ventures, medium-scale Filipino-owned fishing corporations and small marginal fishermen. Pirates continued to prey on hapless fishermen operating in the high seas and other fishing grounds throughout the country. From 1992 to date, pirates have looted their fishermen-victims of fish catch, cash and other valuables amounting to P392 million. The fear of pirate attacks also forced some Filipino fishermen to venture into other safer fishing grounds, even outside the country notably in Indonesian and Malaysian waters. In some instances, this has put them into a worse situation especially when they are apprehended for illegal entry and illegal fishing.

Lastly, the increased risk and prevalence of piracy as well as the threat of maritime terrorism also pose serious economic repercussions for Southeast Asia's highly lucrative tourism industry, which is one of the region's biggest dollar earners and sources of job creation. The global perception of the region as a haven for piracy and terrorism created an atmosphere of uncertainty, reduced confidence and a heightened risk perception (which has been further reinforced by the spate of bombing incidents in Indonesia, notably the Bali and Marriott Hotel bombings; the series of kidnappings in the Philippines particularly those perpetrated by the ASG; and reports about the unabated terrorist activities of the JI). This confluence of events in turn compelled the United States, Canada, Australia and other European countries to issue travel advisories cautioning their citizens against travelling to certain Southeast Asian countries. These advisories also contain warnings against travel in Mindanao and some parts of Metro Manila, citing the series of bombings and kidnappings that have given the country a negative image abroad. The country's efforts to attract more foreign tourists and investments were badly affected by the negative publicity generated by the ASG kidnapping incident in Sipadan and Pandanan Island in Sabah in 2000, and its seaborne raid of the Dos Palmas beach resort in Palawan in 2001. Consequently, the Department of Tourism reported a 24 per cent decline in tourist arrivals in the country in 2003.

Government Counter-measures against Piracy

The Philippine Navy, the Maritime Group of the Philippine National Police (PNP), the Philippine Ports Authority (PPA) and the Philippine Coast Guard are the agencies that primarily enforce all applicable laws regarding piracy and armed robbery against vessels. These agencies and offices have congruent functions to implement such laws albeit with specific limitations in terms of operating areas, equipment and facilities. The Philippine Coast Guard (PCG) is the primary agency in the enforcement of the country's maritime laws and at the forefront in the fight against piracy and armed robbery against vessels. It continues its efforts towards capability-building to enhance its strength as a force against all maritime transgressions including piracy. While primarily tasked for defence against external aggression, the Philippine Navy also plays an important role in maritime law enforcement. The Philippine Navy's role in the counter-insurgency campaign, especially in the fight against the ASG, highlighted its role in the country's anti-piracy efforts. Since majority of the piracy incidents in the country occurred in the coastal areas, the Maritime Group of the PNP has been the most involved agency during armed encounters with the pirate groups. Other government agencies involved include the Philippine Army with its Riverine Group that conducts patrols in coastal areas in Mindanao against the MILF, ASG and the NPA. Meanwhile, the civilian watchdog Bantay Dagat has been vigilant in the campaign against illegal seaborne activities in the municipal waters.

Overall, Philippine maritime law agencies have been steadfast in their campaign to protect the country's vast waters against piracy. From 2003 to June 2004, these agencies neutralized fifteen pirates and apprehended twenty-one others during twelve successful counteraction operations. The country's maritime law enforcement agencies have also embarked on their capability development programmes in view of the growing capability of pirate groups. Through the acquisition of additional floating assets and the upgrading of surveillance, monitoring and communications equipment, these efforts have greatly helped in their counter-piracy efforts. The PCG has also started on a modernization programme anchored on the acquisition of more vessels and the upgrading of its communications and surveillance equipment. Some of its latest acquisitions include eight search-and-rescue vessels from Australia and one donated fiberglass patrol boat.

At the time of writing, the acquisition of the following maritime assets were reported to be in the pipeline:

- Two multi-purpose vessels from Japan to be delivered this year as part of the Philippine Maritime Safety Improvement Project (MSIP);
- Seven 37-metre marine disaster response vessels from Japan to be delivered in 2005; and
- T-Four Dauphin helicopters and one CL-415 seaplane from Canada.

The PCG has also tapped civilian organizations to act as collectors of information to further improve its counter-piracy efforts. An agreement between the PCG and civilian maritime organizations such as, the Masters and Mates Association of the Philippines, the Marine Engineers Officers

Association, United Filipino Seafarers, and the Associate Marine Officers and Seamen's Union of the Philippines have been designated information collection agencies on the activities of pirate and terrorist groups in the country. In line with its anti-piracy campaign, the Philippine Navy has increased its patrols in the country's waters and has established special task forces to counteract piracy, terrorism and other violent maritime threats. In an effort to further enhance its capabilities, the Philippine Navy has also embarked on a fifteen-year modernization programme aimed at acquiring new platforms and upgrade of its bases, communications equipment and training of its personnel. The Philippine Navy is also set to acquire patrol ships and other equipment from the United States to upgrade its capabilities. To further improve its surveillance capabilities, the Philippine Navy also established seven Coast Watch Stations to monitor vessel traffic in the country's vital sea lanes and critical chokepoints.

Other agencies involved in maritime law enforcement have enhanced their collaborative endeavours to further strengthen the government's campaign against the threat. In General Santos City, an agreement was signed among the local government, the PN, PA and the PCG to deploy elements from the Civilian Armed Forces Geographical Unit as escorts onboard fishing boats in Sarangani Bay. Plans are also afoot to deploy sea marshals from the PCG, AFP and PNP aboard passenger/cargo vessels in light of the growing threat of maritime terrorism. These agencies have also cooperated with the International Maritime Bureau-Regional Piracy Centre in Kuala Lumpur, Malaysia. The center monitors the global piracy situation and its state-of-the art database on piracy has greatly helped them in analysing piracy trends and developments worldwide.

At the national level, the government has enacted laws and other initiatives that will address piracy, terrorism and other maritime threats. Significant among them is the creation of the Philippine Centre for Transnational Crimes. Said agency is responsible for the formulation and implementation of a concerted programme of action on law enforcement, intelligence and other agencies for the prevention and control of transnational crimes.

The Philippines and Regional Cooperation

Philippine maritime law enforcement agencies recognize the value of cooperative endeavours in combating the scourge of piracy. As such, the country has been active in regional anti-piracy initiatives. For example, the PCG has increased its cooperation with its foreign counterparts to improve its capabilities in countering piracy and lawlessness at sea through information exchanges, joint patrol exercises, training and other collaborative efforts. Some of these recent endeavours include:

1. Active participating in the Regional Experts Meeting in Combating Piracy and Armed Robbery Against Ships;
2. Signing and implementing bilateral agreements between the PCG and Indonesian Coast Guard on search and rescue and anti-piracy efforts;
3. Signing and implementing an agreement between the PCG and the Korean National Maritime Police Agency for maritime law enforcement training against piracy and trafficking of drugs and firearms; and
4. Conducting joint patrol exercises between the PCG and the Japanese Coast Guard for search-and-rescue and anti-piracy operations.

The Philippine Navy has also increased its cooperation with its foreign counterparts to further improve its campaign against piracy through information exchange, joint naval exercises, and training. For example, the Philippine Navy is involved in several bilateral and multilateral naval exercises with the United States and its ASEAN neighbours, particularly Malaysia and Indonesia where it has common borders. The Philippine Navy also has a border crossing and joint patrol agreement with the Indonesian navy to monitor and secure through coordinated joint patrols the movement of people, goods and services in their common borders against piracy and lawless activities at sea. The country has also signed several bilateral and multilateral agreements with other countries to further strengthen the campaign against piracy and terrorism. Overall, these activities have given Philippine law enforcement agencies opportunities for more intelligence exchange and interaction, foreign training and military exercises. For example, the Philippine Government has signed the U.S.-ASEAN (Association of Southeast Asian Nations) Anti-Terrorism Treaty and the Anti-terrorism Agreement with Malaysia, Indonesia and Cambodia which provide mechanisms for enhancing border security, joint training exercises and sharing of intelligence.

Conclusion and Prognosis

Piracy and sea armed robbery against vessels will remain to be a major security concern for the Philippines in the coming years. The problem is expected to worsen as the country is on the verge of an economic crisis that will force a portion of the population to look to alternative means of livelihood, particularly those in Southern Philippines. The unresolved insurgency and separatism in the country may contribute to the prevalence of piracy as rebels will increasingly look to piracy as alternative financing scheme while conventional sources of funds start to dry up due to efforts to clamp down on terrorism. Meanwhile, as anti-terrorism campaigns heat-up on the ground, terrorists operating in the Philippines may look towards the sea to carry out their political agenda.

The government acknowledges the importance of containing this modern scourge of the sea. Containing piracy will remain to be a primary concern of the Philippine Government, notwithstanding current limitations set by the current force mix. While there is a continuing move to improve capabilities of local maritime law enforcement agencies through a modest program to acquire more assets, these are deemed inadequate given the immensity of the country's numerous waterways. At present, the enhancement of inter-agency as well as bilateral and multilateral cooperation (and coordination) will prove to be an effective force multiplier at a time when the country continues to be beset by a lack of adequate security and financial assets.

Note

[1]   The piracy cases being referred to are those that took place in the high seas.

4

Political Piracy and Maritime Terrorism: A Comparison between the Straits of Malacca and the Southern Philippines

Stefan Eklöf Amirell

Introduction

Since the 11 September 2001 terrorist attacks on the World Trade Centre in New York (9/11), the threat of a terrorist attack targetting the maritime sector has gained considerable attention, both in the international media and in international fora such as the International Maritime Organization (IMO). In comparison with the aviation sector, where security immediately improved considerably in the wake of 9/11, the maritime sector seemed to provide terrorists with a wealth of easy or soft targets. Even though a range of measures have since been implemented in order to improve maritime security, it still seems much easier for terrorists to hijack a ship than an aeroplane.

This chapter will discuss the twin problems of political piracy and maritime terrorism in Southeast Asia. Even though it may often be difficult in practice to separate the two phenomena from one another — and from "ordinary", non-political piracy — the distinction is useful, on a theoretical level, in order to identify the main characteristics of the different threats that maritime crime and terrorism currently pose. Both political piracy and maritime terrorism can be seen as special sub-categories of piracy broadly defined. They differ from most forms of common piracy, however, in that they are in principle perpetrated for public — rather than private — ends.[1] Thus, the main criteria for defining political piracy revolves around the issue of motive: It is not carried out for the purpose of private economic gain, but rather for the purpose of generating funds for political, ideological or religious, struggle — usually an armed insurgency. Admittedly, the distinction may be a fine one, as common banditry is often cloaked in political, ideological or religious pretexts. However, the blurred boundaries between political piracy and "ordinary" piracy — or, more broadly put, between a political struggle and banditry — does not make the distinction less valuable. On the contrary, for practical purposes, it is all the more important to identify the most fundamental motives behind the specific piratical activity in order to identify and deploy the most efficient counter-measures.

Just like political piracy, acts of maritime terrorism are perpetrated in order to promote a political, ideological or religious cause. What distinguishes maritime terrorism from political and other forms of piracy, however, is the focus on violence as a means of creating havoc or instilling fear in a population or the general public. In contrast to other forms of piracy, where the motive is driven by economics, the objective of maritime terrorism is the very violence constituting the attacks.[2] Again, the boundaries may be blurred, but the distinction is useful in order to identify the required responses and levels of security needed.

Political Piracy in the Malacca Straits

Aside from the problem of "ordinary" piracy, the Malacca Straits have in the past few years seen an increase in what can best be described as "political piracy" perpetrated by members of the Free Aceh Movement (GAM, *Gerakan Aceh Merdeka*). The organization, which was founded in 1976, has been fighting an armed struggle for Acehnese independence from the Indonesian central government, and piracy — including the kidnapping of crew members for ransom — seems to have become a source of funding for that struggle in the last few years, at least for some sections of the organization.

According to the International Maritime Bureau (IMB), the first reported incident involving kidnappings for ransom off the Acehnese coast occurred on 25 June 2001. The Indonesian-flagged tanker *MT Tirta Niaga IV* had anchored off the west coast of Aceh to conduct engine repairs when a group of pirates boarded the ship and looted the vessel of cash and valuables. The pirates then abducted the master and second officer and took them ashore. The second officer was released a few days later after negotiations, but the master was held hostage for more than six months before being released, reportedly after a ransom of US$30,000 was paid.[3]

The attack on the *Tirta Niaga IV* seems, at least from the start, to have been an opportunistic attack by coastal villagers with no evidence of GAM involvement. Two months later, at the end of August 2001, however, the *MV Ocean Silver* was attacked by a group of pirates armed with guns and a grenade launcher while passing the east coast of Aceh in the northern part of the Straits of Malacca. Six of the crew members, including the master, were taken ashore and held hostage. The remaining six crew members were left onboard for three days before being rescued by an Indonesian naval vessel. The pirates reportedly demanded a ransom of US$34,000 from the ship owner as a "financial contribution" to the struggle for Aceh's independence.[4]

A GAM spokesman, Ishak Daud, denied that the organization had anything to do with the kidnappings. He is reported to have claimed instead that the incident had been staged by the Indonesian military in order to make GAM look like terrorists in the eyes of the international community and asked rhetorically, "How could we have pirated that ship when the waters of Aceh are daily crawling with war vessels of the Indonesian Navy which has stepped up its patrols?" At the same time, however, he claimed that only GAM — and not the Indonesian Navy — was able to secure the Malacca Straits for the safety of shipping. He also seemed tacitly to acknowledge GAM's involvement in the incident, demanding that ship owners recognize GAM's claim to sovereignty over Acehnese waters: "If they [the shippers] do not want to seek permission from us, then they should not blame the GAM if cases such as experienced by the Honduran-flagged Ocean Silver ship repeat itself again."[5]

In the three years following the attack on the *Ocean Silver*, a number of similar incidents have occurred in the northern parts of the Straits, most of which were close to the Acehnese coast. Other incidents have also taken place further to the south, off the coast of the Indonesian province of North Sumatra, close to the Malaysian side of the Straits. The IMB also recorded five incidents, which involved kidnappings in the Straits in 2002, and another four in the following year, with such figures only probably being the tip of the iceberg.[6] Victimized ships include not only commercial vessels, but also local fishing boats and barter trade boats. Indeed, these pirate activities seem to have become a major threat to fishermen on both sides of the Straits. For example, in the first two weeks of August 2002, six Indonesian fishing boats with forty-six crew members went missing, with kidnappers reportedly demanding US$88,000 for the release of each vessel.[7] In January 2003, a North Sumatran businessman who owned a number of fishing vessels told the *Jakarta Post* that different groups of armed pirates extorted between one and two million Indonesian rupiah (US$110 to $220) in order not to loot fishing boats at sea. Vessels sometimes had to pay up to four million rupiah (US$450) on a single day for all the groups they came across.[8] In the first four months of 2004, moreover, at least thirty vessels, including fifteen Indonesian fishing boats, were attacked off the coast of Aceh and North Sumatra. In May the same year, the director of the North Sumatra Fishery Office, Ridwan Batubara, estimated that 8,000 fishing boats — two thirds of the province's fishing fleet — were not operating because of the threat of piracy.[9]

While most of the attacks on fishing boats are not reported by the IMB, it also seems that many kidnappings of crew members of commercial vessels go unreported. According to the regional director of the IMB's Piracy Reporting Centre in Kuala Lumpur, Noel Choong, ransoms demanded by the kidnappers are usually considered quite "reasonable" by international standards — typically a few thousand dollars for each person — something which encourages ship owners to pay out the kidnapper's ransom rather than report an attack to the authorities or the IMB, thereby further risking the lives of the hostages.[10]

The Indonesian authorities, as we have seen, blamed GAM for the *Ocean Blessing* attack in 2001, as well as for other kidnap-and-ransom attacks in the northern parts of the Malacca Straits. In February 2004, these allegations seemed to have been substantiated as the Indonesian Navy sank a vessel, the *MV Champion XIX*, which had been hijacked, reportedly by GAM rebels.[11] Allegations made by the Indonesian authorities of GAM involvement in piracy and other criminal activities, however, warrant caution, because the Indonesian authorities clearly have an interest in weakening GAM's international legitimacy by associating the organization with a host of criminal activities.[12] According to Noel Choong of the IMB, it is uncertain whether the pirate attacks outside Aceh are the doings of GAM rebels or ordinary bandits. Based on testimonies from former hostages received by the IMB, there is some indication that at least some members

of the organization have been involved in certain attacks.[13] Further
supporting the allegations of GAM involvement are indications that
members of the organization have been involved in a string of kidnappings
and hijackings of vehicles on land, especially in 2001 and 2002.[14]

Criminal activities — including piracy, kidnappings and drug trafficking
— seem to be significant sources of funding for GAM, and analysts have
in recent years speculated that the organization may be undergoing a
process of criminalization. According to Kirsten Schulze, however, the
kidnappings for ransom are almost certainly not endorsed by GAM's
central leadership in Sweden, the strategy of which in recent years has
been to try to gain support from the international community for the goal
of Acehnese independence.[15] It thus seems more plausible that those
responsible for the pirate attacks are, as put by Schulze, "criminal elements
within GAM or groups abusing the GAM label for personal gain".[16]

Moreover, just as GAM's central leadership does not seem to endorse
criminal activities, the organization has been careful not to associate itself
with international terrorist organizations such as the al-Qaeda or the
Jemaah Islamiyah (JI), which is often affiliated with it. GAM's main
ideological foundation is Acehnese nationalism, and Islam, in that context,
is an integral part of the organization's ideology.[17] Islam, however, is
mainly seen as reflecting Acehnese identity and culture, and Islamist
political aspirations — especially in the international context — are
downplayed. The group has rejected allegations that it would have ties to
international terrorist organizations, and, according to Leonard C. Sebastian,
this claim was supported by senior Indonesian military officials in Banda
Aceh in mid-2002.[18] According to Sebastian:

> GAM had rejected the initiative of Osama bin Laden's deputy Ayman
> Al Zawahiri when he visited Aceh in June 2000 with the aim of setting up
> al-Qaeda training bases in Aceh. In a sense, GAM possesses significant
> independent sources of funds, as well as an ideology that is secularist. Its
> intention is to set up an independent Sultanate in Aceh and is unlikely to
> be drawn to al-Qaeda's cause while fighting for independence from
> Indonesian rule. Furthermore, while Aceh may be a devoutly Muslim
> province, its society is pluralistic and minorities are well accepted and
> protected and therefore unlikely to gravitate to the insular Islamic ideologies
> championed by the groups like al-Qaeda.[19]

GAM thus seems unlikely to involve itself in any maritime terrorist
activity, both because of its apparent lack of established connections
with international terrorist organizations and because the movement
tries too hard to court international support for its political cause which

is distinct from the politico-religious projects of the al-Qaeda and the JI. It is even doubtful if such activities qualify as political piracy, or if they simply should be seen as acts of banditry and thus "ordinary" piracy carried out by criminal elements within GAM, or groups abusing the GAM label for personal gain.

The Threat of Maritime Terrorism in Southeast Asia

The Malacca Straits

Most of the concerns regarding a maritime terrorist attack in Southeast Asia have in recent years focused on the southern parts of the Straits of Malacca and Singapore. There appears to be two main reasons for this. First, it is clear that the region is of major strategic importance as a bottleneck for international maritime trade. An attack blocking the Straits of Malacca would force vessels to take the detour around the west coast of Sumatra, something which would have large economic consequences, not least for Europe, Japan and the United States. Second, the threat of "petty" piracy — which for the last twenty-five years has been a relatively minor security concern for commercial vessels in the southern parts of the Straits — seems, at least to some observers, to indicate a greater risk for terror attacks against transiting commercial vessels. The assumption seems to be that the pirates who frequently attack commercial vessels for the purpose of robbing them, might get the idea of perpetrating a terrorist attack, for example by sinking a ship or using it as a floating bomb against a major port city.[20]

Far-fetched as such assumptions may seem — certainly as regards the beer-drinking petty pirates described by Eric Frécon in this volume — a number of developments in the wake of the 9/11 attacks indicate that international terrorists have developed plans for an attack in the Straits of Malacca. Some pieces of evidence seem rather flimsy, such as a video, found by American forces in Afghanistan in 2001, showing the movements of Malaysian naval vessels, or the unfounded allegations, reported by The Economist and other respected news media in 2003, that terrorists had hijacked a chemical tanker in the Straits of Malacca in order to practice navigation — allegedly the "equivalent of the al-Qaeda hijackers who perpetrated the 9/11 attacks going to flying school in Florida".[21] Other pieces of evidence, however, indicate that terrorists indeed seem to have been making plans for mounting a maritime terrorist attack in the Malacca Straits area. In December 2001, Singapore's Internal Security Department arrested thirteen JI members for planning a string of attacks against Western targets in the city-state. According to a report issued by Singapore's Ministry of Home Affairs, one of the group's major plans was to attack a U.S. naval vessel in the Johore Straits. Detailed planning — including topographical maps, operational planning and video footage — had been made for a sea-borne suicide bomb attack using a small vessel against a steaming naval ship in the most narrow part of the Straits. Apparently, the plan had first been conceived in the mid-1990s, but had then not been pursued by the Singapore-based JI members because they lacked the operational capacity to carry out an attack. It was subsequently revived in early 2001, when two unidentified Middle Easterners approached the Singapore group for information about the U.S. military vessels in Singapore.[22]

The arrests in Singapore in the end of 2001 apparently averted the immediate threat of a terrorist attack against U.S. vessels in Singapore, but did little to cripple the JI. On 12 October 2002 — incidentally, only a few days after the al-Qaeda suicide bomb attack on the French super tanker *Limburg* outside the coast of Yemen — the organization mounted its most lethal terrorist attack so far against the Sari Night Club in Bali, killing around 200 people. The Bali bombings shifted much of the focus in the so-called "war on terrorism" from the Middle East to Southeast Asia. At the same time, the attack against the *Limburg* raised concerns over the possibility that terrorists in the region might attempt a maritime terrorist attack in the Straits of Malacca.

If recent information from intelligence sources, as reported in the media, is to be believed, then such a scenario may be more possible than it initially imagined. In August 2004, the director of Indonesia's State Intelligence Agency, Abdullah Makhmud Hendropriyono, said that senior JI operatives in detention had admitted that attacks on shipping in the Malacca Straits had been contemplated in the recent past.[23] Around the same time it was also reported that U.S. intelligence officials had intercepted communications between JI activists revealing a plot to seize a vessel in the area using local pirates. The ship in question was supposed to have been wired with explosives and either directed against another vessel, detonated in a port or used to threaten the busy sea lanes in the area.[24]

However, the fact that no such attack has yet been attempted in the Straits of Malacca indicates that the JI — and other terrorist groups operating in the area — lack the operational capacity to stage such an attack. The most likely target in order to create the greatest possible havoc is a shipment of volatile cargo, such Liquefied Petrol Gas (LPG), Liquefied Natural Gas (LNG) or other refined oil products. Triggering an explosion of LPG or

LNG-laden cargo, however, is relatively difficult, as most vessels carrying such cargoes are relatively modern vessels equipped with robust cargo security systems operated by reputable firms with established safety records. According to the Organization for Economic Cooperation and Development it is thus "relatively unlikely that a terrorist group could successfully rig the explosion of a LPG/LNG vessel's cargo".[25]

Second, it seems difficult, at least today, for the JI and other terrorist groups like it to recruit local pirates to carry out an attack. The arrest of a pirate gang in Riau in February demonstrated that local pirates from the area have recently offered their services for hire to outsiders, but so far, it seems, only to international crime syndicates.[26] Since mid-2004, however, the Malacca Straits states have taken what appear to be decisive measures to combat piracy and other non-traditional threats to maritime security in the Straits. On 20 July 2004, Indonesia, Malaysia and Singapore signed an agreement establishing coordinated patrols — called Operation Malsindo — along the Straits. Just as in 1992, when bilateral agreements between Indonesia and Singapore and between Indonesian and Malaysia also established coordinated patrols, these measures may be likely to bring about some decline in the number of pirate attacks in the area. The efforts have also led to the arrest of a number of alleged pirates and perpetrators of other maritime crimes.[27] Moreover, being driven by economic survival, local pirates are more likely to be enticed by any rewards from the authorities in providing any known information of a terrorist plot as compared to the possible remuneration that terrorists might offer pirates for their services. Overall, the case can be made that the threat of a maritime terrorist attack involving a commercial cargo vessel in the Straits of Malacca does not seem imminent at the moment — although such a scenario should by no means be disregarded in the efforts to provide a secure maritime environment in the area.

The Southern Philippines

Compared with the Straits of Malacca, the problem of piracy is much more endemic in the Southern Philippines. Piracy — as well as smuggling, kidnappings and other forms of banditry — has been rife in the area at least since the end of World War II, when declining state authority combined with the proliferation of surplus military equipment, including arms and boat engines, helped creating new opportunities for smugglers and pirates in the border region between Indonesia, Malaysia and the Philippines. Since 1972, the Southern Philippines have been plagued by insurgency, with rebels demanding independence for the predominantly Muslim parts of the Southern Philippines. In this context, all of the major insurgent groups — the Moro National Liberation Front (MNLF), the Moro Islamic Liberation Front (MILF) and the Abu Sayyaf Group (ASG) — have used piracy as a means of financing their struggle.[28]

Both the MILF and the ASG were formed as splinter groups from the MNLF — the MILF in 1984 and the ASG in the early 1990s — as a result of disaffection with the 1976 Tripoli Agreement between the MNLF and Philippine Government. They both claim to fight for an independent Islamic state in the Southern Philippines and both are known to have ties to international terrorist organizations such as al-Qaeda and JI — although MILF leaders publicly deny having such ties. In spite of the attention, which the ASG has attracted in international media in recent years, it is the MILF, which is the driving force behind political Islam — in its extreme — in the Philippines today. The group has an estimated between 12,000 and 15,000 followers, compared with the ASG's 200 to 500 members. In contrast to the ASG, the MILF has publicly renounced terrorism and has so far not been listed as a Foreign Terrorist Organization (FTO) by the U.S. Department of State. MILF leaders have also constantly denied having any ties to the ASG.[29]

Members of the MILF seem to use piracy mainly as a means of fund raising — that is, political piracy as defined here — but the organization has also been accused of perpetrating maritime terrorist attacks. The most serious attack, which the Philippine authorities blamed on the MILF, was the bombing of the inter-island ferry *Our Lady of the Mediatrix* in Iligan Bay off Mindanao in February 2000, which killed around forty people. The evidence indicates MILF involvement in the attack, although the organization denied responsibility for it, claiming that it does not target civilians.[30] The attack on *Our Lady of the Mediatrix*, however, should be seen as part of a wider trend of increasing terror attacks in the Philippines since 2000, including several bomb attacks on provincial cities and towns in Mindanao. Police investigations point to the involvement of the MILF in several of these attacks, although it is uncertain to what extent the use of terrorism is condoned by the organization's leaders. In a recent report on terrorism and the peace process in the Southern Philippines, the International Crisis Group identified three main explanations to the rising terrorist activity in relation to the MILF. First, the terror attacks may be part of a mixed political strategy, deliberately pursued by the MILF leaders, to put pressure on the Philippine Government and the international community to find a solution to the conflict in the Southern Philippines.

Second, the terror attacks may be the work of more militant factions of the MILF, possibly in alliance with the ASG, JI or other external elements. Finally, the MILF leaders may actually be unaware of, or unable to control, terrorist activities that make use of the organization's territory, resources or followers.[31]

Regardless of which of these three possibilities is closest to the truth, fears of maritime terrorist attacks involving MILF followers deserve to be taken seriously for at least three reasons. First, the MILF does have links to regional terrorist organizations, such as the JI, which has been making plans for maritime terrorist attacks in Southeast Asia. Second, MILF members have been involved in numerous pirate attacks in the past and its members clearly possess the necessary skills to perpetrate a maritime terrorist attack. Third, the organization, or at least some of its followers, has been involved in terrorist attacks, including at least one maritime terrorist attack, in recent years.

The smaller outfit that constitutes the ASG has also been accused of perpetrating maritime terrorist attacks, and here the evidence seems more conclusive than the case of the MILF. The ASG is considered to be a terrorist organization by the United States and has since its formation been more associated with indiscriminate violence and the targeting of civilians than either the MNLF or the MILF. The group is known to have long-standing ties to international terrorist organizations, particularly the al-Qaeda from which it has received training as well as direct financial assistance. The motives for the group's actions, however, are disputed. In contrast to the MILF, the ASG does not have a strategy for creating a sovereign Islamic homeland in the Southern Philippines, and the group has been accused by other Muslim organizations, including the MILF, of violating the fundamental principles of Islam. In addition, the Philippine government sees the group as more of a criminal bandit organization than as a political or religious movement.[32] Both political and pecuniary motives are obviously at play in the case of the ASG, or, as a recent report by the U.S. Department of State put it, the organization "has primarily used terror for financial profit".[33]

The ASG has also to a greater extent than the MILF been involved in maritime terrorist and political pirate attacks. The organization first made its existence and cause known to the rest of the world through an attack on a Christian missionary vessel, the *MV Doulos*, in the port of Zamboanga in Southwest Mindanao in August 1991. The attackers fired a grenade on the ship in retaliation for the missionaries' alleged defamation of Islam, leaving two people dead.[34] Another two attacks, in which members of the ASG were implied, took place in early 1996, when "pirates cum Muslim insurgents" descending from the sea, looted Sempoerna, a small town on the east coast of Malaysian Sabah.[35]

In April 2000, the ASG gained international fame for the abduction of a group of twenty-one people — ten of whom were foreign tourists — from the Malaysian diving resort of Sipadan. Claiming responsibility for the kidnappings, the ASG reportedly demanded that a number of Muslim terrorists, among them the perpetrator of the 1993 bombing of the World Trade Centre in New York, Ramzi Yousef, be released from prison. However, as the group realized that these demands would not be fulfilled, the group eventually released the hostages after protracted negotiations in exchange for ransom money. Through the "mediation" of Libya, around ten million dollars were paid for the release of the foreign hostages, and Malaysian businessmen collected some five million dollars for the release of the Malaysian hostages.[36] The money enabled the ASG to acquire more followers and more weapons. Moreover, apparently strengthened by the success of the Sipadan abductions, the ASG — or at least some of its members — seems to have begun to specialize in kidnapping foreigners and holding them for ransom. For example, in the following year, three Americans and seventeen Filipinos were abducted from a tourist resort in Palawan in the Southern Philippines, and in 2003, six workers — three Indonesians, two Malaysians and one Filipino — were abducted from the Borneo Paradise Eco Farm Resort on the east coast of Sabah. Both of these abductions resulted in the killings of several of the hostages.[37]

Apart from the Sipadan kidnappings, the most spectacular attack involving the ASG in recent years has been the bombing of the *SuperFerry 14* in the Manila Bay in February 2004. Shortly before the ferry left Manila for Baclod and Davao in Mindanao, an ASG member, Rodendo Cain Dellosa, placed a cardboard box with 3.6 kilograms of TNT onboard the ship. The bomb was detonated an hour after departure, causing an explosion which killed over 100 people.[38] Even though the ASG claimed responsibility for the attack, the Philippine authorities initially — possibly because of pressure from the ship owners — rejected suspicions that the explosion was caused by a terrorist attack. In October 2004, however, the police investigation concluded that an explosive device indeed caused the attack. The investigation also revealed that the ferry company, WG&A, had received an extortion letter prior to the bombing. The letter, which was believed to have been signed by the ASG's leader Khadaffy Janjalani, reportedly demanded US$1 million from the ferry company for the unhampered use of the waters of Mindanao.[39]

As has been suggested in the media, in spite of the devastation and large number of civilian casualties, the bombing of the *SuperFerry 14* does not necessarily prove that the ASG under Janjalani's leadership recently has been moving away from kidnappings and extortion to a more politically motivated struggle involving terrorism as a major strategy.[40] Just as in the case of the kidnappings during the past four years, the main motive behind the ferry bombing seems to have been related to extortion activities and not to any particular political goal. If this is indeed is the case, then the Philippine authorities seem to be correct in treating the ASG not as a political organization, but rather, as a criminal bandit gang. In the same vein, Eric Gutierrez has suggested the label "entrepreneurs in violence" to describe the ASG's followers. The description implies that the ASG's members excel in violence, but do not have any serious political goals. For these reasons, the organization is also susceptible to infiltration by outsiders, such as, for example, other insurgent groups, various criminal organizations and local warlords — all of which, at one time or another, may have use for the group's services and expertise in violence.[41]

Conclusion

Much has been said about the possible nexus between piracy and (maritime) terrorism in the Straits of Malacca. However, as far as hard evidence or even credible indications go, there is little to suggest that the threat is imminent. There is nothing which indicates that the GAM members who seem to be involved in piracy and kidnappings in the northern parts of the Straits of Malacca are linked to international terrorist organizations. In addition, GAM's strategy to date has been not to associate itself with other organizations, criminal and/or terrorist in nature. There is even less to suggest that the petty pirates of the southern part of the Malacca Straits and the Singapore Straits would be linked to international terrorists.

By contrast, the indications that the problems of piracy and terrorism are linked to one another are much more conclusive in the case of the Southern Philippines. In contrast to the Straits of Malacca area, there is ample evidence that local insurgent groups — particularly the MILF and the ASG — have links to groups such as the JI and the al-Qaeda. Both groups have been involved in violent acts that qualify as political piracy, but border on maritime terrorism because of the indiscriminate use of violence against civilians. Even though both groups have so far confined their activities to the Philippines in principle, their international connections and ideological foundations should raise concerns that they might try to mount a maritime terrorist attack in other adjacent Southeast Asian waters.

   In spite of the great interest in, and worries over, the threat of maritime terrorism in Southeast Asia, the February 2004 attack on the *SuperFerry 14* in Manila Bay has attracted very little attention outside the Philippines. Worries over a possible connection between piracy and terrorism in Southeast Asia remain focused on the Straits of Malacca. This bias seems mainly to be motivated by the Straits' importance as a major international shipping lane and the fact that an attack in the area — in contrast to the Southern Philippines — would have far-reaching consequences for the global economy. However, in terms of the individual and collective human suffering of a society, the maritime violence in the Southern Philippines has so far been more serious than in the Straits of Malacca region.

Notes

1   "Piracy" will, for the present purposes, be defined broadly as an act of violence carried out upon the ocean or unappropriated lands or within the territory of a state through descent from the sea by a body of men or women acting independently of any sovereign political entity. This definition is adapted from Henry A. Ormerud, *Piracy in the Ancient World* (Liverpool: The University of Liverpool Press and London: Hodder and Stoughton, 1924), p. 60. Regarding the distinction between political piracy and other forms of piracy, see Samuel P. Menefee, "Terrorism at Sea: The Historical Development of an International Legal Response", in *Violence at Sea*, edited by Eric F. Ellen (Paris: ICC Publishing S.A., 1986), p. 192.

2   The definition of the concept of "terrorism" is a contestable one. For an interesting discussion, see for example, C. A. J. Coady, "Terrorism and Innocence", *The Journal of Ethics* 8, no. 1 (2004): 37–58. For present purposes, however, it is enough to establish that terrorism, in contrast to other forms of piracy, is defined by its use of terror — that is, creating havoc and fear.

3   *Piracy and Armed Robbery against Ships: Annual Report 1st January – 31st December 2001* (United Kingdom: ICC-International Maritime Bureau, 2002) p. 19; and John S. Burnett, *Dangerous Waters: Modern Piracy and Terror on the High Seas* (New York: Plume, 2002) p. 324.

4   *Kompas*, 30 August 2001.

5   *Agence France Presse*, 3 September 2001.

6   See *Piracy and Armed Robbery against Ships: Annual Report 1st January – 31st December 2002* (United Kingdom: ICC-International Maritime Bureau, 2003), pp. 26–47; *Piracy and Armed Robbery against Ships: Annual Report 1st January – 31st December 2003* (United Kingdom: ICC-International Maritime Bureau, 2004), pp. 27–44.

[7]   *Kompas*, 14 August 2002. See also *New Straits Times*, 4 November 2003, about attacks against Malaysian fishermen from Hutan Melintang in Southern Perak.

[8]   *Jakarta Post*, 13 January 2003.

[9]   *Jakarta Post*, 10 May 2004.

[10] Interview by the author, Kuala Lumpur, 16 January 2004.

[11] See *Jakarta Post*, 14 February 2004.

[12] Incidentally, there have also been allegations that sections of the Indonesian military have been involved in pirate attacks in the northern parts of the Malacca Strait as well as allegations that security officials extort money from fishermen in North Sumatra in order to provide protection from pirate attacks; see for example *The Star*, 1 December 2002, and *Jakarta Post*, 13 August 2002.

[13] Interview by the author, Kuala Lumpur, 16 January 2004. The Director of the IMB, P. Mukundan, likewise concluded that the attack on the Malaysian tanker *Penrider* in August 2003 may have been conducted by "criminals posting as GAM rebels"; see Mukundan, P. "Terrorism and Piracy Threats: Scourge of Piracy in Southeast Asia — Any Improvements in 2004?". *Regional Outlook Forum* (Singapore: Institute of Southeast Asian Studies, 2004), p. 4.

[14] Kirsten Schulze, "The Free Aceh Movement (GAM): Anatomy of a Separatist Organisation", *Policy Studies* 2 (Washington D.C.: East-West Centre Washington, 2004), p. 28.

[15] Ibid., pp. 28–29.

[16] Ibid., p. 29.

[17] Ibid., p. 7.

[18] Leonard C. Sebastian, "The Indonesian Dilemma: How to Participate in the War on Terror Without Becoming a National Security State", *After Bali: The Threat of Terrorism in Southeast Asia*, edited by Kumar Ramakrishna and See Seng Tan (Singapore: World Scientific, 2004), p. 365.

[19] Ibid.

[20] See for example, "Peril on the Sea", *The Economist*, 4–10 October 2003, pp. 61–62. See also Adam J. Young, and Mark J. Valencia, "Conflation of Piracy and Terrorism in Southeast Asia: Rectitude and Utility," *Contemporary Southeast Asia* 25, no. 2 (2003), for a critical perspective on the blurring of the piracy and maritime terrorism in Southeast Asia.

[21] "Going for the Jugular", *The Economist*, 12–18 June 2004, pp. 53–54, and "Peril on the Sea", *The Economist*, 4–10 October 2003, pp. 61–62. The source for the allegation concerned the hijacking of the *MT Dewi Madrim* on 26 March in the 4 October article was a dubious report by Aegis Defence Services, a London-based defence and security consultancy; for a further discussion on the issue, see the chapter by Carolin Liss in this volume.

[22] *White Paper: The Jemaah Islamiyah Arrests and the Threat of Terrorism*. Ministry of Home Affairs of the Government of Singapore (Singapore: Ministry of Home Affairs, 2003), pp. 29–30.

[23]   A. M. Hendropriyono, "RI-S'pore ties: Opportunity Lost", *Jakarta Post*,
       25 August 2004.
[24]   Philip Sherwell, Massoud Ansari and Marianne Kearney, "Al Qaeda terrorist
       'plan to turn tanker into a floating bomb' ", *The Telegraph*, Internet edition,
       12 September 2004. <http://www.telegraph.co.uk/news/main.jhtml?xml=/
       news/2004/09/12/wterr12.xml&sSheet=/portal/2004/09/12/ixportal.html>.
[25]   *Security in Maritime Transport: Risk Factors and Economic Impact*. Organization
       for Economic Cooperation and Development (Paris: Directorate for Science,
       Technology and Industry, Organization for Economic Cooperation and
       Development, 2003) p. 12. See pp. 8–12 for an assessment of this type of threat.
[26]   See Tom McCawley, "Sea of Trouble", *Far Eastern Economic Review*, 27 May
       2004, pp. 50–52. In 2003, the Indonesian magazine *Latitudes* also reported that
       pirates in Riau had begun to offer their services for hire. See Tantyo Bangun,
       "Private Services", *Latitudes* 33 (October 2003): 25.
[27]   See Fadli and Endy M. Bayuni, "Show of Force Launched to Protect Vital
       Strait", *Jakarta Post*, 21 July 2004, and "Navy Seizes 128 Boats off Batam",
       Jakarta Post, 6 September 2004. For the anti-piracy measures implemented in
       1992, see Stefan Eklöf, *Pirates in Paradise: A Modern History of Southeast Asia's
       Maritime Marauders* (Copenhagen: NIAS Press, 2005).
[28]   In the 1980s, MNLF rebels were accused of looting fishing vessels and extorting
       money from fishermen in order to finance their struggle. The MNLF pirates
       were known as *ambak pare* — "jump, buddy" — from the order they allegedly
       used to give to their victims. See "A Tide of Pirates", *Asiaweek*, 27 May 1988,
       p. 28.
[29]   See Charles Donnelly, "Terrorism in the Southern Philippines: Contextualising
       the Abu Sayyaf Group as an Islamist Secessionist Organisation", a paper
       presented at the 15th Biennial Conference of the Asian Studies Association of
       Australia, Canberra, 29 June–2 July 2004, pp. 4–5; "Southern Philippines
       Backgrounder: Terrorism and the Peace Process", *International Crisis Group
       (ICG) Asia Report* no. 80, 13 July 2004, p. 1. For the list of Foreign Terrorist
       Organizations, see the U.S. Department of State's "Patterns of Global Terrorism
       2003: Appendix B", <http://www.state.gov/documents/organisation/
       31946.pdf>.
[30]   *Global Nation*, 26 February 2003 <http://www.inq7.net/globalnation/sec_new/
       2003/feb/26-03.htm>.
[31]   "Southern Philippines Backgrounder", p. 8.
[32]   Donnelly, "Terrorism in the Southern Philippines", 2004, p. 2, 4 and 5; and
       "Southern Philippines Backgrounder", p. 22.
[33]   "Patterns of Global Terrorism", p. 114.
[34]   Dépêche EDA (Eglise d'Asie), no. 121-16/11/1991, 1991, <http://
       eglasie.mepasie.org/1991/novembre/philippines/121/depeche8_1/>.
[35]   James Warren, "A Tale of Two Centuries: The Globalisation of Maritime Raiding
       and Piracy in Southeast Asia at the end of the Eighteenth and Twentieth

Centuries", ARI Working Paper, no. 2 (Singapore: Asia Research Institute and National University of Singapore, 2003) p. 18. The ASG is implied, because the perpetrators reportedly were insurgents armed with heavy weapons and were Tausug; an ethnic group from which the ASG draws a large number of its followers.

[36] Penny Crisp, "A Religious War Comes to Paradise", *Asiaweek*, 5 May 2000, pp. 20–22, and Deidre Sheehan, "Buying Trouble", *Far Eastern Economic Review*, 7 September 2000, p. 29.

[37] "Patterns of Global Terrorism", p. 114; Karl B. Kaufman, "Kidnappers Execute 5 Captives from Malaysian Resort; 1 Escapes", *Manila Times*, Internet edition, 29 October 2003 <http://www.manilatimes.net/national/2003/oct/29/top_stories/20031029top5.html>.

[38] Simon Elegant, "The Return of Abu Sayyaf", *Time Asia*, Internet edition, 23 August 2004 <http://www.time.com/time/asia/magazine/article/0,13673,501040830-686107,00.html>.

[39] "Arroyo Orders Arrest of Abu Leaders Linked in Ferry Blast", *Sun Star*, Internet edition, 12 October 2004 <http://www.sunstar.com.ph/static/net/2004/10/12/arroyo.orders.arrest.of.abu.leaders.linked.in.ferry.blast.html>.

[40] See Elegant, "The Return of Abu Sayyaf".

[41] Eric Gutierrez, "New Faces of Violence in Muslim Mindanao", *Rebels, Warlords and Ulama: A Reader on Muslim Separatism and the War in Southern Philippines*, edited by Kristina Gaerlan and Mara Stankovitch (Philippines: Institute for Popular Democracy, 2000), pp. 358–59.

5

Piracy and Armed Robbery at Sea along the Malacca Straits: Initial Impressions from Fieldwork in the Riau Islands

Eric Frécon

Introduction

The Franco-Spanish singer and political activist Manu Chao is very often a victim of piracy, but of the Internet kind rather than in the maritime realm. His famous Latin song "Welcome to Tijuana", which like many popular songs today, is constantly pirated over the Internet in infringement of the laws defending intellectual property rights. Although Manu Chao makes reference to the town of Tijuana bordering between the United States and Mexico, or between "the Empire and the new Barbarians" as Jean-Christophe Rufin describes, it is a reference that can easily be applied to the issue of modern piracy in Southeast Asia.[1] Indeed, to borrow his illustration, the Malacca Straits delineates a border between two particular worlds: On the one hand, the ordered world based on a nations-states system and, on the other hand, the underworld of criminal activities challenging state governance. It is probably against this background, that industrialized societies in the region such as those in Singapore and Malaysia, would regard modern-day pirates as a "sea hooligan[s]" and even a harbinger of "coming anarchy"[2] developing in this kind of "grey area", especially in the Malacca Straits.[3]

For this reason, the aim of this chapter is to offer another view of maritime piracy that is driven by actual field observations; specifically, from the "maritime ghettos" around the Indonesia archipelago. Hopefully, this endeavour may allow us to draw a more nuanced picture of modern Southeast Asian piracy beyond the wealth of statistics on this phenomenon. This chapter delivers its findings from preliminary field research carried out in the Riau islands in Indonesia where pirates are often suspected to reside. The author has carried out his research by making field observations of suspected pirates in their living environment, conducting interviews with residents and collecting testimonies.

The reports from the International Maritime Organization (IMO) and from the International Maritime Bureau (IMB) provide useful "clues" to the field researcher and have helped to frame the work of this chapter. To a large degree, the statistics are quite correct in making the impression that a new generation of pirates is hauling up "Jolly Roger" over the Southeast Asian seas. Firstly, while the total number of reported incidents piracy and (more correctly) armed robbery against ships decreased in the first six months of 2004, from 234 during the corresponding period of 2003 to 182, the Malacca Straits showed an increase, up to 20 attacks from 15 reported in the same period in 2003.[4] Pirates seem to withdraw into areas closer to their bases but some of them still go out of their den to other locations, where security is still lax. Today, the two main hot spots are generally off Aceh and off the Riau islands, at the entrance and the exit points of the Straits. Secondly, pirates seem to prefer to attack vessels that are underway rather than at berth or at anchor. This could be an outcome of the recently established IMO International Ship and Port Facility Code (ISPS). In Asia, they often attack especially vessels controlled by Indonesian or Singaporean companies. Thirdly, the IMB has reported the highest number of piracy-related killings in a decade. The latest piracy report reveals that 30 crew members were killed in attacks — twice as many as for the same period of 2003. Some experts depict pirates as being more and more desperate and attacks are involving more groups of heavily armed people and sometimes including several boats.

Some Social and Demographic Insights of Pirates

Today, regional pirates tend to be young in age against the traditional or legendary stereotypes of such individuals as being much older in their years. To be sure, there are "veteran" pirates though they seem to be disappearing from the scene for various reasons such as imprisonment, retirement through old age and death.

Imprisonment

Against the common perception about the absence of proper law enforcement against pirates in Indonesia, the Indonesian police do actually catch pirates and send them to jail from time to time. For example, there is an individual the author interviewed, named Mr Wong whom many people regard as the most notorious of Indonesian pirates until he was arrested in 1999 at a hotel on Batam Island. He was sentenced to six years of solitary confinement in Indonesia and was accused of having supervised the disappearance of several vessels in the seas of Southeast Asia. Mr Wong was transferred to the old reformatory prison establishment of Pekanbaru, in Sumatra. The conditions of detention were so severe that Mr Wong, who is nearing sixty, is constantly sick until today. When the author first met Mr Wong in 2002, he wanted to forget his past life as a pirate. The "shady business partners" of Mr Wong, who lead the triad from their office in East Asian cities, are even more mysterious and seem to have left him alone.[5]

In the first semester of 2004, there was an increase in attacks across Asia only on small vessels owned or controlled by companies from Indonesia or Singapore. On the other hand, big Japanese, Korean and Chinese vessels were less attacked. Moreover, there are fewer ships being hijacked in the Malacca Straits for conversion into *kapal hantu* or "phantom ships" in the South China Sea.[6] Among other things, this could be attributed to China's effort to deal with piracy off the Chinese coast arising from its participation in the World Trade Organization since the 1990s, in addition to the general stepping-up of counter piracy measures by the international community through greater cooperation and the use of technology during this period.

For these reasons, organized criminal syndicates and individuals such as Mr Wong may have been compelled to reduce the scale of their activities. Still, such pirates continue to benefit from the impasse in regional cooperation over matters such as "hot pursuit" between the national maritime patrols of the littoral states straddling the Malacca Straits, the continued corruption among the police authorities and their collusion with organized crime, and the lack of harsh laws and penalties for pirates who are caught.

Retirement

This case is maybe more frequent than imprisonment. Two former pirates the author met in Riau islands ceased their activities when the police became increasingly a threat. One of them is Marcus Uban whose clan lives in a charming housing complex in Batam. Uban is what many would regard as a "hooligan" who with time has become extremely successful at his trade. In an affable tone, he told the author about his "bohemian" years during which he set out to attack cargo ships in the Malacca Straits. Marcus Uban tells his story:

> In 1987, I left Timor to look for work in Jakarta. But I did not find any and I had to try my luck in Batam where I became a pirate in order to earn my living. Just like me, many came from miserable *kampung*. Singapore was rich; we were poor. So, we went to pillage the areas in the vicinity of Singapore (*laughs*). We targetted cargo ships. Fishermen? They don't have money (*laughs*)! If by chance the crew dared to resist a little, we used pistols and machine guns. Not *kris* (dagger) or rocket-launchers. But, [even then], we did not kill the people; we did not even hit them.

A few years later, the adventure ended for Uban as he further explains:

> Now, my companions have all left Indonesia because of the police who were looking for us. Many have switched to the smuggling of cigarettes from *Batu Merah* in Batam for example. As far as I am concerned, I am through with all that. I want to become a good man. I opened a karaoke outlet and I also have a hand in running a business in professional boxing.[7]

The second pirate, Yono, was a former chief of a small pirate gang. With his money, he decided to build his house near other retired pirates, in the residential district of the island where current pirates also reside. Now, Yono manages a taxi-boat business rather than a pirate outfit, even if pirates do work for him as his taxi-boat drivers during the day. Hence, it appears that there are other alternative jobs for former pirates. However, the piratical trade can be a hard habit to break. Like other old and former pirates, Yono has a hand in encouraging the rise of a younger generation of pirates. The author was told that in 2002, a group even came from as far as Palembang, from the south of Sumatra, to become apprentices.

The Demise of Old Pirates

In this island, where former and current pirates live in different districts, Nasrul[8] is renowned as a legend, a kind of "Robin Hood" of the sea among the community. From what the author was told, he used to burgle rich vessels after which he would distribute the plunder among people in the coastal villages. The village mosque and the footbridges have thus been built thanks to his booties from robbery at sea. Nasrul was the respected chief of the main pirate gang and of the village during the early nineties until his recent demise. Subsequently, both his wife and son left the island. People say that a rival gang murdered him after he talked with British journalists. In the village, most of the inhabitants, except a rival gang, miss him.

The Influx of New Pirates

Some of the young pirates the author interviewed in the Riau islands were eighteen years of age when they began to attack vessels in 2002. Their motivations at the time were specific: To rob ships. It is hard to imagine that these pirates live less than ten kilometres from Singapore, in their poor coastal village. The relative disparities in development and wealth between Singapore and Riau can be a hard reality for them to bear, especially if one aspires towards the good life. Like many other people, they have become tired of the Indonesian Government's broken promises of reaping the dividends of the "Asian miracle" and distributing them to the people. The adjacent island of Batam, for one, was expected to become, to borrow the analogy from Manu Chao once more, a new "Eldorado" at one time.

Instead, from the disenfranchised masses of the Asian economic boom, about 40,000 illegal immigrants swarmed shanty residences, according to a pastor who has been travelling in the Riau archipelago for many years. The atmosphere in this "Indonesian Far East" is a heavy and sombre one. The luxurious Novotel hotel seems to eclipse that of *Tanjung Uma*; a shanty village famous for its illegal immigrants. Most significantly, it is located close to Nagoya, formerly known as *Lubuk Bajak*; the "pirate mire". This mysterious island is also on the edge of a massive population explosion. In fact, the population is reported to have jumped from 38,000 inhabitants in 1990 to 500,000 around 2001.[9]

Deprived of the benefits of any economic growth, they are forced to turn towards petty crimes such as pick-pocketing and prostitution. For the price of a cheap beer, visitors can seek the sexual services of young women in the Riau islands. In addition to the burgeoning sex trade, there are a string of illegal activities related to organized crime.[10] Within the context of such an environment and factoring in the heavy shipping that passes through the region, groups and individuals with a maritime background

— their forefathers were fishing people or sailors — have a tendency to turn to piracy to supplement their income from other sources; legitimate or otherwise. In the end, it appears that the waters of the Malacca Straits continue to play out a modern version of brigandry of the Middle Ages, when robbers plied desolate roads and forests to prey on unsuspecting travellers.[11] Today, these robbers ply their trade at sea along vital SLOCs (Sea Lines of Communication) such as the Malacca Straits.

The Pirate Den of Kampung Hitam (Black Village)

On the island mentioned above, the pirates live in the small village of *Kampung Hitam* (Black Village). Even under the cover of a tourist, it is very difficult to ask people indirectly about piracy and armed robbery at sea. According to them, there are no more pirates to speak of. The common reply is usually *"Dulu saja!"* ("Only before!"). This reflects the continuing existence of an "omerta" or "law of silence" that governs the secrecy of triads and those who know them. Obviously, the statistics tell us that pirates still exist but almost no one dares to speak about it, except for an eighteen-year-old male, who went by the nickname "Zorino" and who grew up in Kampung Hitam.

Through the help of Zorino's local knowledge, the author has found that the island can be divided into two realms: A peaceful and orderly section, and a notorious suburban area. The main village falls into the former category. It looks like a peaceful locality, quieter than other islands of the Batam district. Like everywhere else in Indonesia, the main market area, with a road cutting through it, is colourful and the stalls bustle with life. Near the market, small beautiful houses accommodate former pirates who have now found other professions.[12] This picturesque scene would almost make one forget that pirates actually exist on this island.

However at the end of the market road, after a small post office, a left turn leads one to a pirate den. Here lies a bay divided into three parts: One for the police, another for local prostitutes, and the last one for pirates and smugglers. A small police office can be found at the exit of the bay. In its current state, this police station is a crude cabin facing the Straits. The local police are, no doubt, fully aware of the criminal activities that exist on the island and along the Straits. In fact, in order to reach the Straits, pirates have to pass their view on their way out. Some people the author spoke to have also commented that until a few years ago, policemen actually collected a small "tax" from boats sailing around the island. In order to conduct a maritime patrol, the police only have at their disposal two very small sampans with only one outboard motor, when, in comparison, pirates often have two or three. Often shabbily dressed without proper uniforms, the policemen spend their time idling in front of their police station or to make visits to the brothels of *Pulau Babi* [Pig Island], rather than clamping down upon pirate activities.

This small island is in the middle of the bay, along *Sungai Buaya* [Crocodile River]. Apart from some of its gaming rooms which are open during the day, Pulau Babi looks just like any other village built on stilts; with the different being the numerous brothels that service Singaporean visitors on weekends. There, they sit down at the tables of pirates who come here for leisure, between two boarding attacks. Nasrul once lived on this island. Now, this place seems more desolate than it once was.

Along the coast, fishermen, pirates, and the chief of the village are neighbours. The community is closely knit as everyone is quite familiar with each other. When the tide is low, fishing for prawns become a worthy enterprise. However, on a moonless night, they turn towards attacking vessels crossing the Straits, just ten minutes from Pig Island. Indeed, lights of Singapore shine in the background. The Philip Channel is very near to Kampung Hitam, on the other side of the bay. This helps to explain why piracy is a favourable trade. In this Indonesian "Far East", vessels are equivalent to stage coaches passing vulnerably through a canyon. Ships are perpetually under threat as pirates can surge forth from the nearby islands and mangroves with relative ease at the time of their choosing.

To be sure, there are families seeking to earn a decent living reside in this village with their children. Life is not easy. Most of them try to ply the trade of fisherman although it is more and more difficult because of pollution or fishing and maritime traffic. One night, a fisherman, nicknamed "Moustache", caught only four small squid and a small fish on his small boat in the Philip Channel. Moustache sold it only for one Singapore dollar at the local market the next day. On other days when he is not fishing, Moustache works as a taxi-boat driver. However, some of his colleagues incarnate into pirates for the next attack. Indeed, it is difficult to imagine these individuals and their families depending solely on the the salary from a taxi-boat business. To begin with, there are hardly any passengers to eke out a decent income.

It serves to mention that a government official actually manages this district where pirates live and symbolizes the strange attitude that the Indonesian authorities have regarding piracy in their backyards. He told the author that his task was to inform his office in Jakarta if problems such as piracy get out of hand. However, he appeared to display an indifferent attitude towards the reality that pirates were operating under his watch. He even admitted that his own daughter had married a pirate chief. Thus, it is quite clear that he has not made any reports to Jakarta to date. According to Romain Bertrand, a French researcher, this instance would imply that Jakarta is actually tolerant of small-scale piracy.[13] The national or provincial government appears to allow for such robberies provided that maritime muggers do not destabilize the area on a scale that terrorists such as the *Jemaah Islamiyah* (JI) or separatist rebels (such as Free Aceh Movement or GAM) possibly could. However, even if they are not as dangerous as terrorists or separatists, pirates do disrupt maritime trade. Hence, they are often regarded as notorious criminals to be taken seriously.

Among the other coastal criminals, procurers and smugglers manage their own business from Pulau Babi or from the pirate district. Sometimes, there are a few connections with the pirates. For example, an old Chinese woman accommodates pirates and prostitutes — or *anak malam* [children of the night] — in her guesthouse. Not so far from this house, by night, illegal immigrants carefully board small wooden boats in their attempt to enter Singapore. Some people the author spoke to, described horrific stories related to sentences or punishments in cases of recidivism. Like piracy, prostitution and illegal immigration are foremost concerns for regional governments. All of these issues are connected to the surrounding poverty. If you are poor, you could become a pirate or an illegal immigrant. Both activities often originate from the same social background, commonly in the vicinity of Batam. Therefore, piracy represents only one aspect of the criminality in Kampung Hitam (as in the Riau islands). A few years ago, pirates came from other regions and islands and resided temporarily in Kampung Hitam from where they attacked vessels. According to Uban, pirates were usually from Indonesia while their ringleaders were often Chinese in ethnicity.[14] But many pirates have now come back to their *kampung* or native town like Palembang in Sumatra. This could be described as the end of the "Golden Age" of Kampung Hitam since the death of Nasrul.

Among the pirates who continue attacking vessels, most of them are around their thirties. They are also often single and tend to work as taxi-boat drivers or fishermen. Some of them are former seamen and they live among the rest of the mainstream community as well as prostitutes and smugglers.

Younger pirates, often around their late teenage years, have come to replace their older counterparts. Most of these individuals have not completed their basic education. For example, one of them by the name of Rosa, plays *sepak takraw* — Malay-Thai colloquial term for a regional sport called "kick ball" — with his friends daily. He often goes prawn fishing with Zorino. He also spends part of his day building his own house. Sometimes, he goes at night to a harbour of Batam where he steals cables, which may yield around 80,000 rupees in profit.

Another former friend of Zorino works as taxi-boat driver and pirate. Last year, he went with another companion to Malaysia where he stole boat engines. He was eventually caught and imprisoned. The Malaysian police also injured his accomplice with a bullet wound in the leg. Now, he has come back to Kampung Hitam where he is ready to attack other vessels while the Indonesian police look the other way. In general, these pirates tend to work for gangs. In Kampung Hitam, the number of such gangs is known to be on the decline. Nevertheless, around five gangs, each of them composed of between seven to eight pirates, continue to attack unsuspecting vessels.

The *Orang Buton*, who originated from the Southeast of Sulawesi, currently form the main gang in the pirate den. Buton people — who carry the reputation of being a courageous but socially reserved group — are considered to be close ethnic relatives of the Bugis who themselves used to be pirates in previous centuries, made famous in Joseph Conrad's novel *Karain*. Today, the Buton people have turned to piracy only because they do not have access to any form of employment. Because of the transmigration and the Indonesian Government's "Batam Plan" for the massive industrial development of the island, large numbers of migrants coming from the rest of the Indonesian archipelago become disappointed with their expectations after their arrival.[15] Subsequently, they began grouping together in dilapidated housing, like the Buton pirates in the den.

This particular gang is managed by Robi, who was married to the daughter of the chief of Kampung Hitam. All the members of this gang live in Robi's house. The villagers are not in much in contact with these pirates. The brother-in-law of a villager named Arif worked with Robi. Arif lives in the middle of Kampung Hitam. He knows almost everyone and his neighbours are the village chief and the chief of another gang, named Bong. This individual, an ethnic Chinese who is relatively old in his years, was actually a rival of Nasrul and decided to stay in Kampung Hitam. He told everybody he had to use a wheelchair since a motorcycle crash. In fact, he broke his leg when his tie broke during a piracy boarding attempt. In his house, a few individuals — among them the son of the village chief — drink and idle about together daily.

Bong worked for a Singaporean named Chen who used to ferry pirates by boat to a small island as a kind of "pirate logistician". By chance, fishermen in the Anambas islands confirmed this story. About two years ago, these villagers accommodated the Chen's gang for a few months. The pirates lived in the village and went sometimes on a deserted island, near the village, in order to monitor the maritime traffic nearby and prepare for attacks between the Anambas islands, Malaysia and Bintan, in the South China Sea. This arrangement came into being especially when more attacks were reported in South China Sea. A few years ago, according to the village chief, this gang also stole a statue from a temple on Kusu Island, off Singapore. Next to this house, the chief of another gang lives with his family. A good friend of Zorino also happens to be his neighbour. Sometimes, he sees speedboats leaving the *kampung* by night in order to attack ships in the Straits. Arif, who lives nearby, tells me that pirates often bring back stolen safes, which they try to open back in the village.

The local policemen do not disturb the pirates and their chiefs so long as these groups do not explicitly challenge their authority. These so-called policemen only protect prostitutes; they manage their own business while keeping a low social profile. This seems to be the price of keeping the domestic peace. That is why, for example, a pirate named Dewi can live in the pirate district although the police of Batam wants to arrest him. To be sure, the policemen are sometimes not only tolerant but also accomplices in piracy activities. Certain brave individuals have told the author that some policemen are in reality the bodyguards of the two key characters — who happen to be brothers — of the pirates' shady schemes. Like Barberousse himself in the Mediterranean Sea five centuries ago, one of them adds his political shrewdness to the courage of his warrior brother, nicknamed Deddy. All the islands, including Kampung Hitam, the main village and the market, is in Deddy's hands. Together with his brother, Deddy owns several discos in Batam and CD shops in the market.

Deddy plays the equivalent of a lord over his serfs who, in this case, are the inhabitants he physically abuses when he is angry. Invoking the analogy of the Middle Ages once more, Deddy's status is approximate to an overlord far removed from the central power of Jakarta, making him (and his brother) the *de facto* chiefs of a quasi-feudal system, based on terror and submissiveness in this island only a few kilometres to the south of Singapore. Even pirates cannot escape their control, as they are compelled to keep Deddy and his brother informed of their operations.

This "dark alliance", to use the phrase of an Indonesian journalist in his reference to Mr Wong and his activities, invokes the third phase in Philip Gosse's "cycle of piracy", which identifies three steps in the pirate process in the context of the Mediterranean, Atlantic and Indian Oceans throughout history.[16] First, the poor and marginalized sections of the population tended to band together in isolated groups and resort to armed robbery at sea. Second, these groups become structured networks with greater degrees of organization over time. Finally, these groups and networks become established communities — and in some cases, even become nation-states — which in some cases, jettisoned their illegitimate activities such as piracy and participated in mainstream economic and political affairs. Barberousse, who amassed greater power through his activities over time, is a good case in point in the context of the Mediterranean Sea. Today, the links between certain local potentates and pirate bands, especially in Indonesia have become a significant concern. However, the authorities in Jakarta may find themselves in an increasing bind if it continues to tolerate the modern incarnation of Gosse's third phase in modern Indonesia.

How Pirates Actually Board Ships: Some Field Notes

Before the Attack

It is very difficult to ascertain the exact frequency of pirate attacks stemming from Kampung Hitam. Indeed, there are many different motivations or causes that explain why pirate decide suddenly to attack. This includes the availability of information from various sources, which is required in order to help them plan and execute an attack. In some cases, pirates are able to tune into the VHF (Very High Frequency) radio network of commercial shippers. The village chief also informed this author that pirate often know exactly where a ship and its cargo is located by tapping into a ship's Automatic Identification System (AIS). Therefore, one French Master explained to the author,

> When I enter the Malacca Straits, I know that there are pirates, especially along the coast of Sumatra. Indeed, it takes at least 24 hours to cross the Malacca Straits, around 950 km long. This is a significant advantage for the pirates who always attack by night. Consequently, my crewmen close all the doors. I also increase the speed of my ship and I switch off the AIS![17]

When it is just about sunset — and especially when the moon has not yet come out — pirates spend their time together by drinking, consuming illegal drugs such as morphine and womanizing with the female inhabitants on islands such as nearby *Pulau Babi*. A fisherman from Kampung Hitam explains: "It is at eight o'clock [in the evening] that the pirates begin to work. They come with an additional motor on their shoulder. They mount it on their *sampan*. Thus, they can easily catch up with the cargo ships that cross the Straits".

Before that, they try to catch fish while they survey the traffic. This is one of the reasons why it is so difficult for naval patrols to catch pirates in the act. A villager explained that, one day, pirates hesitated to attack a particular ship they had been trailing because they were deterred by what appeared to be crewmen posted astern on duty. Indeed, these pirates may not have been very astute or well trained. On balance, they preferred not to take excessive risks. In the end, it turned out that instead of posting actual crewmen, the master of the vessel that had been trailed had put cardboard silhouettes to dissuade pirates from attacking. The pirates should have seen through this charade from the onset, instead of hesitating from making an attack.

During the Attack

In the end, the pirates did attack. In general, boarding incidents at night are a delicate affair, because the pirates do not have the luxury of navigating with the aid of any Ground Positioning System (GPS) or ship floodlights, which would expose their position. The backwash, caused by the propellers of the ships they are trailing, also makes the act of climbing aboard a ship extremely perilous. Pirates negotiate the act of boarding with the help of grapnels or big gaffs equipped with a sickle at the end; more suitable for collecting coconuts than for boarding.[18]

Once aboard, they move towards the captain's cabin or quarters, and threatening him once found — with weapons at their disposal such as pistols or *parang* (machetes) — and force him to lead them to any available money and valuables on board. They take their booty and make a quick get-away on their motorboats moving towards Indonesian waters. Overall, the *modus operandi* of a ship-boarding attack is relatively risky for pirates. Interestingly, many pirates find strength and confidence in the various "ghosts" and "spirits" they beseech. For example, off the coast of the island of Malaysia's Penang, some pirates attribute their ability to traverse these waters undetected to *Puja*, a local spirit. They believe that Puja allows them to suddenly vanish in a cloud of smoke. The author has come to hear that even the local policemen of Penang believe this to be true of their pirate adversaries.

After the Attack

In general, pirates usually return to their den by the early morning. There, they drink again and spend the money they have accrued very quickly. They also use this opportunity to share the booty they have collected. The author has heard of cases where pirates settle their quarrels over the share of the booty with pistols. They then spend the rest of the day resting and wait for the next attack at nightfall. In sum, this is the life in a pirate den but it is only one case among various others. An island in the east of Bintan accommodates other gangs near Kijang, in the area where numerous attacks were reported in 2003, which this chapter does not cover.

Final Comments

The author's preliminary field investigation of Kampung Hitam confirms that pirates still haunt the Malacca Straits and that pirates appear more and more idle and desperate. Besides, it conveys the impression that piracy is, more often than not, committed by small groups that are not necessarily linked to large organizations or triads. The weekly reports of the IMB show that most attacks are opportunistic and petty in nature that are carried out along coast and near to land. According to the IMO Working Group on the Malacca Straits formed in 1993, such kinds of attacks are consistent with Low Level Armed Robbery (LLAR), unlike Medium Level Armed Assault and Robbery (MLAAR) or Major Criminal Hijacking (MCH), which tend to involve much larger and more structured transnational gangs.[19]

Consequently, the Asian pirate of the third millennium is nowhere near the sophistication of a space-age pirate as depicted in the fictional character of Captain Harlock. On the contrary, the simplicity of Asian piracy is still comparable to ancient times. Indeed, the Mediterranean pirate cycle ended in the nineteenth century with a regional reaction: Faced with the sons of Barberousse, William Eaton, the American Consul in Tunis, and American authorities were shocked that

> seven kings of Europe, two Republics and a continent relied on North African buccaneers [were] unable to eliminate these highly placed savages, whose entire fleet [did] not match the might of our vessels.[20]

A few years later, the then U.S. supported European initiatives to put an end to several centuries of Berber piracy, with much difficulty.

Nearly two centuries later, history appears to be repeating itself again; this time in Southeast Asia. In April 2004, the U.S. authorities have taken a hard stance against piracy once more as reflected in the U.S. Admiral Thomas Fargo who proposed the establishment of a Regional Maritime Security Initiative (RMSI), which — in its initial offering — intended to have the U.S. Marine and other military units patrol the waters of the Malacca Straits to counter piracy and the possible threat of maritime terrorism.[21] However, even such draconian measures, if they are put in place, will probably not be sufficient. As this chapter suggests, the location of pirates and the reasons for their trade has become public knowledge. It is very likely, that piracy will continue to exist at a significant level as long as unemployment remains a significant problem. Regional governments, non-governmental organizations aiming to redress some of Indonesia's socio-economic problems, as well as Indonesia's large business firms that have a stake in Batam and Riau, have to make a greater effort in alleviating some of the factors that feed into the worsening of the piracy situation.

As a last and passing comment, one of the factors we could exclude is the threat of a connection or "nexus" between pirates and terrorists, which the author believes to be a weak assertion. In the case of Kampung Hitam, this village does not even have a *pesantren* (Koranic school) like those found in Ngruki on the Indonesian island of Solo. The basis of radical or extremist Islam sweeping the village is simply not there to start with.[22] It appears that from the possible threat of maritime terrorism, pirates (and the success of their attacks) can inspire terrorists into similar action, but it is very likely that pirates have no real interest in helping terrorists towards this end. Most obvious of all, pirates attack vessels for economic reasons. As such, staying alive, evading capture and sustaining their trade are important imperatives. Pirates may be less educated than the members of al-Qaeda or the JI (many of whom are known to be relatively well-schooled) and they infringe too many Islamic laws (such as the drinking of alcohol, to become suitable allies with such terrorists). That is why this hypothetic alliance would be discreditable for the militant Islamists who seek their goals through terrorism.

Notes

[1]   Jean-Christophe Rufin, *L'Empire et les Nouveaux Barbares* [The Empire and the New Barbarians] (Paris: Lattès, 1992).

2   Robert Kaplan. "The Coming Anarchy". *Atlantic Monthly* 273, no. 2 (February 1994): 44–76.
3   James Holden-Rhodes and Peter Lupsha, "Horsemen of the Apocalypse: Grey area Phenomena and the New World Disorder", *Low Intensity Conflict & Law Enforcement* 2, no. 2 (Autumn 1993): 212.
4   ICC International Maritime Service, "Fatal attacks on the increase, ICC reports shows", in *ICC Commercial Crime Services*, 26 July 2004 <http://www.icc-ccs.org> (accessed 9 August 2004).
5   Personal interview with the author, 26 March 2002.
6   *Piracy and Armed Robbery against Ships: Annual Report, 1 January – 31 December 2004* (Kuala Lumpur: IMB Regional Piracy Centre, 2005), p. 9.
7   Personal interview with the author on 25 February 2002.
8   Most of the proper nouns are false, in order to protect the anonymity of the protagonists.
9   *Le monde des affaires à Singapour* [Business World in Singapore] (Paris: FNEGE, 2001), p. 12.
10   For example, in the town of Tanjung Pinang, Bobby exerts much of his influence over illegitimate businesses and criminal activities within Bintan from *Club 5*, a proprietary of his.
11   "I conventionally term 'the new Middle Ages' the fall of the legitimate principle of power and the legal principle of the monarchies and democracies and their replacement by the principle of strength, of vital energy, of unions and spontaneous social groups." Alain Minc quoting Berdiaev in *Le Nouveau Moyen Age* [The New Middle Ages] (Paris: Gallimard, 1993.)
12   It is common local knowledge that tourists from Singapore visit Batam island for shopping and recreation during the weekends. It is also common knowledge that a significant number of male Singaporean visitors come to visit their girlfriends or mistresses they have met here. Indeed, the people in the village told the author that several large private homes actually belong to Singaporean businessmen.
13   Romain Bertrand, *"L'Affaire de la prise d'otages de Jolo: un exemple de criminalisation du politique en Asie du Sud-Est"* [The Case of the Hostage Crisis in Jolo: An Example of Political Criminalisation in Southeast Asia], *La Revue internationale et stratégique*, No. 43, Autumn 2001, pp. 41–47.
14   Personal interview with the author on 25 February 2002.
15   Batam Industrial Development Authority, 2005, <http://www.batam.go.id>.
16   Andreas Harsono, "Dark Alliance Rules the High Seas", *World Source Online*, 13 April 1999, <http://www.icij.org/investigate/harsono.html>; and Philip Gosse. *Histoire de la Piraterie* [History of Piracy] (Paris: Payot, 1952), pp. 13–14.
17   Personal interview aboard the container vessel *Debussy* in March 2004.
18   Personal interview with Mr Mak Joon Nam, a then researcher with the Malaysian Institute of Maritime Affairs in Kuala Lumpur on 9 April 2002.

[19] International Maritime Organization, *Report of the IMO Working Group on the Malacca Strait Area* (London: IMO, 1993), p. 15. According to the IMO, the LLAR "is generally carried out in the vicinity of land from small high-speed craft by groups of petty thieves armed with machetes, clubs and, occasionally, low velocity weapons such as pistols and shotguns. The vast majority of the attacks by such groups are carried out at night, generally between 2200 hrs and 0400 hrs. The perpetrators are judged to come from criminal and fishing communities based close to the area of attack", as in Kampung Hitam.

[20] Armel De Wismes, *Pirates et corsaires* [Pirates and Corsairs] (Paris: France – Empire, 1999), p. 80.

[21] According to the U.S. Pacific Command, the RMSI, in its currency is intended to be a long-term, multi-national approach to counter transnational threats, including terrorism, maritime piracy, illegal trafficking — narcotics, weapons, human, and illicit cargo — and other criminal activities in the maritime domain through a U.S.-supported partnership of willing nations to enhance capabilities and leverage capacities through unity of effort to identify, monitor, and intercept transnational maritime threats consistent with existing international and domestic laws. "Regional Maritime Security Initiative", U.S. Pacific Command, <http://www.pacom.mil/rmsi/>.

[22] The author has come to believe that if a *pesantren* did exist in Kampung Hitam, the village chief and its policemen would come to know about it and inform the central authorities in Jakarta which takes a strong position against the threat of terrorist groups such as the JI. Concerning the JI and its possible influence, see Barry Desker, "The Jemaah Islamiyah (JI) Phenomenon in Singapore", *Contemporary Southeast Asia* 25, no. 3, pp. 489–507; and also Rémy Madinier, "Asie du Sud-Est: les Chimères de l'Islam Radical" [Southeast Asia: The Chimeras of Radical Islam], *Outre-Terre — Revue Française de Géopolitique* no. 6 (2003): 109–14.

6

The Politics of Anti-Piracy and Anti-Terrorism Responses in Southeast Asia[1]

Mark J. Valencia

Introduction

Since the events of 11 September 2001, the fear of linkages between pirates and "terrorists" in Southeast Asia has been reflected in the mass media and government policy statements, both within and outside the region.[2] But some argue that piracy and terrorism have different causes, motives, objectives and tactics, and thus require different responses.[3] This chapter explores the politics of anti-piracy and terrorism efforts in and for Southeast Asia, including the conflation of the two phenomena.

Regarding conflation of piracy and terrorism, opinions continue to be sharply divided. Brian Jenkins, a terrorism expert and senior advisor at the RAND Corporation says: "I don't think that it is appropriate to blend the increasing problem of piracy with the potentially more dangerous consequences of terrorism."[4] Similarly, Captain P.K. Mukundan, Director of the IMB, agrees that there

> was nothing to show that terrorists and pirates have joined up. There is a
> terrorist threat to the Straits of Malacca, and that is fair comment, but that

will be done by terrorists not pirates. There are politically motivated groups attacking ships off the northern coast of Sumatra and the Southern Philippines as well as Somalia, but their objectives are different to piracy.

Admiral Thomas Fargo, the then U.S. Commander-in-Chief of the Pacific and the proposer of the controversial Regional Maritime Security Initiative (RMSI) — which surfaced in the media in April 2004 — to combat piracy, terrorism and WMD smuggling, has stated that "U.S. intelligence services have found no evidence that pirates operating in the Straits of Malacca have links to terror networks in Southeast Asia."[5] Even Malaysia's Internal Security Department Deputy Minister Chia Kwang Chye has said "while the threat of piracy against ships continues to cause concern, there is no proof that pirates have terror links."[6] While some alarmists point to the kidnappings off Sumatra and the disappearance of tugs in Indonesia as evidence that pirates and "terrorists" are joining hands, officials in Malaysia and Indonesia explain the kidnappings as a means for the Gerakan Aceh Merdeka (GAM) — the separatist movement in the province of Aceh in North Sumatra — to raise money for its struggle, and that the tugs are being stolen to be used for smuggling.[7]

On the other hand, there has been a rise in kidnap and ransom cases in the northern Malacca Straits.[8] These incidents have been attributed to the GAM. In June 2004, the Indonesian Navy killed three GAM rebels who were trying to hijack a Pertamina tanker, the MV Pematang, near Behala Island, off North Sumatra.[9] And the head of the International Maritime Organization (IMO), Elthimios Mitropoulos said international action may be necessary to counter the threat from a "nexus of terrorism and piracy in the Malacca and Singapore Straits".[10] Meanwhile Singapore, led by Tony Tan, Singapore's Deputy Prime Minister, maintains a drumbeat of concern regarding both terrorist attacks in the Straits and the linkage with pirates.[11]

A compromise view has been expressed by Peter Chalk, another RAND analyst, who acknowledges that there is no hard evidence tying terrorists and pirates but believes such co-operation is logical. "Pirates and criminal syndicates could 'contract out' their maritime expertise to terrorists, hijacking a ship to be used for smuggling, or as a weapon or to cause a collision. They could also provide training in ship boarding or even their operation."[12]

Piracy and Terrorism: Similarities and Differences

Clearly there is some overlap in the definitions of piracy/sea robbery and "terrorism" in that they both can and often do involve violence at sea.

"However, piracy and sea robbery are illegal acts committed for private gain while terrorism is an illegal act committed with the intent of influencing a government or a polity, i.e., it has a political objective." And "piracy on the high seas is a universal crime and can be repressed by any nation while repression of terrorism on the high seas is legally confined to particular nations and circumstances."[13]

Moreover the tactics of piracy and terrorism are usually different, although there may be some overlap at the "high end" of piracy. Piracy/sea robbery encompasses a wide spectrum of criminal behaviour ranging from in-port pilferage, to hit-and-run attacks, to temporary seizure of the ship, to long-term seizure, and, at the "high end", to permanent theft of the ship. This spectrum corresponds to an escalating scale of risk and return. As the risk and potential return increase, so do the threat and degree of violence. Indeed, the more that is at stake the more the attackers are willing to use violence. Additionally, as the risk, return, and the potential for violence increase, so does the apparent degree of organization of the attackers. A significant portion of piracy incidents worldwide occur in Southeast Asia, and according to Chalk, "the violence of attacks appears to be increasing, including hijacking, hostage taking, and the use of firearms."[14]

Seizing a ship, especially if it is already underway, requires boats, grappling hooks, and enough people with the means to control the crew. This necessitates some coordination and organization. Significant capital investment is required for boats and arms, training (or finding experienced people for boarding), coordinating a large group, and possibly for obtaining inside information regarding what a particular vessel is carrying.

The most serious form of piracy is hijacking or permanent seizure. Those seizing the boat for its cargo and the ship itself must do something with the crew. In permanent seizures the pirates need a contact to sell the cargo, and a location where the boat can be disposed of, or in some cases repainted, re-flagged and returned to service. Because the potential return of the attack is so high, the necessary organization so extensive, and the ultimate disposal of the crew necessary, hijacking is at the high end of the spectrum of risk, potential return, violence, and level of organization. And it obviously raises concerns that terrorists could undertake similar actions for political purposes.

Terrorism at sea includes the twin threats of attacks on shipping and the threat of ships being used as weapons, and the threat of ships being used to deliver concealed weapons of mass destruction (in containers or within the ship's superstructure). Some secessionist groups have resorted to piracy to raise funds for their struggle. Actual examples include the ransom kidnappings undertaken purportedly by members of the Abu Sayyaf Group (ASG) in the Southern Philippines and those by alleged members of GAM, in which crew members were attacked and held for ransom in waters off Aceh.[15]

Piracy: Cause and Consequences

Piracy is an economic crime done for financial gain, and therefore the principal causes can be sought in prevailing economic conditions. The Asian economic crises deeply impacted Southeast Asian countries, creating an incentive for those at the lower end of the economic scale to turn to illegal sources of income. This economic collapse also triggered widespread political instability, most notably in Indonesia, creating an environment where people could more easily pursue illegal methods of income generation. "Indeed, economic collapse, combined with endemic governmental corruption and loose political control, creates an environment in which piracy may be ignored or even tacitly enabled by corrupt military elements who may share in the 'booty' ".[16] Another factor encouraging piracy in Southeast Asia is the relative security provided by the permeable, poorly controlled and in some areas, uncertain international boundaries which allow pirates to easily cross borders to escape pursuit.

The dangers of piracy include a direct threat to the lives and welfare of the citizens of a variety of flag states; a direct economic impact in terms of fraud, stolen cargoes, delayed trips, and increased insurance premiums; the undermining and weakening of political stability by encouraging official corruption; and the potential to cause a major environmental disaster when the helm is left unattended during a pirate attack.

Terrorism is distinct from piracy in a very straightforward manner. While piracy is a crime motivated by greed and thus predicated on immediate financial gain, terrorism, and its maritime manifestation, "political piracy" or maritime terrorism, is motivated by political goals beyond the immediate act of attacking or hijacking a maritime target. Terrorist acts also have the potential to cause systemic economic dislocation. Indeed, the effect of a major attack on a transshipment hub such as Singapore would be felt globally. For example, the aspect of tanker transportation most economically sensitive to terrorism is insurance. Oil and liquefied natural gas (LNG) supplies could be adversely affected by a spike in insurance premiums. Worse, coverage could be withdrawn from certain areas if the terrorism or war risk were to be considered unacceptably high. Since the Bali bombing, war-risk status has applied to Indonesian ports, but not as yet to passage through the archipelago.[17]

But maritime terrorism remains rare. The reasons for a low rate of maritime terrorism as compared to piracy are:[18]

1. Most terrorists are "land-lubbers" with little maritime experience;
2. Operating at sea requires special equipment and skills;
3. Fixed land targets offer a greater ease of access;
4. Despite 9/11, terrorists are traditionally tactically conservative and tend to opt for the course of least resistance; and
5. Attacking a vessel on the high seas is less likely to attract international attention than more media-accessible land targets.

Nevertheless, the perceived threat of maritime terrorism has increased in recent years due to:

1. lax port security, poor coastal surveillance, a profusion of targets, and a trend towards "skeleton crews";
2. the opportunity for mass casualty attacks such as LNG carriers/terminals, refineries, petrochemical installations, and cruise ships; and
3. increased tactical sophistication as exemplified by the events of 9/11.

However, Indonesia's Chief of Intelligence Hendropriyono said "Jemaah Islamiah terrorists now in detention have admitted that attacks on the Malacca shipping lane have been contemplated in the recent past."[19] To be sure, piracy and terrorism do overlap in the tactics of ship seizures and hijackings, and the conditions, which allow them to thrive, for example, poverty, political instability, permeable international boundaries, and ineffective enforcement. However, the political objectives of terrorists distinctly separate their motivation from that of pirates. Indeed, terrorists want to call attention to their cause and to inflict as much harm and damage as possible. Pirates want to avoid attention and will inflict only as much harm and damage as is necessary to accomplish their mission. It is highly likely that most pirates would avoid linkages with terrorists because the repercussions of association could put them out of business.

Although the circumstances that allow piracy and terrorism to develop and grow are similar, the root causes are different. For pirates, the motivating factor is economics; for terrorists it is generally political and religious ideology stemming from perceived injustices, both historical and contemporary. Thus while the tactics of combating maritime terrorism and piracy may be similar, long-term solutions may require different approaches.

The Politics of Current Counter Measures

The 1988 SUA Convention

The Achille Lauro incident indirectly led to the IMO sponsorship of the 1988 Rome conference from which emerged support for a Convention for the Suppression of Unlawful Acts Against the Safety of Maritime Navigation Convention (SUA).[20] SUA was meant to "fill many of the jurisdictional gaps highlighted when the acts endanger the safety of international navigation and occur on board national or foreign flag ships while underway in the territorial sea, international Straits or international waters. The convention requires states to criminalize such acts under national law and to cooperate in the investigation and prosecution of their perpetrators".[21] Although the convention was developed largely in response to the 1985 Achille Lauro incident and with the objective of combating terrorism, it can also be an anti-piracy and anti-sea robbery measure.[22] Indeed, "if a person seizes control of a ship by force, or threat thereof, or performs an act of violence likely to endanger the ship's safe navigation, the person has committed an offence under the convention, regardless of the motive.[23]

However there has been some reluctance of ASEAN states to ratify SUA although members now include Myanmar, the Philippines, Singapore and Vietnam. Most ASEAN states are unwilling to commit to prosecute persons caught in their waters for acts committed in another country's waters. In addition, for countries with a recent colonial history and relatively newly won independence, as well as ineffective navies and disputed or porous maritime boundaries, the convention can be seen as underscoring their inability to fulfil their obligations, or even compromising their national sovereignty. Adding to their suspicion is an Intertanko-backed proposal to establish a neutral flag fleet that would patrol the Malacca Straits and be allowed to pursue pirates across national maritime borders.[24] This could be perceived by the Straits states as "internationalizing" the Straits. Thus some Southeast Asian states feel the SUA Convention only makes sense for those countries with effective maritime forces and unchallengeable maritime boundaries.

It has been argued that in order to enforce the provisions of the 1982 United Nations Convention on the Law of the Sea concerning piracy, the military vessel of one state might be allowed with the courtesy of the coastal state to continue the pursuit of a pirate ship across territorial sea boundaries. However, these arguments have not been convincing enough to undermine the doctrine of territorial sovereignty enjoyed by coastal states. But if "piracy" and "terrorism" are fused into a general threat to maritime security, developing countries may find support of SUA as well as outside "help" easier to accept and to "sell" to their domestic polity. So it may be in the interest of Singapore and foreign Straits users to conflate piracy and terrorism to persuade reluctant developing countries to allow them to assist in the pursuit of pirates and terrorists in their territorial and archipelagic waters.

U.S. Initiatives

Since the terrorist attacks of 11 September 2001, the United States has viewed Muslim extremists in Southeast Asia as potential threats to shipping moving through the region. The worst scenario is that a supertanker will be hijacked or attacked and sunk in the narrowest portion of the Malacca Straits, thus seriously disrupting or detouring commercial traffic including the imports of oil to East Asia, and potentially constraining U.S. naval mobility and flexibility as well. And the United States seems to have little confidence in the ability of most of the Southeast Asian countries to prevent such a disaster.

Thus the United States undertook, in cooperation with India, a proactive attempt to control both piracy and terrorism in the Straits of Malacca. "Tankers and LNG carriers using the Straits are considered particularly vulnerable to 'ramming' and boarding because they are slow moving and carry valuable and potentially dangerous cargo, and the Straits has high economic importance, high traffic volume and limited space for maneuvering."[25] This effort used U.S. and Indian warships to escort commercial vessels of "high value", transiting the Straits. However, naval patrols by major powers may not be the most effective or politically acceptable way to combat either piracy or terrorism. Indeed, the conflation of the two phenomena may actually be a disadvantage to the United States.

First, these patrols have created suspicion in parts of Southeast Asia regarding the real goals of the Indian and U.S. naval presence in the Straits of Malacca. Indeed, this effort may well be viewed in some quarters as an attempt to internationalize the Malacca Straits. Second, in the wake of the Cold War and the events of 9/11, the United States and India have developed a new political and military relationship. Indeed, it appears that Washington is interested in a military alliance with India. Apparently, India agreed to the joint patrols in return for the resumption of arms sales to India, specifically the "Fire Finder" radar system.[26] "This political context suggests that the Indian and U.S. naval presence in the Straits is not just to combat piracy and terrorism, but is part of a broader attempt to assert a U.S.-friendly Indian naval presence in the region."[27] Thus for the United States, the joint patrols can be seen as the beginning of a larger military engagement with India.[28] "And for India, the joint patrolling of the Malacca Straits is evidence and endorsement of its claim that its security interests stretch up to and include the Straits."[29]

Although this may be seen by some as a reasonable attempt to create a security order in the region, others such as Indonesia and China could well view this development as a threat to their regional authority and influence. When one considers the current U.S. military and political actions in the Muslim world, such actions by the United States and historically dominant India may not be universally viewed as positive, or constructive, by Muslim Southeast Asia. Indeed the potential ability of these patrols to curb piracy and terrorism may not outweigh their potential to undermine security relations in the region.

Concerns over terrorism are driving closer cooperation among the police forces and intelligence agencies in Southeast Asia, but are also triggering distrust and cautious monitoring by neighbouring countries. All the while, a wary eye is being cast on U.S. involvement in the region, with lingering fears that Washington will use terrorism as an excuse to impose its political will upon Asian nations. Countering this requires even more cooperation and a more grounded basis for a regional block — something some nations are mooting — but distrust and inherent competition continue to undermine such initiatives.

There are also practical issues regarding the effectiveness of U.S. and Indian naval anti-piracy/terrorism patrols in the Malacca Straits region. Of significant concern is the arrest authority of foreign naval vessels in waters under another country's jurisdiction. Commercial ships may exercise their rights to transit through international straits, and accordingly naval vessels may escort those ships under the transit passage regime. But their authority is generally limited to their own flag vessels. Enforcement is largely left to the navy, which possesses the hardware of enforcement but lacks the power of arrest. This role deviates from international practice "in which navies typically operate on the high seas leaving patrolling of territorial waters to coast guard-type bodies". "Perhaps the purpose of the

U.S./Indian naval escorts is simply to deter would be pirates and terrorists by the sheer intimidation of their presence, regardless of their legal authority, or to act as the eyes and ears of local maritime security forces."[30]

There is also a question regarding the appropriate size of the pursuit craft. "In the shallow waters where most pirates operate, high-speed patrol craft are of more practical value.[31] Pirates tend to be highly mobile groups that operate based on intimate local knowledge of the waters and can easily lose larger pursuers in the maze of islands in Southeast Asia.

The U.S. Proliferation Security Initiative (PSI) and the Regional Maritime Security Initiative (RMSI)

The PSI is a Bush Adminstration proposed effort to suppress traffic in weapons of mass destruction (WMD). Under U.S. pressure, a group of "like-minded" countries have agreed to selective interdiction of ships and aircraft bound to or from "rogue nations" carrying materials or technology used to manufacture or deliver WMD. Such interdictions are controversial.[32]

In April 2004, the United States proposed the RMSI in a bid to bolster security for Southeast Asia. The announced purpose was "to operationalize the PSI by facilitating intelligence sharing and law enforcement activities to monitor, identify and intercept suspected vessels in national and international waters".[33] The initial focus was to be the Malacca Straits. It was hoped this multilateral initiative would "blunt criticism of U.S. policy against terrorism as unilateral and unidimensional".[34] But the proposal had the opposite effect and split the Malacca Straits countries. Malaysia and Indonesia publicly opposed it, emphasizing that the responsibility for the security of the Straits is theirs alone.[35] Although Malaysia said it would support the PSI and discuss the RMSI, it reserved to itself decisions on interdiction.[36] It also referred to the Five Powers Defence Arrangement as a proper vehicle to deal with the threat of "piracy" and "terrorism", although reiterating that each country would deal with the problems in its own waters.[37] Basically, Indonesia, Malaysia and others are concerned that a U.S. presence in the Malacca Straits will attract terrorist attacks and enhance the ideological appeal of extremist elements.[38]

However, Singapore supported the proposal and scrambled to find "like-minded" countries. Indeed, Singapore's Defence Minister Teo Chee Hean appealed to governments concerned to "have a firmer commitment to multinational consultation and collaboration".[39] And Singapore's Deputy Prime Minister Tony Tan appealed to countries outside the region including Japan, to help patrol the Malacca Straits.[40] He added that "it is not realistic to unilaterally confine such patrols only to countries in this part of the world." Singapore would also like to involve the United Nations in such patrols, an anathema to Indonesia and Malaysia, which strongly oppose internationalizing the Straits. To implement the multilateral concept, Singapore proposed a joint naval exercise in the Malacca Straits for August to include India, Japan, South Korea and the United States.[41] But after China conveyed its displeasure to India and the United States, Japan and South Korea declined to participate.

Singapore currently allows the U.S. Navy to use its port for repair, refuelling and replenishment, and U.S. military jets to stopover there. Moreover, Singapore and the United States are in the process of developing a strategic framework agreement on security and defense, which will "include co-operation in counter-terrorism, prevention of trade in WMD and joint military exercises".[42] This has raised concerns in Indonesia and Malaysia that the arrangement could lead to the establishment of a U.S. military base.

Malaysia's Foreign Minister responded to Singapore's position by saying that "Singapore cannot unilaterally invite the United States to patrol the Straits."[43] Malaysia said it would only heighten its control of security in the "Straits only if there are specific and accurate intelligence reports on terrorist threats". Indonesia reacted by downplaying the security situation in the Straits while asserting it had the capacity to handle the situation. Indonesian Navy Chief Admiral Bernard Kent Sondakh said: "There is a grand strategy to paint a bad picture over our waters, as if the Indonesian Navy is not strong and the crimes at sea are increasing. ... Indeed, if we can't show the ability to guard the Straits of Malacca, the international forces may get in."[44] He also ordered his commanders to shoot dead armed pirates or terrorists operating in the Malacca Straits. In so doing, he asserted that "From now on we will show to the world that the Indonesian Navy alone is capable of safeguarding the Malacca Straits" — and added — "don't try and accuse us of violating human rights."[45]

As a pre-emptive reaction, Malaysia proposed joint anti-terrorism training, coordinated patrols and increased intelligence sharing.[46] Defence Minister and Deputy Prime Minister Najib said: "I stress that we must tighten co-operation among Malaysia, Indonesia, and Singapore as it is our responsibility to convince the international community that the Straits will not be exposed to possibilities" of a terrorist attack.[47] Indonesia made a similar proposal as part of its larger proposal for an ASEAN Security Community. In June 2004, Malaysia and Indonesia agreed to create a joint task force with troops operating under their own national commands, thus avoiding the sovereignty issue.[48] Each country will supply up to seven ships with about 100 crew. And on 20 July 2004, seventeen vessels from the Indonesian, Malaysian and Singaporean navies began joint patrols of the Malacca Straits.[49] The new initiative contains a "hand off" arrangement if the vessel being pursued enters the territorial waters of another country, but it does not allow for the naval vessel of one country to enter the territorial waters of another.

Despite the coordinated patrols, sharp differences persist. Admiral Sondakh still considers the concerns with terrorism as overblown and suggests that some governments, including the United States, want to control the Straits.[50] In contrast, Singapore's Defence Force Chief Major General Ng Yat Chung said that "The marrying of terrorism and piracy is of course a very bleak scenario for us and that is something we should not rule out."[51]

Other regional countries' reactions to the U.S. proposal were strong and varied. Surprisingly, Australia reacted coolly to the U.S. proposal to patrol the Malacca Straits.[52] It stressed that any military presence there should be that of the coastal states — Indonesia, Malaysia and Singapore. On the other hand, India, supposedly responding to a request by the three littoral states, offered to provide security in the Straits.[53] There is a precedent in which India and Indonesia held joint patrols off the Andaman islands to suppress poaching, smuggling and drug trafficking. Thailand expressed support for the U.S. proposal to increase technical and intelligence support for the littoral states but did not support the deployment of U.S. troops.[54] Even France chimed in agreeing that the United States should play a role in suppressing piracy in the Malacca Straits, but cautioning that "U.S. naval vessels should not enter Malaysian or Indonesian territorial or archipelagic waters without permission."[55]

China's view was significant. It has a particular dependence on, and thus a security interest in imports of Middle Eastern oil through the Malacca Straits. China opposes the RMSI proposal. A Chinese scholar publicly argued that insertion of U.S. warships in the Straits could be a violation of Article 38 of the Law of the Sea, which stipulates that "the regime of passage through Straits used for international navigation shall not in other respects affect the legal status of the waters forming such Straits or the exercise by the States bordering the Straits of their sovereignty or jurisdiction over such waters and their air space, seabed, and subsoil."[56]

Moreover China appears to be interested in assisting the littoral countries in safeguarding the Malacca Straits.[57] Senior Colonel Wang Zhongchun, a Deputy Director of Beijing's National Defence University, under the People's Liberation Army, proposed that China and ASEAN start with "substantive co-operation in such areas as anti-terrorism intelligence exchange, co-operation and co-ordination in handling legal cases, and deportation of suspects. Subsequently we can include counter-terrorism, piracy, and fighting maritime criminal activities." Given the rising tension between China and the United States over Taiwan,[58] competition for influence in Southeast Asia and control over the Malacca Straits may not be far behind.

The Way Forward?

The RMSI has three components: "A sea situation picture of the traffic in the Malacca and Singapore Straits, a decision making structure to decide on steps to be taken when clandestine activity is ongoing, and a standby maritime force to act on that decision."[59] Some of the components are already in place. According to Joshua Ho, the most efficient way to create a real-time picture of the maritime situation is to link existing or planned systems such as Singapore's Vessel Traffic Information System (VTIS), Port Klang's Vessel Traffic Management System (VTMS), Straitsrep and the IMO-mandated Automatic Identification System (AIS). VTIS monitors traffic in the Singapore Straits; VTMS monitors vessel activity in and around Port Klang. Straitsrep is a joint Indonesia-Malaysia-Singapore mandatory ship reporting system implemented in December 1998 under the IMO. And AIS will identify ships and their position to shore stations, other ships and aircraft, and exchange data with the VTS Authority.

These existing elements are a result of binding agreements between the states and IMO, perhaps making the proposal more politically palatable to both the coastal states and the Straits users. However U.S. naval ships cannot be used to interdict vessels in the Straits under existing IMO agreements. Clearly, there is a need for more naval patrols and escorts like that provided previously by the United States and India in the Malacca Straits, and now provided by Singapore in and out of its port, more anti-piracy drills, and increased monitoring and readiness.[60] But for RMSI to be successful, the three littoral states must take the initiative and carry most of the load, with perhaps the United States backstopping with technology, training, and intelligence.

Meanwhile, the United States has shown no signs of "backing off" its proposal at the time of writing. The United States officially proposed the RMSI at an ARF meeting in Yogjokarta in May 2004. But it was opposed, especially by Malaysia.[61] At ASEAN's meeting of Foreign Ministers in

June, an "ARF Workshop on Maritime Security", was tabled as a counter to the U.S. proposal. Nevertheless, U.S. Secretary of Defence Donald Rumsfeld emphasized the importance of the RMSI at the June 2004 Shangri-La Dialogue organized annually by the International Institute of Strategic Studies, while promising to "consult with friends and allies regarding its implementation".[62]

Japanese Initiatives

On 12 March 2002, at Japan's initiative, maritime authorities and experts from 14 other Asian countries convened in Tokyo to discuss ways of combining piracy in the region.[63] Also in August 2002, the Japanese Coast Guard and the Royal Brunei Marine Police conducted a joint anti-piracy exercise in waters offshore Brunei.[64] On 23 October, Japan dispatched a Coast Guard patrol boat (the *Yashima*) for training in the South China Sea and joint training with the Indian Coast Guard. The *Yashima* made port calls in India and Singapore and patrolled nearby waters.[65] In March, after an anti-piracy conference of the region's coast guards in Manila, Japan and Philippine Coast Guards led an anti-piracy training exercise.[66] In July, the *Yashima* participated in a training exercise in Malaysia and Japan is assisting Indonesia in drafting a coast guard code.[67] Although Japan continues to propose multilateral joint patrols, Southeast Asian nations have so far not accepted this proposal. The lingering memories of Japanese wartime behaviour make this proposal difficult for Southeast Asian governments and their publics to accept. Moreover, Japan's interpretation of Article 9 of its Constitution restricts Japanese defence to Japanese citizens or Japan-flagged vessels, and rejects collective self-defence, casting doubt on Japan's ability to be of much direct help.

Conclusion

The objectives of piracy and terrorism are usually different. The motivation for piracy is economic while that for terrorism is predominantly political and religious ideology.[68] Yet the simplistic conflation of piracy and terrorism has been encouraged by the facts that the motivation of the offender is irrelevant under the SUA Convention and that both piracy and terrorism occasionally use similar tactics (ship hijacking), the similar political and economic circumstances under which both piracy and "terrorism" tend to thrive, and the responses of the United States which tend to lump the two phenomena. On the one hand this conflation may enhance cooperation of indigenous states in prevention efforts. But on the other hand, their different perspectives on "terrorism" and sovereignty may undermine such cooperation.

Although the indigenous capacity in Southeast Asia is insufficient to combat the problem, naval patrols by outside maritime powers or even "neutral" flags are perceived as a challenge to national sovereignty. Naval patrols by India and the United States in the Malacca Straits are perceived in some Southeast Asian quarters as part of a much broader regional security plan whose scope goes well beyond combating piracy and terrorist threats in the Straits. Japanese proposals for similar joint patrols have also raised suspicion of "ulterior motives". And the U.S.-led PSI and the RMSI proposal have created considerable stress and nervousness in the region. Sovereignty concerns and the ASEAN tradition of "non-interference" in internal affairs may also explain the reluctance of some Southeast Asian nations to ratify the SUA Convention.

Furthermore, the practical effectiveness of U.S. or Japan-led patrols is questionable. The arrest authority of foreign naval vessels exercising rights of transit through international straits is unclear. Beyond this legal jurisdictional issue, the sheer size of the vessels used, while menacing, may actually inhibit their effectiveness in pursuing pirates and would-be terrorists using small high-speed craft who have intimate knowledge of the surrounding waters. Moreover, traditionally, it is not the role of the military to function as police. The U.S. Coast Guard might be a more acceptable and effective substitute.[69]

Because of the overlap in operational similarities, short-term counter-measures such as enhanced patrols, intelligence sharing and coordination, as well as ship defence will be useful for countering both piracy and terrorism. Indeed, "for the Malacca Straits, the three Straits states and the principal users could enter an agreement under Article 43 of the 1982 UNCLOS to cooperate in securing the obligation of Straits states to suppress and prevent piracy and terrorist attacks on vessels in the Straits and the obligation of user states to provide the Straits states with the technology, equipment, and training to do so."[70] In this context, the relevant ministers of the three Straits states have agreed to seek financial support to enhance security in the Malacca Straits.[71]

However, long-term solutions aimed at eliminating the root causes of piracy and terrorism may have to be fitted to the particular problem. To attack the problem of piracy at its root, there should be more concerted efforts at assisting both state economic development and maritime enforcement capacity building in Southeast Asia. Indeed, piracy is largely driven by poor economic conditions, and by addressing that issue, a major cause of piracy can also be addressed. However, the organized crime syndicates responsible for major ship hijackings may not be curtailed by economic development, because the potential returns of hijacking are so high. Thus these "high end" criminals must be denied bases and the transnational criminal networks that enable syndicates to transfer stolen cargo and ships must be disrupted. Also by promoting state development efforts, and assisting the building and strengthening of coast guards and internal security and intelligence *apparati*, these crime syndicates may be dealt with more effectively.

Addressing the threat of maritime terrorism *qua* terrorism is more problematic, and involves more complicated and sensitive questions of religion, ideology, sovereignty and foreign policy. It should be remembered that although ship hijacking or attack by terrorists in Southeast Asia is a serious potential threat, it is so far just that and not yet a reality. Perhaps standard anti-terrorist approaches such as disrupting the finances and leadership of the sponsoring organization may be effective in the short term. But by helping these states develop their own surveillance and enforcement capacities, long-term, and longer-lasting, solutions will be possible. A relevant example may be the U.S. project to create a Yemeni coast guard complete with high-tech equipped gunboats and training.[72] Ultimately, however, some nations may have to provide greater cultural and religious "space" for dissident groups. Thus, to combat the threat of piracy and maritime terrorism, both indigenous countries and external maritime powers should focus on what has created the threat as well as its symptoms.

Notes

1   This chapter draws heavily from Mark J. Valencia, "Piracy and Terrorism in Southeast Asia: Similarities, Differences and their Implications", in *Piracy in Southeast Asia*, edited by Derek Johnson and Mark J. Valencia (Singapore: ISEAS, 2005); and Adam Young and Mark J. Valencia, "Conflation of Piracy and Terrorism in Southeast Asia: Rectitude and Utility", *Contemporary Southeast Asia* 25, no. 2 (August 2004): 269–83.
2   R. Halloran, "What if Asia's Pirates and Terrorists Joined Hands?" *South China Morning Post*, 17 May 2003; "China Gives 'Guarded' Response to Indian Warships in Malacca Straits", *BBC Monitoring International Reports*, 18 July 2002; "Sea Lane, Oil Rigs a 'terror target' ", *CNN.com*, 19 September 2002; "Piracy Watchdog Points Finger at Aceh Separatists", *Straits Times*, 4 February 2003; B. Garekar, "Piracy in Malacca Straits Linked to Indonesia's Instability",

Straits Times, 27 January 2003; D. Osler, "Target: tankers", *Lloyd's List*, 6 February 2003; V. Ho, "No Let Down in Global Attacks by Pirates", *Kyodo News Service*, 24 July 2003.

3 See for example, Young and Valencia, "Conflation of Piracy and Terrorism in Southeast Asia", pp. 269–83.

4 Rene Ahmad, "Pirates and Terrorists not Natural Allies", *Straits Times*, 29 June 2004.

5 "No Proof that Pirates have Terror Links", *Straits Times*, 24 June 2004.

6 Tony Emmanuel, "Pirates may not be Linked to Terrorists", *New Straits Times*, 30 June 2004.

7 John Burton, "A Terror Attack in Asia's Busiest Shipping Lane could Wreak Havoc", *Financial Times*, 8 May 2004.

8 The editor of this publication notes the author's preference for the "Malacca Strait" as a singular noun. However, as stated in the introductory chapter, this publication adopts the plural noun "Malacca Straits" and it serves as a political and geographical shorthand for the Malacca Strait and Singapore Strait combined as one collective waterway.

9 Donald Urquhart, "Alarm over Surge in Kidnap-Ransom Cases — IMB Centre Urges Indonesian Authorities to Take Immediate Action", *Business Times*, 16 June 2004.

10 Donald Urquhart, "Terror-piracy Nexus: IMO Seeks Global Action", *Shipping Times*, 21 May 2004.

11 John Burton, op. cit., *supra* n. 7.

12 Peter Chalk, "Contemporary Maritime Piracy in Southeast Asia", *Studies in Conflict and Terrorism* vol. 21, 16 March 1997, p. 89.

13 Natalino Ronzitti, "The Law of the Sea and the Use of Force against Terrorist Activities", in *Maritime Terrorism and International Law*, edited by Natalino Ronzitti (Dordrecht: Martinus Nijhoff, 1990), pp. 1–15.

14 Chalk, *supra* n. 12.

15 "Piracy Watchdog Points Finger at Aceh Separatists", *The Straits Times*, 4 February 2002; "China gives 'Guarded' Response to Indian Warships in Malacca Straits", *BBC Monitoring International Reports*, 18 July 2002.

16 Chalk, *supra* n. 12, p. 93.

17 "US Interdiction Poses Legal Problems", *Oxford Analytica*, 30 June 2003.

18 Chalk, *supra* n. 12.

19 "Indonesia says Militants Considered Malacca Strikes", *Reuters*, 25 August 2004.

20 Convention for the Suppression of Unlawful Acts Against the Safety of Maritime Navigation, 1988, <www.imo.org/conventions/contents.asp?topic_id=259&doc_id=686>.

21 Ashley Roach, "Initiatives to Enhance Maritime Security at Sea", in "Military and Intelligence Gathering Activities in Exclusive Economic Zones: Consensus and Disagreement", edited by Mark J. Valencia and Kazumine Akimoto, *Marine Policy Special Issue*, v. 28, no. 1 (January 2004): 41–67.

22   Jay L. Batongbacal, "Trends in Anti-piracy Cooperation in the ASEAN Region",
      in *Combating Piracy and Ship Robbery*, edited by Hamzah Ahmad and Akira
      Ogawa (Tokyo: The Okazaki Institute), 2001, p. 125. International Chamber of
      Commerce (ICC) and International Maritime Bureau (IMB), "Piracy Report,
      20 October 2002", <www.iccwbo.org/home/news_archives/2002/stories/
      piracy%20report%20Oct2002.asp>; Roach, "Initiatives to Enhance Maritime
      Security at Sea", *supra* n. 21, p. 3.
23   ICC-IMB, "Piracy Report, October 2002".
24   "Experts Want Force to Pursue Pirates", *Lloyd's List*, 28 February 2002; Marcus
      Hand, "Security — Co-operation Call to Ward Off Malacca Straits Attacks",
      Lloyd's List, 20 February 2003.
25   Michael Evans, "US Plans to Seize Suspects at Will", *The Times* (London),
      11 July 2003.
26   Charles Dragonette, *Office of Naval Intelligence Analysis Department Worldwide
      Threat to Shipping Mariner Warning Information*, 21 February 2002.
27   Ibid.
28   Sudha Ramachandran, "India Signs on as Southeast Asia Watchdog", *Asia
      Times Online*, 5 April 2002, <atimes.com/ind-pak/DD05Df01.html> (Accessed
      on 6 June 2005).
29   Ibid.
30   Ibid.
31   Chalk, *supra* n. 12, p. 96.
32   For an elaboration of the pros and cons of the PSI, see Mark J. Valencia, "The
      Proliferation Security Initiative: Legal and Political Implications", paper
      presented to the Honolulu Conference on the Regime of the Exclusive Economic
      Zone: Issues and Responses, Ship and Ocean Foundation, Tokyo, December
      2003.
33   "U.S. Embassy Claims Senior Admiral 'mischaracterized' ", *New Straits Times*,
      6 April 2004.
34   John R. Bradley and William Choong, "Asia Must Guard its Seas from Terrorists,
      U.S. official warns", *Straits Times*, 22 April 2004.
35   John Burton and Shawn Donnan, "US Plan to Guard Straits of Malacca not
      Welcome", *Financial Times*, 6 April 2004.
36   "Malaysia to Monitor Restricted Export Items", *The Star*, 20 January 2004;
      "America still Ready to Ride Along if Need be", *The Korea Herald*, 10 June 2004.
37   "FPDA to Include Anti-terror Exercises", *Business Times*, online edition,
      Singapore, 9 June 2004.
38   "Keep Yanks out", <http://www.abs_cbnnews.com/News Story.asps?
      oid=52831>.
39   "Multilateral Responses Needed to Deal with New Security Threats: Teo Chee
      Hean", *Channelnewsasia.com*, 22 April 2004, <www.channelnewsasia.com/
      stories/singaporelocalnews/view/81405/1/.html> (Accessed on 6 June 2005).

[40] Siti Rahil, "Singapore Seeks Joint Patrols of Malacca Straits, Involving Japan", *Kyodo News*, 20 May 2004, <home.kyodo.co.jp/all/display.jsp?an= 20040520156> (accessed on 6 June 2005).

[41] Huma Siddiqui, "India, America, S'pore joint naval exercise in August", *The Financial Express*, 16 April 2004.

[42] Chua Mui Hoong, "S'pore on Track in Foreign Security Accord", <http:// Straitstimes, asia1.com.sg>.

[43] "S'pore can't Invite US to Patrol Straits: KL", *The Straits Times*, 12 May 2004; "KL to Tighten Security in Straits of Malacca on Specific Intelligence Reports", *Channel NewsAsia*, 20 May 2004, <www.channelnewsasia.com/stories/ southeastasia/view/85982/1/.html>, (accessed on 6 June 2005).

[44] Achmad Sukarsono, "Indonesia being Tested over Malacca Straits — Report", *Reuters*, 19 July 2004.

[45] "Indonesia Orders Pirates, Sea Terrorists Shot on Sight", *Reuters*, 18 June 2004.

[46] "Malaysia Seeks to Boost Security Co-operation among Neighbors", *Financial Times*, 16 June 2004.

[47] John Burton, "Anti-terrorism Patrols Planned for Malacca Straits", *Financial Times*, 19 June 2004.

[48] Sukarsono, *supra* n. 44.

[49] Supriyatin, "Malacca Straits Nations Start Co-ordinated Patrols", *Reuters*, 20 July 2004; "3 Nations Join to Protect a Vital Oil Lifeline", *International Herald Tribune*, 20 July 2004.

[50] "3 Nations Join to Patrol a Vital Oil Lifeline", *International Herald Tribune*, 20 July 2004.

[51] Ibid.

[52] Rob Taylor, "US Warned: Stay out of the Pirate Straits", *Sunday Times*, 16 June 2004.

[53] Natwar Singh, "India Ready to Protect Malacca Straits", *PTI*, 1 July 2004.

[54] "Bangkok Backs US in Straits Initiative", *The Nation*, 25 June 2004.

[55] Balan Moses, "France Wants US Warships out of Straits", *New Straits Times*, 9 June 2004.

[56] Ji Guoxing, "US RMSI contravenes UN Convention of the Law of the Sea", *PacNet*, 29, 8 July 2004, <www.csis.org/pacfor/pac0429.pdf>.

[57] Lee Kim Chew, "China could Play Part in ASEAN's Maritime Security", *Straits Times*, 20 June 2004.

[58] John M. Glionna, "U.S., China Set to Host Major War Exercises", *Honolulu Advertiser*, 20 July 2004, p. A5.

[59] Joshua Ho, "Guarding the Region's Waterways", *Today online*, 24 June 2004.

[60] Shepli Rekhi, "Terrorists may be Rehearsing at Sea", *Straits Times*, 18 April 2004.

[61] "ASEAN Ministers to Focus on Security in Annual Talks", *Kyodo News Service*, 25 June 2004.

62 "Rumsfeld: Asia Maritime Security Plan", *Reuters*, 3 June 2004.
63 "Asian Nations Begin Talks in Japan on Measures to Combat Maritime Piracy", *BBC Monitoring Asia Pacific*, London, 12 March 2002.
64 "Brunei: Hijack Drama on High Seas", *Borneo Bulletin*, 15 August 2002.
65 "Japan to Send Coast Guard Boat on Anti-terrorist Mission", *BBC Monitoring Asia Pacific-Political*, London, 18 October 2002.
66 "Philippines, Japan Lead Multilateral Anti-piracy Exercises", *BBC Monitoring Asia-Pacific*, London, 7 March 2003.
67 Donald Urquhart, "Malaysia Acts to Create National Coast Guard, IN will Use the Japan Coast Guard as its Model", *Business Times*, Singapore, 8 July 2003.
68 There are no hard and fast lines separating economic and political motives, for one can often support the other, but most pirates are not politically motivated.
69 Bruce B. Stubbs, "Piracy and Terrorism", *Washington Times*, Letters, 10 July 2003.
70 Marcus Hand, "Security — Co-operation Call to Ward off Malacca Straits Attacks", *Lloyd's List*, 20 February 2003.
71 David Osler, "Malacca Straits Security on Agenda", *Lloyd's List*, 23 September 2002.
72 Jerry Frank, "Washington Backs Yemen in Piracy and Terrorism Fight", *Lloyd's List*, 21 August 2002.

7

Private Military and Security Companies in the Fight against Piracy in Southeast Asia

Carolin Liss

[T]he most telling effect on modern buccaneers may well come not as a result of high-sounding pontifications from international bodies. It may well result from the availability of well trained and equipped commercial marine security forces operating out of North America, Europe, Africa and Southeast Asia — driven as the pirates are by the pursuit of profit.[1]

Introduction

We live in an increasingly privatized world. Private education, private airlines, private telephone companies, and private healthcare are only a few examples of the increasing impact of privatization on our daily lives. Designed to stay competitive in the global market, private companies promise cheaper rates and better service for the customer. Today, these companies offer services for every aspect of life, including the security and military sectors. It should, therefore, be far from surprising that so-called Private Military Companies (PMCs) and Private Security Companies (PSCs) are also employed to secure the world's oceans. In the last ten years an increasing number of private companies surfaced and expanded, offering services ranging from maritime terrorism and piracy response training for law enforcement personnel, to recapturing hijacked vessels and rescuing kidnapped crew members.

This chapter attempts to give an insight into this growing business, focusing on services offered to address modern day piracy.[2] Despite the global character of the topic, this article concentrates on the Asian region, where most pirate attacks have been reported in recent years. The first part of the article gives a brief overview of piracy in Southeast Asia, including the South China Sea, based on data published by the International Maritime Bureau's (IMB) Piracy Reporting Centre (PRC). The second part looks at the rise of PMCs/PSCs in recent years, with particular focus on companies offering anti-piracy services. The following part then examines the obstacles as well as favourable conditions in the maritime world that hinder or are beneficial for the services offered by PMCs/PSCs in regard to piracy. Here, the author also discusses concerns about PMCs/PSCs and the services they offer, resulting from their internal structure, information policy and the nature of operations they conduct. The chapter concludes by suggesting that PMCs/PSCs will most likely play an increasingly important role in maritime security in general and in the fight against piracy in particular. However, it is stressed that the services they advertise and their work practices should be regarded with a certain dose of scepticism.

Piracy in Southeast Asia

Since the early 1970s, incidences of piracy and crime on the high seas have steadily increased in Southeast Asia and in recent years, the region has become one of the global hot spots of vessel attacks. Even though attacks on merchant ships increased in the area in the 1970s and 1980s, they were often still small in scale and rarely involved physical injuries to those who were attacked.[3] This changed in the 1990s, when modern day pirates began operating on a larger scale and across regional borders. By the late 1990s, more than half of all reported attacks on vessels worldwide occurred in Southeast Asia, or more precisely in the Straits of Malacca, the South China Seas, the sea north of Java, and in the waters surrounding the Sulu Archipelago. The modern day pirates, armed with parangs or modern guns, operate in fast motorboats, and prey on fishers, barter traders, cruising yachts, and, increasingly, commercial shipping.[4]

According to data from the IMB-PRC, the number of actual and attempted pirate attacks[5] reported in the 1990s range from 90 attacks in 1994 to as many as 469 reported incidents in 2000. In 2001, the number slightly declined to 335 reported attacks, rising again to 370 in 2002 and 445 in 2003.[6] In the first half of 2004, the number of reported attacks fell to 182, from 234 incidents reported in the same period in the previous year.[7] The real number of attacks, however, may in fact be much higher. According to Noel Choong, the Regional Manager of the PRC, more than 50 per cent of all pirate attacks on commercial vessels remain unreported for a variety of reasons.[8] Furthermore, attacks on fishing boats and other small craft are rarely reported to the IMB or the local authorities, and therefore do not find their way into these statistics. However flawed, the IMB-PRC's reports indicate that modern day pirates are increasingly prepared to use violence to further their aims, with the number of pirates armed with guns and other small arms on the rise. Injuries to the crew, assaults, and killings occur regularly in pirate attacks in the region. Worrisome is also the latest increase in hostage taking of crew members and vessels for ransom.[9]

The vast majority of pirate attacks in Asia today are simple hit-and-run robberies, committed by what can best be described as common sea-robbers. Such attacks are often brief affairs, lasting no longer then fifteen to thirty minutes, and require a minimum level of organization and planning. The attacks usually take place either in territorial waters, at anchorage or in ports.[10] These sea robbers attack commercial vessels as well as small crafts such as fishing boats and yachts. In cases in which the pirates confront the crew onboard directly, these simple robberies can involve a high level of violence.[11]

A second group of pirates can be characterized by a higher level of organization and sophistication compared to the hit-and-run sea-robbers. These organized pirate gangs or syndicates predominately attack medium sized vessels, including cargo ships, bulk carriers and tankers. Organized pirate gangs adapt their own methods to a rapidly changing world, becoming increasingly technologically sophisticated in the process.[12] Two different types of pirate attacks by organized gangs can be distinguished, so-called long-term and permanent seizures. Long-term seizures are attacks in which a vessel and its crew are held hostage for a limited time. In these cases a vessel is attacked whilst underway, the crew overpowered and the ship diverted from its course. In some cases, the ship is repainted and the name changed by the pirates in order to avoid detection. However, while the crew is held hostage, the ship is brought to a safe location to unload the cargo, after which the crew and the vessel are released.[13] An even higher level of organization and sophistication is required for permanent seizures.[14] In these cases the entire vessel is literally hijacked by pirates. It is a method used by organized crime syndicates to acquire a ship, which is then turned into a so-called "phantom ship".[15]

Responses to piracy in Southeast Asia have been manifold and diverse. Local, as well as international authorities, have addressed the problem in various ways, including the launch of coordinated patrols in the Malacca Straits involving the navies of Singapore, Malaysia and Indonesia in July 2004.[16] National, regional and international organizations, most notably the IMB and the International Maritime Organization (IMO), have through their work increased awareness of modern day piracy and have initiated and promoted a number of countermeasures. Yet another less widely discussed response to the increase in piracy comes from the private sector, or more precisely from PMCs or PSCs.

Private Military and Security Companies in the Fight against Piracy

Private Military and Security Companies: An Overview

The U.S.-led war in Iraq in 2003 has brought to world attention the existence and involvement of private companies in wars and post-war reconstruction efforts unlike any other conflict before. Media reports of the horrific deaths of four employees of Blackwater USA in Fallujah,[17] and the coverage of private contractors' alleged involvement in the abuse of Iraqi detainees at Abu Ghraib prison,[18] heightened public awareness of the nature of work conducted by the private military industry in conflict zones. Peter Singer, author of the book *Corporate Warriors: The Rise of the Privatised Military Industry (2003)*, suggested elsewhere:

> ...the Iraq War is where the history books will note that the [private military] industry will take full flight. Iraq is not just the biggest U.S. military commitment in a generation but also the biggest marketplace in the short history of the privatised military industry. In Iraq, private actors play a pivotal role in great-power warfare to an extent not seen since the advent of the mass nation-state armies in the Napoleonic Age.[19]

Singer's statement also shows that outsourcing of military services is hardly a new phenomenon. Looking at history one finds numerous examples of private military actors, known as mercenaries, *condotierri* or *dogs of war*, to mention just a few,[20] in past conflicts and wars around the world.[21] However, in the past fifteen years, PMCs or PSCs have arisen as a new breed of private military actor. PMCs/PSCs are private business companies, offering a large variety of services in the military and security sector. There has been an ongoing debate how to distinguish between PMCs and PSCs. Some observers have suggested that PMCs provide active security services, including military training, while PSCs offer more passive services, such as logistics support for military operations.[22] Yet, as Singer argues, these distinctions are difficult to put into practice.[23] Today, this is increasingly so, as companies expand and merge, with many of the smaller companies bought by their larger counterparts, resulting in single companies offering an ever expanding range of services. However, as this article is concerned mainly with anti-piracy services — services mostly provided outside areas of active armed conflict or war[24] — the author will use the term PSC[25] for the remainder of this chapter.[26]

The number of PSCs and the variety of services they offer have grown rapidly in the post-Cold War environment. One of the major reasons for the growth of the privatized military industry was the changing nature of conflict after 1989. With the end of the Cold War, the number of internal and regional armed conflicts — formerly held in check by the two Cold War superpowers — increased. Many of these conflicts, predominantly in the developing world, were fought over control of natural resources and the wealth and power resulting from the exploitation of these resources. These conflicts were "often intermixed with ethnic, religious, and tribal antagonisms",[27] and were characterized by the involvement of transnational crime syndicates, regional or local warlords, rebel groups, terrorists and insurgents.[28] The emergence of these conflicts coincided with a general unwillingness of *Western* states to intervene in these conflicts. As J. L. Taulbee states:

> The negative experiences with intervention in the early 1990s undercut the [United Nations] Security Council's ability to interfere on humanitarian or other grounds without explicit consent from the parties in conflict. The political will to intervene has become dependent upon estimates of potential casualties and costs, not strategic value or humanitarian issues...Defence services provided to other states such as training, procurement and certain tasks associated with UN peacekeeping operations, have been increasingly delegated to private companies.[29]

Furthermore, with the end of the Cold War, a global down-sizing of major armies began, particularly so in the former Soviet Union but also in the United States and the United Kingdom, leaving an abundance of well-trained and experienced soldiers available either to set up or be employed by PSCs. Also, the reduction in size of the military at a time when numerous conflicts in different parts of the world emerged, led the U.S. Government to increase military outsourcing in order be able to respond to these conflicts.[30] However, the latest increase in demand for PSCs services, fostering the establishment of even more PSCs, is linked to the war against terrorism and the U.S.-led intervention in Iraq since 2003.[31]

Apart from the U.S. Government, PSCs are today employed by various other governments, the UN, humanitarian NGOs and multinational corporations, but have also been known to assist rebel groups and international criminal syndicates.[32] Like their clients, PSCs are now based all around the world, with many new companies emerging in the developing world, and a number of large established companies, often based in the United States or Britain, opening branch offices in different corners of the earth, including Southeast Asia. Active throughout the globe, PSCs offer services ranging from logistics support, risk analysis, training of military units, and intelligence gathering, to the rescue of hostages and the protection of assets and people in conflict zones.

Proponents of PSCs have pointed out that private companies can offer more effective military services at more competitive prices than state militaries and can respond to crises more rapidly. Also, it has been stressed that PSCs have successfully operated in post-conflict areas providing, for example, de-mining services.[33] However, with the increasing employment of PSCs, a number of concerns about the nature of work provided by these companies surfaced. These concerns mostly centred on the lack of transparency and public oversight of operations and business practices of PSCs and the question of whether or not the protection of national security and the provision of military services should remain within the domain of governments, rather than the profit motivated private sector. Furthermore, some observers have argued that the employment of PSCs allow *Western* governments "to pursue policies in tough corners of the world with the distance and comfort of plausible deniability".[34]

These concerns were fuelled by reports of scandals surrounding the work conducted by a number of PSCs. Allegations included overcharging, the prolonging of conflict in order to increase their own profits, involvement in criminal activities,[35] and the acceptance of payment in the form of mining or oil concessions in exchange for their services.[36] One example of a controversial PSC operation is the intervention of Sandline International — a British company set up by the infamous Colonel Tim Spicer — in

Papua New Guinea (PNG) in 1997. Sandline was hired by the PNG Government after local military efforts failed to recapture the world's largest copper mine on Bougainville island, seized by a local rebel group. The government offered Sandline US$36 million to help recover the island from the rebels and restore the mine back into operation, as the rebels had shut down the mine to prevent further pollution of their island and to demand a larger share of the revenue for the local population. Spicer's arrival in PNG, accompanied by seventy ex-soldiers, provoked the army to rebel and stage a coup, leading ultimately to the government's collapse. Spicer was arrested for illegally importing arms, but was later allowed to return to the U.K. after he agreed to be questioned by a government commission of enquiry.[37]

The example of Sandline's involvement in PNG shows that PSCs are active in Asia and Southeast Asia, even though PSC operations are often thought to be largely confined to Africa and the Middle East. In Southeast Asia, increasing globalization and the intensification of the global economy have brought about many changes in the post-Cold War era. These include not only the transformation of economies and polities, but also the development and dissemination of radical political and religious ideologies into and within the region. In this period, the region experienced a resurgence of religious fundamentalism together with a sharpened sense of maintaining ethnic identities and boundaries, enhancing previous regional conflicts in several Southeast Asian nations.[38] Since the Asian economic crisis of 1997, poverty, uncertainty and political dissatisfaction with central governments and regimes spread ever more widely in Southeast Asia. Moreover, with the collapse of the Soviet Union and the end of Soviet and American-supported proxy wars in Asia, Africa and Latin America, the international arms market suddenly became saturated with automatic weapons. Light arms from the Soviet Union, Cambodia, China and Afghanistan have been sold for relatively low prices in countries such as Myanmar, Indonesia and the Philippines and are readily available to pirates, drug lords, crime syndicates, and terrorist groups.[39] With the beginning of the war against terrorism and the more recent terrorist attacks in the region — including the October 2002 bombings on the Indonesian island of Bali — the feeling of insecurity and the sense of threat, especially to foreign interests, have increased significantly. All these developments heightened the demand for services offered by PSCs. Work conducted in the Asian region has therefore been diverse and has included:

- The rescue of a businessman kidnapped in East Timor for US$220,000 by Onix International;
- Demining services conducted by the French company COFRAS in Cambodia;
- The employment of Strategic Communication Laboratories, a firm specializing in psychological warfare operations, by the Indonesian Government to train its forces to respond to religious or secessionist violence more effectively;[40]
- The training of the Royal Malaysian Police in close protection, hostage rescue and crisis management by TASK International in preparation for the 1998 Commonwealth Games;[41] and
- The establishment and training of the Filipino police counter-terrorism force by Grayworks, a Filipino company — which also sends its specialists on missions into conflict areas, such as the southern part of the archipelago, with the forces they train.[42]

These examples of PSCs involvement in Asia may seem a far cry from maritime security issues. However, the history, past operations, and current state of PSCs are important in regard to maritime security, as it is, to a large extent, the same (or similar) companies and individuals, which were discussed above that offer maritime security and anti-piracy services in the Asian region today.

PSCs in the Maritime Sector

New York and London — Three established companies have formed a unique new company to address the challenges of marine security in the wake of the September 11th terrorist attacks on the United States, it was announced here today by top executives of the three companies involved in the new venture.[43]

While the involvement of PMCs in Iraq since 2003 is now widely discussed, not many people are aware that PSCs are active players employed to secure the world's oceans, or more precisely, commercial vessels, yachts, cruise ships, oil platforms, container terminals and ports. Being part of the overall phenomenon of the privatization of military and security services discussed above, the majority of companies presently operating in the maritime sector emerged after the end of the Cold War. However, their number increased considerably after the 9/11 terrorist attacks. To address the security challenges in the maritime sector, PSCs offer a wide range of services. These include International Ship and Port Facility Security Code (ISPS-Code) training courses, risk and vulnerability assessment and consulting, the training of naval and maritime security forces, insurance fraud and cargo crime investigation and prevention, crisis management and much more. Some examples of the range of services conducted by PSCs in the maritime sector include:

- The training of U.S. Navy recruits by Blackwater USA at their 5,200-acre training facility in North Carolina;[44]
- The training of the British Royal Navy in the use and maintenance of their nuclear-powered submarines;[45]
- The employment of Gurkha escort guards, provided by the British company Anglo Marine Overseas Services, aboard cruise vessels in high risk areas;[46] and
- The employment of Trident Maritime, a British based company headed at that time by Colonel Spicer,[47] following the Liberation Tigers of Tamil Ealam's devastating attack on the Bandaranaike International Airport in the Sri Lankan capital of Colombo in July 2001. In the aftermath of the attack, Lloyd's of London introduced a hefty war risk surcharge on shipping to Sri Lanka, threatening the shipping dependent nation with a serious loss of trade. In order to improve security and ultimately reduce the impending surcharge, Lloyds suggested that the government hire Trident Maritime to conduct a security survey of the countries airport and seaports, and to implement the recommendations given by the company.[48]

Anti-Piracy Services

Most PSCs active in the maritime sector also offer services to address the growing piracy problem in Asia and other parts of the world. Their services, however, are not sought after only by clients based in piracy prone regions, but also by insurance companies and banks located in major cities around the globe. Many PSCs offering anti-piracy security are part of, or linked to, larger PSCs or transnational corporations outside the security industry. While many of the larger companies are based in the United States and Great Britain, a number of them have recently established branch offices in the Asian region. One example is Global Marine Security Systems Company (GMSSCO), (formed by Hart Group Limited, Tufton Oceanic Limited, and Energy Transportation Group, Inc)[49] which is reported to have recently opened an office in Singapore. Moreover, a number of smaller companies have been established in the region, such as Background Asia, with headquarters in Singapore. Many other companies are based in other parts of the world, yet they offer anti-piracy services covering the Asian region. These include in Britain, Gray Page Limited,[50] in Germany MarineServe GmbH (MSG),[51] in Israel G.S.SEALS,[52] in the USA the Trident Group[53] and in Australia the Australian National Security Service (ANSS),[54] to mention just a few.

The security services offered by these companies range from risk consulting to the "detention and elimination of threatening parties".[55] While not all companies offer all anti-piracy services, with some solely providing risk consulting or vessel tracking services, most seem to offer many or most of the major anti-piracy services. These include:[56]

a) *Risk Assessment and Consulting*: Almost all companies offer risk consulting services, either consisting of general political risk reports published and updated regularly, or client-specific risk assessments. These range from port or vessel threat assessments and pre-employment screening to crisis management planning. Companies such as Control Risks Group (CRG),[57] which are solely offering consultancy services, stress on their corporate websites that their role is strictly advisory.[58]

b) *Training of Crews, Port Authority Personnel or Military and Law Enforcement Units, Vessel Tracking*: Almost all companies also seem to offer ISPS training courses and surveillance services rendered through twenty-four hour monitored vessel tracking systems. Security-awareness training courses for crewmembers, including piracy response and prevention training are also offered. More advanced training for law enforcement officers or military personnel is also available from selected companies. Enterprising Securities for example offers such courses, which include "anti-piracy interdiction" training. The courses are held either in the United States or at other international locations, including the Philippines.

c) *Provision of (Armed) Guards on-board Vessels or Vessel Escorts*: A large number of companies offer to provide escort vessels or armed/ unarmed guards for commercial vessels or yachts to prevent and react to piracy or terrorist attacks. Securewest International[59] for instance offers armed and unarmed Gurkha security officers to protect commercial and military shipping in port and at sea.

d) *Crisis Response, Investigation and Recovery of Hijacked Vessels and Cargoes, and the Rescue of Kidnapped Crew Members*: Many companies today offer crisis response, with some extending their services to the investigation and recovery of hijacked vessels and stolen cargoes. Two companies specializing in investigations and the recovery of hijacked vessels are Gray Page Limited and Pilgrim Elite Limited,[60] both based in the UK. Furthermore, some companies also offer to assist in the negotiation process in cases of kidnapped crew members, with some even offering to rescue hostages in cases where negotiations have failed.

e) *Fisheries Protection*: Perhaps the least attention has so far been paid to the services provided in the fisheries sector. For example, Hart Nimrod (Bermuda) and Global Fishing Licenses Limited — both members of the Hart GMSSCO Group — offer assistance in the establishment of "Fisheries Management and Protection Programmes", which promise "protection for local fishermen against illegal foreign fishermen and the preservation of the territorial limit for exclusive use of local fishermen", as well as "anti pollution, piracy, smuggling and terrorist capabilities".[61]

Hence, PSCs offer preventive as well as post-attack services, addressing all types of pirate incidents on commercial vessels and pleasure crafts. Hit-and-run robberies, maybe even attacks by organized pirate gangs or syndicates, may be prevented through better training of the crew or the presence of armed or unarmed guards onboard a vessel. Victims of hijackings can rely on crisis management assistance during the event, or employ a company to relocate and/or recover the hijacked vessel or stolen cargo afterwards. Furthermore, PSCs services may even help prevent attacks on fishermen, which are often very violent in nature. There is, however, an important difference between the services advertised by PSCs on their Internet websites and the services actually put into practice for a customer. The questions that now arise are what the factors favouring the employment of PSCs in the maritime sector are; and what the difficulties and problems that the industry and their clients may face are.

PSCs: Favourable Conditions, Obstacles and Overall Problems

Favourable Conditions

As discussed above, the security environment changed considerably after the end of the Cold War, and particularly so after the 9/11 terrorist attacks. With a heightened fear of a maritime terrorist attack,[62] governments began to look at the world's oceans with grave concern, resulting in the implementation of the ISPS code and other new safety and security regulations in the maritime sector. This has enhanced the emergence of a new security consciousness in the shipping industry, with many becoming aware that security improvements were necessary to sufficiently protect their assets, investments and crews.[63] As government authorities and agencies were unable to provide security, training, and technical security equipment on a scale that is now sought by the maritime industry or is required as part of new regulations, these changes undoubtedly offered an unprecedented opportunity for PSCs.[64]

Yet, there has been wide concern about whether or not the implementation of the ISPS code and other new regulations will substantially increase security, with many observers arguing that everything may look good on paper, but that in reality nothing will change.[65] Even if the new regulations are to be successful, the maritime environment would still remain one of the least controlled and regulated sectors, a legacy of the old maritime tradition of the freedom of the ocean. This lack of effective control leaves ample opportunity for *grey-zone* and outright illegal activities, and provides pirates and terrorists with room to conduct their business. William Langewiesche even suggests that:

> It is not by chance that the more sophisticated pirate groups and terrorists seem to mimic the methods and operational techniques of the ship owners. Their moral and motivations are different, of course, but all have learned to work without the need for a home base and, more significantly, to escape the forces of order not by running away, but by complying with the laws and regulations in order to move about freely and to hide in plain sight.[66]

These overall conditions provide PSCs with the opportunity to offer a wide range of services. It remains, for example, comparatively simple to re-register a hijacked vessel, making it very difficult to locate the vessel once it is given a new identity. This, as a result, gives PSCs the opportunity to offer investigation and vessel recovery services. Additionally, companies such as Gray Page Limited, offer not only to recover hijacked vessels but also "specialise in lifting the corporate veils between off-shore registered companies to provide title to assets such as vessels to which beneficial ownership has been concealed through the use of non-disclosure domiciles."[67]

Some PSCs also offer pre-employment and crew background checks, as document fraud remains a major problem in the maritime industry. The Seafarers International Research Centre at Cardiff University found, for instance, more than 12,000 cases of forged certificates of competency in a survey of fifty-four maritime administrations.[68] Background checks conducted by PSCs may not only increase the overall safety on vessels but may also, in some cases, prevent the employment of crewmembers likely to collaborate with pirate gangs. Also, the lax controls in the maritime world may allow PSCs to conduct their work more freely and discreetly than in other environments. This provides on one hand room for less reputable companies to act and operate outside the law.[69] On the other hand, it allows companies to operate unhindered and to complete their operations swiftly and effectively. The striking similarities between the maritime industry and the privatized military and security industry in regard to secrecy as well as to lax controls and oversight, could also be beneficial for PSCs, as potential clients do not have to fear that any information about their own operations and business practices will be revealed or made public.

Not only the nature of the maritime environment may be favourable for PSCs to find and conduct business, but also the questionable reputation and low resources of some of the authorities and law enforcement agencies in the Asian region. The reputation of some officials, particularly so in countries like Indonesia or the Philippines, to accept bribes to either turn a blind eye, or assist in certain tasks, may for example, aid PSC employees to operate in the region.[70] Next, an incentive for ship or cargo owners, banks or insurance companies to hire a PSC may be the general difficulty for outsiders to deal effectively with authorities in Asia, and a lack of faith that local authorities will successfully handle the case and act in the victim's interest . The employment of a PSC, on the contrary, promises the use of highly experienced and motivated individuals, working solely in the client's interest. The relatively low level of training and the poorly maintained equipment of some navies and other law enforcement agencies in some Asian countries such as Indonesia, may not only increase these suspicions, but also offer other employment opportunities for PSCs.[71] These include assistance in maintaining and operating existing and new equipment, as well as the training of units by experienced personnel in specialized skills such as terrorist or piracy counter-manoeuvres.[72]

Obstacles

The same maritime environment that provides the favourable conditions for PSCs discussed above also poses and creates obstacles for these companies. For example, while crew background checks may be useful in screening out potential criminals, being able to get reliable information on the life, training and former experiences of, for instance, a Filipino citizen from a remote island, can be difficult and therefore too expensive for a ship owner. The unwillingness of the maritime sector to invest in the safety of their assets and the people they employ, may indeed be the biggest obstacle faced by PSCs. Despite the growing concern about security within the maritime industry, there seems to remain a reluctance to spend additional money[73] to increase safety.[74] Furthermore, the overall financial loss resulting from most pirate attacks remains rather low, and industry observers such as Captain Mukundan, Director of the IMB, have, for example, pointed out that the employment of armed/unarmed guards onboard vessels, is likely to have only a very limited effect in deterring pirates or terrorists.[75] The extra costs for employing armed guards may therefore not be justifiable in the eyes of ship owners who have to stay commercially competitive.[76]

Furthermore, reputable PSCs have to act within the legal boundaries set by the states they are operating in. This can be a difficult and complex task as a vessel does not only move between various states and jurisdictions, using the right of innocent passage, but also sails under the flag of yet another state. The lack of clear maritime laws and borders may also hamper PSCs services, for example, in regard to fisheries protection. While it seems a viable solution to protect local fishermen from foreign fishing boats and attacks by illegal poachers, such incidents often occur in waters where the maritime boundaries are not legally agreed upon by all parties concerned.[77]

PSCs also have to compete with local authorities and institutions like the IMB's PRC for contracts. While a number of government offices, NGOs and other institutions offer political risk analysis, the IMB also regularly publishes reports on piracy and armed robbery at sea. Furthermore, it has a proven track record of successfully assisting victims in the recovery of hijacked vessels and stolen cargo.[78] The IMB has also the advantage of providing these services most likely substantially cheaper than private companies.[79] Commenting on the role of PSCs in response to piracy, Captain Mukundan, for one, believes that they can play an important role in the training of crew members, teaching them, for example, how to act in hostage situations. He adds that in many other aspects the services offered by PSCs are controversial, and that he is not convinced that a PSC has indeed ever succeeded in recovering a hijacked vessel.[80] In the end, Captain Mukundan's views may, in the eyes of PSC staff, only be a statement of a commercial competitor. However, his scepticism towards PSCs is shared by many others and may be based in part on the internal structure and set up of such companies, as well as on concerns regarding the nature of services they provide.

Internal and Overall Problems

In interviews the author conducted with various PSC employees, most of them commented on the large number of PSCs now offering maritime related services. They also raised their concerns about the ability of the majority of these companies to actually deliver what they promise. The rising number of PMCs offering maritime related services can be in part attributed to the fact that a relatively low amount of capital is required to set up such an enterprise. Many PMCs hire personnel and acquire necessary equipment on a case-to-case basis, once a contract with a client is signed. This allows the companies to run their business with limited expenses. Many companies, therefore, only consist of an office, a very limited number of permanent staff, and, usually, an impressive presence on the Internet. While this type of company set-up can be beneficial for the client — as resources are bought and staff hired specifically for the client's needs — it also allows companies to rapidly dissolve and recreate themselves if need be.[81] Also, it allows the establishment of PSCs by a wide variety of people. Information provided by companies about their background, the company itself and the services they have conducted in the past, as well as information about the people they hire if required, is usually sparse. As Frank Hopkins writes:

> There are many shingles out for 'maritime security', including several with a shingle but no credential or track record. They would like to sign you up as a client or sell you stock in their company, either way is fine, as long as they get your money. There are others who have even initiated relationships with legitimate security firms or army suppliers, but sail under false flags as far as credentials and experience [are concerned]. There are many very professional websites, behind which we were unable to find a professional organization.[82]

However, the level of information about these companies, their founders and employees vary considerably. Some companies, such as Enterprising Securities,[83] provide hardly any information at all while other companies such as Gray Page Limited, offer brief background information about its founders and staff. Gray Page is not only in this regard rather the exception, as the company is set up and run mostly by people without a military background. The majority of PSCs operating in the maritime sector seem to be founded by and to employ mostly ex-military or ex-law enforcement personnel, with the credentials and reputation of the company often linked closely to the past military experiences of its founding members and employees. Therefore, most companies advertise to employ former members of elite special forces from around the globe, with *vast experience*. To be sure, whether or not this experience is in the maritime sector or related to the services and tasks they are now employed for by the company — including for example knowledge about the vulnerabilities of a ship — remains often unclear. To bridge the exisiting gap in background information and to win a potential client's trust, all these companies go to great lengths in stressing the high moral standing of their employees. A good example is Securewest International's use of Gurkha soldiers' reputation to reflect on the company and the companies' operational abilities, as they employ former soldiers from the British Army Brigade of Gurkhas. They are described in the company's brochures not only as "the bravest of the brave" but also as "the most likable people you will ever meet".[84] Other companies often use descriptions such as *of good character* or *men with highly tested character* to describe the personnel they employ if needed.

Furthermore, to accomplish many of the services advertised, PSCs require good connections and relationships with government authorities in the Asian region, as well as a reliable network of informants. A certain level of diplomatic skill is also needed to maintain these relationships as well as an assured depth of knowledge of the maritime sector. While most of the companies emphasize their *excellent relationships* with law enforcement agencies and government officials, these claims are difficult to assess due to the lack of information given about such companies.

The lack of information about a company's track record and real experience in the services they advertise is a characteristic common among all PSCs operating in the maritime sector. All stress on their websites that the services and operations they conduct for a client remain confidential. While this is understandable in some cases, it offers companies the easy option of claiming to have conducted a wide range of services, as no one is able to verify the information given. One example that comes to mind is the vast number of companies claiming to be experienced in, or claiming to have recovered, hijacked vessels. While a vessel can be anything from a rubber dinghy to a supertanker, the number of hijacked vessels would be enormous if all these claims were true.[85] The lack of information about the track records of PSCs, is also an indicator for another more serious problem. PSCs conduct their operations for a specific client and are bound to follow their client's interests. If a hijacked vessel is recovered for example, information about the hijacking and the culprits is only given to local authorities with the client's consent.[86] Therefore, if the client has no interest in, or does not believe it fruitful to inform law enforcement agencies, the perpetrators are left untouched and are able to continue their line of business.

All these factors can certainly arouse suspicion in the wider maritime community and make it increasingly difficult for a potential customer to choose among these companies. The difficulty of choice for a reliable company, however, is not unique to PSCs, but the choice becomes more crucial in regard to PSCs, as the consequences of hiring an unreliable company can be problematic at best or disastrous at worst — not only for the customer. A ship owner for example, has to trust a company to choose the right kind of people to be employed as armed guards on one of his vessels.[87] The choice of employees as well as the general objectives of PSCs can, in some instances, result in the use of what may be regarded as excessive violence. Talking about a case in which his company provided an armed escort for a yacht in Indonesian waters, a manager of a PMC stated in an interview that the instructions to his employees were clear: "Shoot first, ask questions later." Anyone approaching the vessel without providing satisfactory identification would be shot at.[88] While there have been numerous attacks on yachts in Indonesian waters which involved a high level of violence from the attackers, others were simple hit-and-run attacks conducted by a number of local coastal inhabitants attacking a yacht to steal food and small belongings in times of need.[89] To shoot in these circumstances can be unnecessary, not to mention other incidences in which local fishermen may simply approach the yacht without any malicious intent. However, these extreme actions on the side of PSCs are possible and remain unaccounted for, as they will most likely occur at sea and out of sight of authorities or witnesses. Furthermore, the *pirates* conducting such *attacks* will most likely be local fishermen or other inhabitants of small local villages. The chances that any serious action will be taken in inquiring what happened to these people, or if the actions taken by the PMC employees were justified, unfortunately remain slim. Equally important, weapons in the hands of guards on a large commercial cargo vessel or a tanker, can have devastating consequences if handled in a careless or inconsiderate, over-eager fashion.

The question of reliability, however, does not only concern obvious issues such as weapons on board a vessel, but many other aspects of services provided by PSCs, including the rescue of hijacked crew members or vessels, which exceed the scope of this discussion. However, controversies that may arise from risk consulting conducted by PSCs are perhaps less obvious and are therefore worth briefly looking at. By relying on political risk analysis reports from PSCs, one relies on information provided, in many cases, by the very companies that sell solutions to security threats, such as piracy. The secrecy surrounding the work of PSCs and the methods of research they employ, make it difficult for outsiders to verify the information presented in these reports. The findings of PSC reports, however, are not always only accessible to PSC clients, but regularly find their way into the mainstream media. It is therefore important for the reader to keep in mind that PSCs are foremost commercial enterprises, aiming at maximizing financial profit for the company and its shareholders. The extensive publicity in the case of the attack on the vessel *Dewi Madrim* in the Malacca Straits is one example.[90] Countless newspapers in various parts of the globe, discussed over months the links between terrorist and pirate attacks, using the example of the attack on the *Dewi Madrim*. The source of information for these articles was allegedly a commercially available, but expensive, report published by Aegis Defence Services Ltd,[91] a London based PSC managed by its shareholders, among them, as Chairman and CEO, Lt-Col Tim Spicer.[92] The following excerpt from *The Economist* is a typical sample:

> But according to a new study by Aegis Defence Services, a London defence and security consultancy, these attacks represent something altogether more sinister. The temporary hijacking of the DEWI MADRIM was by terrorists learning to drive a ship, and the kidnapping (without any attempt to ransom the officers) was aimed at requiring expertise to help the terrorists mount a maritime attack. In other words, attacks like that on the DEWI MADRIM are the equivalent of the al-Qaeda hijackers, who perpetrated the September 11th attacks going to flying school in Florida.[93]

Investigations into the attack on the *Dewi Madrim* by the IMB, however, came to the conclusion that terrorists were not involved.[94] Information from the manager of the vessel, and a telephone conversation with the ship's captain, in fact showed that no-one was kidnapped and that the attackers made no attempt to learn how to *drive* the vessel.[95] Asked in an interview about these discrepancies, Dominic Armstrong, Managing Director of AEGIS Research and Intelligence, stated that the AEGIS report was simply misquoted in regard to the kidnapping.[96] Obviously, it is out of AEGIS' control what newspapers publish and it should be the responsibility of journalists to verify their sources — even if the price of the AEGIS report at US$5,800 makes this an expensive task. However, it remains that Mr Armstrong confirmed in the interview that his company had not spoken to the manager of the vessel or anyone who was onboard the ship during the attack.[97]

Conclusion

PSCs today offer preventive as well as post-attack services to address every kind of modern day piracy incident. Some of the services advertised and some of the companies are, however, still in the formative stages and only time will tell if this commercial alternative to provide anti-piracy solutions will be accepted. Given the increased security awareness in the maritime sector and the overall trend of outsourcing in the military and security sectors, the chances of PSCs growing in numbers and prospering in the maritime sector seem good. Greater business opportunities in the maritime realm could then in turn contribute to the general growth of the privatised military and security sector. In fact, by offering a broad spectrum of services addressing maritime security and terrorism issues, PSCs no longer have to rely on actual wars or armed conflicts to prosper at a time when the number of major armed conflicts is in decline.[98] However, as discussed above, there are a number of problems and controversial issues that are inherent in the private maritime security industry and if the employment of PSCs in this sector is to increase, then improved regulation and oversight of these companies is needed. The examples discussed above also suggest that potential clients should choose the PMC they wish to employ carefully, and that a certain dose of scepticism may be appropriate for clients and the public when relying on information published, or allegedly published, by some PSCs. In future studies, the research methodologies of PSCs is an issue that certainly warrants further attention. In regard to piracy, it is important to keep in mind that while PSCs may assist in preventing individual pirate attacks and help victims in dealing with the aftermath of an attack, they do not address the underlying causes of modern day piracy itself.

Notes

[1]   Frank Hopkins, "Piracy Part III: To Give no Quarter", *Soldier of Fortune*, May 2000, p. 72.

[2]   The research for this chapter is drawn from certain aspects of the author's ongoing research on contemporary maritime piracy in Southeast Asia. However, her research on the relatively new phenomenon of PMCs and PSCs offering services for the maritime sector is yet to be completed at the time of publication. This chapter is therefore a work in progress.

[3]   Exceptions were attacks on Vietnamese Boat People in the Gulf of Thailand, which often featured a high level of violence and cruelty.

[4]   James Francis Warren, "A Tale of Two Centuries: The Globalisation of Maritime

Raiding and Piracy in Southeast Asia at the End of Eighteenth and Twentieth Centuries", paper presented at KITLV Jubilee Workshop, Leiden, 14–16 June 2001, pp. 13–17.

5   While there are a variety of different definitions of piracy that often only consider attacks on the high seas, the PRC employs a more inclusive definition. It includes in its analysis any "act of boarding any vessel with the intent to commit theft or any other crime and with the intent or capability to use force in the furtherance of that act". See: ICC International Maritime Bureau. "Piracy and Armed Robbery against Ships. A Special Report. Revised edition — March 1998", International Chamber of Commerce, 1998, p. 2.

6   ICC International Maritime Bureau, "Piracy and Armed Robbery against Ships. Annual Report. 1 January–31 December 2003", International Chamber of Commerce, 2004, p. 5.

7   "Twenty per cent drop in acts of piracy in first half of 2004", Channelnewsasia.com, 26 July 2004 <http://channelnewsasia.com/stories/afp_world_business/print/97563/1/.html> .

8   Noel Choong, Regional Manager IMB Piracy Reporting Centre. Interview by author, 23 October 2002. Piracy Reporting Centre, Kuala Lumpur. Some ship owners for instance are reluctant to report attacks, as they fear that an investigation will delay their vessel even further, resulting in additional costs for the owner. Many also do not want to be regarded as unreliable carriers of freight or fear rising insurance rates. Governments and law enforcement agencies in the region are also often reluctant to disclose the number of attacks in their respective countries in order to preserve its reputation as a safe place for trade and passage. See for example: "Piracy in Southeast Asia", CSS Strategic Briefing Papers, Vol. 3, Part 2, Centre for Strategic Studies, June 2000.

9   A prominent case was the attack on the tanker Penrider, in which three members of the crew were taken hostage. See for example: Kate McGeown, "Aceh rebels blamed for piracy", BBC News, 8 September 2003 <http://newsvote.bbc.co.uk/mpapps/pagetools/print/news.bbc.co.uk/2/hi/asia-pacific/3090136.stm>.

10 ICC International Maritime Bureau, "Piracy and Armed Robbery against Ships. A Special Report. Revised edition — March 1998", p. 3 and p. 7.

11 Reports of lost yacht equipment, hijacked yachts, injury or even death of yacht owners and their crew appear from time to time in newspapers or other reports. To the best of my knowledge, systematic data-collection of attacks on yachts and fishing vessels remains to be undertaken.

12 Today, the gathering of intelligence and the conduct of surveillance with modern technical equipment are common practice among organized pirates to target selected ships and cargoes.

13 ICC International Maritime Bureau, "Piracy and Armed Robbery against Ships. A Special Report. Revised edition — March 1998", pp. 35–36.

14   Permanent seizures appear to be a phenomenon particular to the Far East region and increasingly Indonesian waters. In the past, many hijacked vessels have been found in southern Chinese ports. However, the number of hijacked medium sized vessels has, according to IMB data, declined in recent years.

15   In those cases, the vessel's original cargo is disposed of and the original crew either killed, thrown overboard, or put into life rafts and left to their own devices. The ship is then registered under a different name. Equipped with a new identity, the vessel is then offered to an anxious shipper to transport his cargo. The cargo, however, will never arrive at its destined port, as the vessel is diverted and the cargo off-loaded in another port and sold to another consignee. The vessel is then once again re-registered under a different name and the play begins once again. ICC International Maritime Bureau, "Piracy and Armed Robbery against Ships. A Special Report. Revised edition — March 1998", pp. 32–35.

16   The joined patrols starting in July 2004 were named Exercise Malsindo, with Malsindo beeing an acronym for Malaysia, Singapore and Indonesia. Mohd Haikal Mohd Isa, "Troika Coordinated Patrol, Positive Move to Ensure Straits Safety", *Bernama*, 29 July 2004.

17   Jay Price and Joseph Neff, "Security Company Broke Own Rules", *Newsobserver.com*, 22 August 2004 <http://www.newsobserver.com/news/v-printer7story71552996p-7741192c.html>.

18   Hans de Vreij, "Privatising the Iraq War", *Radio Netherlands*, 14 May 2004 <http://www.rnw.nl/hostspots/html/irq040514.html>; David Isenberg, "Corporate Mercenaries. Part 1: Profit Comes with a Price", *Asia Times*, 19 May 2004 <http://atimes.com/atimes/Middle_East/FE19Ak01.html>.

19   Peter Warren Singer, "Warriors for Hire in Iraq", *The Brookings Institution*, 15 April 2004 <http://www.brookings.edu/views/articles/fellows/singer20040415.htm>. See also Peter Warren Singer, *Corporate Warriors: The Rise of the Privatized Military Industry* (Cornell: Cornell University Press, 2003).

20   The names and labels for such private actors have changed over time, depending on the location and character of conflict and the nature of the private actor's involvement. However, the label chosen for private actors, depended, and still depends, largely on the commentator's point of view. The limits of this article will not allow a full discussion of the debate about whether or not the label "mercenary" can be applied to employees of modern PMCs. However, various authors convincingly point out the differences between mercenaries and PMCs/PSCs. See for example: Singer, *Corporate Warriors*, pp. 40–48. See also: David Shearer, *Private Armies and Military Intervention* (Adelphi Papers, New York: Oxford University Press, 1998), pp. 13–22.

21   For a detailed discussion see the second chapter "Privatized Military History", in Singer, *Corporate Warriors*, pp. 19–39.

22   Doug Brooks, "Messiahs or Mercenaries? The future of International Private

Military Services", in *Managing Armed Conflicts in the 21st Century*, edited by Adekeye Adebajo, Chandra Lekha Sriram (Portland, Oregon: Frank Cass Publishers, 2001), pp. 129–30.

23 Singer, *Corporate Warriors*, pp. 89–91.

24 In a United Kingdom Parliament Select Committee on Foreign Affairs report concerned with the regulation of PMCs, the capabilities of PMCs are divided between Non-Lethal and Lethal Capabilities, with anti-piracy capabilities placed in the Lethal section. The United Kingdom Parliament, Select Committee on Foreign Affairs Minutes of Evidence, Chapter 1 — Introduction, <http://www.publications.parliament.uk/pa/cm200102/cmselect/cmfaff/922/2061321.htm>.

25 It is, however, important to note that these PSCs have little in common with domestic security companies providing, for example, security guards for condominiums or shopping centres.

26 David Shearer suggested that in contrast to PMCs, PSCs "tend to be confined to specific areas, notably those in which foreign investment is located, and their role limited to protecting installations against banditry and other crimes". See Shearer, p. 24. This description could indeed be applied to some of the work conducted by companies in regard to piracy. However, as I will discuss later in the paper, some services offered do not fit into this description and anti-piracy services are also in some cases offered by large, more diversified companies.

27 See Michael T. Klare, *Resource Wars. The New Landscape of Global Conflict* (New York: Henry Holt and Company, 2001), p. ix.

28 Singer, *Corporate Warriors*, pp. 50–53.

29 James L. Taulbee, "Mercenaries, Private Armies and Security Companies in Contemporary Policy", in *Global Society in Transition. An International Politics Reader*, edited by Daniel N. Nelson and Laura Neack (The Hague: Kluwer Law International, 2002), p. 87.

30 Deborah Avant, "Think again: Mercenaries", *Foreign Policy*, July/August 2004 <http://www.foreignpolicy.com/story/cms.php?story_id=2577>.

31 Isenberg, "Corporate Mercenaries. Part 1: Profit Comes with a Price".

32 Singer, *Corporate Warriors*, p. 52. Peter Singer, "Should Humanitarians Use Private Military Services?", *Humanitarian Affairs Review*, Summer 2004 Issue <http://www.humanitarian-review.org/opload/pdf/singerEnglishFinal.pdf>.

33 Brooks, "Messiahs or Mercenaries?", pp. 131–32.

34 International Consortium of Investigative Journalists, *Making a Killing: The Business of War* (Washington, DC, The Center for Public Integrity, 2003) Chapter 1, "Making a Killing: The Business of War", p. 1, <http://www.publicintegrity.org/bow/>. Furthermore, the links between governments and PSCs also remain a critical issue, because many of these companies are politically very well connected, a fact that is very beneficial for the companies in order to win or receive contracts. See for example: David Isenberg, "Corporate Mercenaries

Part 2: Myths and Mystery", *Asia Times*, 20 May 2004 <http://www.atimes/Middle_East/FE20Ak02.html>.

[35]   One of the better-known examples is the involvement of DynCorp employees in the trade and rape of woman and children in Bosnia and Kosovo in 2000. See: International Consortium of Investigative Journalists, *Making a Killing. The Business of War*, Chapter 2, "Privatizing Combat, the New World Order", p. 10.

[36]   Singer points out that the payment in the form of mining or oil concessions can have a long-time impact on the client nation, as a potentially valuable resource and profits from it are lost for the state in question for years after the conflict has ended. Singer, *Corporate Warriors*, pp. 166–67.

[37]   For a more detailed report see: International Consortium of Investigative Journalists, *Making a Killing. The Business of War*, Chapter 3, "Marketing the New 'Dogs of War' ", p. 2 and pp. 7–8. And David Isenberg, "Soldiers of Fortune Ltd.: A Profile of Today's Private Sector Corporate Mercenary Firms", (Washington: Center for Defense Information, 1997) <http://www.cdi.org/issues/mercenaries/merc1.html>; and Klare, *Resource Wars*, pp. 195–98.

[38]   Peter Chalk, *Grey-Area-Phenomena in Southeast Asia: Piracy, Drug Trafficking and Political Terrorism* (Canberra: Strategic and Defence Studies Centre, Australian National University, 1997), pp. 7–11. He also points out that these developments were also fuelled by the increasing marginalization of certain ethnic or religious groups across the region, who suffered from state sponsored administrative and economic neglect as a result of development programmes which had as their prime purpose the furthering of the interests of the dominant community. Ibid, pp. 17–18.

[39]   The trade in light arms has an enormous impact on the countries involved, affecting political stability, the economy and further fuelling what is an already thriving drug-related black economy. See: Peter Chalk, "Light Arms Trading in SE Asia", *Jane's Intelligence Review*, March 2001, pp. 42–45.

[40]   Singer, *Corporate Warriors*, pp. 13–14 and p. 80.

[41]   David Isenberg, "Security for Sale", *Asia Times*, 14 August 2003 <http://www.atimes.com/atimes/Front_Page/E>.

[42]   The company is based in the North Cotabato Province, the Philippines, and is involved in diverse activities, ranging from the protection of a Dole fruit plantation in North Cotabato to involvement in the fight against terrorist and separatist movements in the Southern Philippines. David Pugliese, "Canada's Guns for Hire on Terror's Front Lines", *The Ottawa Citizen*, 2 November 2002 <http://www.sandline.com/hotlinks/canada_story.html>.

[43]   "Global Marine Security Systems Company launched by Industry Experts", *Global Marine Security Systems Company*, Press Release, 2 November 2001. The three companies in question are Hart Group Limited, Tufton Oceanic Limited, and Energy Transportation Group Inc. Please refer to the *GMSSCO* website at <http://gmssco.com>.

44   Barry Yeoman, "Soldiers of Good Fortune", *Mother Jones*, May–June 2003 Issue
     <http://www.motherjones.com/news/feature/2003/05/ma_365_01.html>.

45   Singer, *Corporate Warriors*, p. 12.

46   Mark Bruyneel, "Reports in 2000. April–June" <http://home.wanadoo.nl/
     m.bruyneel/archive/modern/2kreporu.htm>.

47   Today, *Trident Maritime Inc* is, according to information on its homepage, a
     wholly-owned subsidiary of *Techno-Sciences Inc*. See: *Trident Maritime* homepage
     at <http://www.technosci.com/trident/index.php>.

48   For more details see: International Consortium of Investigative Journalists,
     Making a Killing. The Business of War, "Marketing the New 'Dogs of War'".

49   *GMSSCO* <http://gmssco.com>.

50   *Gray Page Limited*, <http://www.graypagelimited.com>.

51   *MSG MarineServe*, <http://www.marineserve.de>.

52   *G.S.SEALS*, <http://www.gsseals.com/profile.htm>.

53   *Trident Group*, <http://www.gotrident.com>.

54   *Australian National Security Service*, <http://anss.com.au/Introduction-to-
     ANSS.htm>.

55   *GMSSCO* homepage.

56   The following services are provided by numerous companies. The companies
     the author choose to give examples for particular services are only random
     samples. The author does not want to imply that these companies are more
     reliable than others, or offer particular expertise that other companies do not
     offer.

57   *Control Risks Group*, <http://www.crg.com>.

58   However, *CRG* has recently joint forces with *Port Maritime Security International
     (PMSi)*, which offers training for *CRG's* clients.

59   *Securewest International*, <http://www.securewest.com/home.ikml>.

60   *Pilgrim Elite Ltd*, <http://pilgrimelite.co.uk>.

61   *GMSSCO* homepage.

62   Indicators of this heightened awareness and fear are the large number of
     newspaper articles discussing the likelihood of a maritime terrorist attack, as
     well as the increasing number of academic papers and books looking at the
     issue. One prominent example in Singapore is: Michael Richardson, *A Time
     Bomb for Global Trade: Maritime-Related Terrorism in an Age of Weapons of Mass
     Destruction* (Singapore: Institute of Southeast Asian Studies, 2004).

63   The protection and safety of crews, however, is unfortunately mostly not the
     main concern of ship owners.

64   There is a broad range of technical anti-piracy products on offer today. These
     include electrical fences for vessels and non-lethal weapons such as shoot-able
     glue.

65   See for example: William Langewiesche, "Anarchy at Sea", *The Atlantic Monthly*,
     September 2003, pp. 76–77.

66   William Langewiesche, *The Outlaw Sea* (New York: North Point Press, 2004), p. 7.

67   *Gray Page Limited* homepage.

68   Sam Vaknin, "On Maritime Piracy", <http://www.knowledgerush.com/kr/jsp/db/view.jsp?columnId=138&contentType=column>. See also: "IMB Calls for Clamp-down on Fake Maritime Documents", *International Chamber of Commerce*, 17 January 2001 <http:www.iccwbo.org/ccs/news_archives/2001/imb_fakes.asp> (accessed 25 August 2004).

69   This is of particular concern in cases where PSC personnel are armed and/or involved in operations such as the recovery of hijacked vessels and yachts, or the rescue of kidnapped crew members.

70   For the Philippines, see for example: Lt Antonio F. Trillanes IV PN, "Corruption in the Philippine Navy Procurement System", March 2002 <http://www.pcij.org/HotSeat/trillanes4.html>.

71   The Center for Defense Information in Washington, D.C., states that only about 20 to 25 per cent of the Indonesian Navy's inventory is operational. See: Center for Defense Information, "Indonesia", Washington, D.C. <http://www.cdi.org/issues/Asia/indonesi.html>.

72   PSCs may even be used as a means for one state, or a group of states, to provide assistance (for example training) to another state, without the providing state being directly involved and responsible for it. This may make it easier for the receiving state to agree to the assistance offered. However, the negative impact of heavy reliance on outside training and assistance can be an over-dependence on the very people and companies that provide these services. See: Singer, *Corporate Warriors*, pp. 96–97. This kind of indirect assistance could, for example, include an anti-piracy training course for a Navy unit, and may be a way for Asian countries to overcome their reluctance to accept direct assistance from other countries.

73   The ISPS Code, for example, requires a Ship Security Officer (SSO) for specific vessels. The cheapest way, and the one chosen by many companies, to fulfil this requirement is to appoint the captain/master as SSO, as no additional personnel needs then to be hired. The downside is that the already busy captain/master has to handle these additional duties. There was even a fair amount of resistance from ship owners when it looked like a commission of the European Union might decide that the SSO on board a vessel must be someone other than the captain/master on ships registered in the European Union. However, the EU Commission eventually decided against it. See: James Brewer, "European Blow to ISPS Compliance", *Lloyd's List*, 12 March 2004, p. 5. Alternatively, please see: C.R. Kelso, "Surprise SSO Ruling is Entirely Sensible", *Lloyd's List*, 17 March 2004, p. 7.

74   Alex Morrison, Security Manager GMSSCO. Interview by author, 20 May 2004. Alexandra Point, Singapore; and Alex Duperouzel, Managing Director

Background Asia. Interview by author, 3 September 2004. Six Battery Road, Singapore. Some also claim that only a major maritime attack (a major terrorist attack or a pirate attack resulting in a major oil spill or collision of vessels) or increased insurance rates will enhance the willingness of the shipping industry to invest into better security.

[75]   Captain P. Mukundan, Director IMB. Interview by author, 21 June 2004. Maritime House, Barking, Essex.

[76]   *Background Asia* suggests the employment of ten guards on a vessel for a passage longer than twenty-four hours. They also provide an indication of the expected costs, stating "a basic team of 10 men would be about US$30,000–40,000 per month and would probably be deployable on vessels in dangerous passages for 25 days a month." See: Background Asia "Piracy and Terrorism", September 2003, pp. 4–5. The report can be downloaded from the company's homepage: <http://www.backgroundasia.com>.

[77]   One example would be the northern part of the Malacca Straits, an area with numerous attacks on fishing vessels. The border issue in the northern part of the Malacca Straits is not yet resolved between Indonesia and Malaysia. Mak Joon Num, Maritime Security Expert. Conversation with author, 1 September 2004. ISEAS, Singapore.

[78]   See for example: "IMB Search Leads Thai Authorities to Hijacked Tanker", International Chamber of Commerce, 21 May 2002 <http://www.iccwbo.org/home/news_archives/2002/stories/thai-piracy.asp>; or see "Piracy Reporting Centre Foils another Hijack on the High Seas", International Chamber of Commerce, 16 June 2000 <http://www.iccwbo.org/ccs/news_archives/2000/hijack_foiled.asp>.

[79]   The IMB does not have shareholders and therefore does not pay out dividends. While some of the IMB's work is conducted free of charge, financial arrangements depend on their clients preferences, with some preferring to pay on a time and cost basis while others prefer to be charged upon the success of an operation. Captain P. Mukundan, Director IMB, "RE: FW: Piracy Questions". Email to the author, 1 September 2004.

[80]   Captain P. Mukundan, Director IMB. Interview by author, 21 June 2004. Maritime House, Barking, Essex.

[81]   This is also the case for PMCs offering non-maritime related services. See: Singer, *Corporate Warriors*, pp. 73–75.

[82]   Hopkins, "Piracy Part III: To Give no Quarter", p. 57.

[83]   *Enterprising Securities*, <http://www.enterprisingsecurities.com/index.html>.

[84]   *Securewest International* homepage.

[85]   However, the author believes that there are a small number of companies, which have been able to recover hijacked vessels.

[86]   Joe Corless, Operations Director Gray Page Limited. Interview by author, 23 June 2004. Baltic Exchange, London.

87   The consequences can, obviously, be more serious in cases where PMCs are involved in wars or armed conflict.

88   Interview conducted by the author.

89   Sethuraman Dinakar and Harry Maurer, "The Jolly Roger Flies High, as Piracy Feeds the Hungry'. *Business Week International Edition*, 24 May 1999.

90   The *Dewi Madrim* was attacked on 26 March 2003 in the Malacca Straits. In the event, ten armed pirates boarded the *Dewi Madrim*, broke open the port bridge door and took the duty officer and A/B hostage. The pirates then gathered all crew members and tied them up. The perpetrators stayed on board for about one hour and there are conflicting reports about who navigated the vessel at that time. The pirates eventually left the vessel with the ship's cash, equipment and some of the crews' personal belongings. None of the crewmembers was injured in the attack. See for example: ICC International Maritime Bureau, "Piracy and Armed Robbery against Ships. Annual Report. 1 January – 31 December 2003", *International Chamber of Commerce*, 2004, p. 30.

91   At the time the author's research was conducted, *Aegis Defence Services Ltd* had four divisions including Risk Analysis (through Research and Intelligence), and Maritime Security. The maritime sector was covered by Hudson Trident, which was either wholly owned by *Hudson Marine Management* (<http://www.hudsontrident.com>) or a 50/50 joint venture between *AEGIS* and *Hudson Marine Services* (<http://www.aegisdef.com>) (as of 15 September 2004). Since then, however, the structure and website of the company have changed. AEGIS is at present (September 2005) a specialist risk management company comprising three divisions: Research and Intelligence, providing risk analysis and assessment, Technical Services, providing risk mitigation, and Security Services, providing risk management. (Information provided to the author by AEGIS.)

92   *Aegis Defence Services Ltd* homepage <http://aegisdef.com>. Also accessible through <http://www.aegisworld.com>.

93   "Peril on the Sea", *The Economist*, 2 October 2003 <http://economist.com/business/displayStory.cfm?story_id=2102424>. The text in brackets is included in the original article.

94   Captain P. Mukundan, Director IMB. Interview by author, 21 June 2004. Maritime House, Barking, Essex.

95   Capt. Chan Kok Leong, General Manager GBLT Shipmanagement Pte. Ltd. Interview by author, 13 February 2004. Beach Road, Singapore. And telephone conversation with the vessel's captain, 13 February 2004.

96   Dominic Armstrong, Managing Director of AEGIS Research and Intelligence. Interview by author, 22 June 2004. 118 Piccadilly, London. He also stated in an interview during a CNN programme called *Insight* that "a ship called the [DEWI MADRIM]...was taken by pirates, and instead of going to the safe room and just stealing the cash, they went to the bridge. They steered the ship

for an (hour), changing speed, changing direction then installed their own radio VHF equipment. At the end of the hour, they left. Now that is only one reported incident. Many incidents may have gone unreported, or just taking place, but that is an example of the maritime equivalent of a Florida flight training school." "Security Experts Worry over Combination of Piracy & Terrorism on High Seas", *CNN Insight*, Aired 17 June 2004, rush transcript <http://www.cnn.com/TRANSCRIPTS/0406/17i_ins.00.html>.

[97] Dominic Armstrong, Managing Director of AEGIS Research and Intelligence. Interview by author, 22 June 2004. 118 Piccadilly, London.

[98] A number of institutions, including the Stockholm International Peace Research Institute and the Canadian Project Ploughshares, report that the number of armed conflict has been on the decline. See: Charles J. Hanley, "War Making Headlines, but Peace Breaks Out", *Associated Press*, 29 August 2004 <http://story.news.yahoo.com/news?tmpl=story&cid=515&e=1&u=/ap/20040829/ap_on_af/war_and_peace>.

References

ICC International Maritime Bureau. "Piracy and Armed Robbery against Ships. A special report. Revised edition — March 1998". International Chamber of Commerce, 1998.

ICC International Maritime Bureau, "Piracy and Armed Robbery against Ships. Annual Report. 1 January–31 December 2003". International Chamber of Commerce, 2004.

"IMB Calls for Clamp-down on Fake Maritime Documents". International Chamber of Commerce, 17 January 2001 <http://www.iccwbo.org/ccs/news_archives/2001/imb_fakes.asp> (accessed 25 August 2004).

"IMB Search Leads Thai Authorities to Hijacked Tanker". International Chamber of Commerce, 21 May 2002 <http://www.iccwbo.org/home/news_archives/2002/stories/thai-piracy.asp> (accessed 15 September 2004).

International Consortium of Investigative Journalists. *Making a Killing. The Business of War*. Washington, D.C. The Center for Public Integrity, 2003 <http://www.publicintegrity.org/bow/> (accessed 24 November 2003).

Isenberg, David. "Corporate Mercenaries. Part 1: Profit comes with a Price". *Asia Times*, 19 May 2004 <http://atimes.com/atimes/Middle_East/FE19Ak01.html> (accessed 1 September 2004).

Isenberg, David. "Corporate Mercenaries Part 2: Myths and Mystery". *Asia Times*, 20 May 2004 <http://www.atimes/Middle_East/FE20Ak02.html> (accessed 21 May 2004).

Isenberg, David. "Security for Sale". *Asia Times*, 14 August 2003 <http://www.atimes.com/atimes/Front_Page/E> (accessed 12 November 2003).

Isenberg, David. "Soldiers of Fortune Ltd.: A Profile of Today's Private Sector Corporate Mercenary Firms". Washington, D.C.: Center for Defense Information,

1997 <http://www.cdi.org/issues/mercenaries/merc1.html> (accessed 26 August 2004).

Kelso, C.R. "Surprise SSO Ruling is Entirely Sensible". *Lloyd's List*, 17 March 2004, p. 7.

Klare, Micael T. *Resource Wars. The New Landscape of Global Conflict* (New York: Henry Holt and Company, 2001).

Langewiesche, William. "Anarchy at Sea". *The Atlantic Monthly*, September 2003, pp. 50–80.

Langewiesche, William. *The Outlaw Sea* (New York: North Point Press, 2004).

McGeown, Kate. "Aceh Rebels Blamed for Piracy". *BBC News*, 8 September 2003 <http://newsvote.bbc.co.uk/mpapps/pagetools/print/news.bbc.co.uk/2/hi/asia-pacific/3090136.stm> (accessed 26 July 2004).

Mohd Haikal Mohd Isa. "Troika Coordinated Patrol, Positive Move to Ensure Straits Safety". *Bernama*, 29 July 2004.

"Peril on the Sea". *The Economist*, 2 October 2003 <http://economist.com/business/displayStory.cfm?story_id=2102424> (accessed 1 September 2004).

"Piracy in Southeast Asia". *CSS Strategic Briefing Papers*, Vol. 3, Part 2, Centre for Strategic Studies, June 2000.

"Piracy Reporting Centre Foils Another Hijack on the High Seas". International Chamber of Commerce, 16 June 2000 <http://www.iccwbo.org/ccs/news_archives/2000/hijack_foiled.asp> (accessed 15 September 2004).

Price, J. and J. Neff. "Security Company Broke Own Rules". *Newsobserver.com*, 22 August 2004 <http://www.newsobserver.com/news/v-printer7story 71552996p-7741192c.html> (accessed 23 August 2004).

Pugliese, David. "Canada's Guns for Hire on Terror's Front Lines". *The Ottawa Citizen*, 2 November 2002 <http://www.sandline.com/hotlinks/canada_story.html> (accessed 13 November 2003).

Richardson, Michael. *A Time Bomb for Global Trade: Maritime-Related Terrorism in an Age of Weapons of Mass Destruction* (Singapore: Institute of Southeast Asian Studies, 2004).

"Security Experts Worry over Combination of Piracy & Terrorism on High Seas". *CNN Insight*, Aired 17 June 2004. A rush transcript is available at <http://transcripts.cnn.com/TRANSCRIPTS/0406/17i_ins.00.html> (accessed 9 September 2005).

Sethuraman, Dinakar and H. Maurer. "The Jolly Roger Flies High, as Piracy Feeds the Hungry". *Business Week International Edition*, 24 May 1999.

Shearer, David. *Private Armies and Military Intervention*. Aldephi Papers (New York: Oxford University Press, 1998).

Singer, Peter Warren. *Corporate Warriors. The Rise of the Privatized Military Industry* (Cornell: Cornell University Press, 2003).

Singer, Peter. "Should Humanitarians Use Private Military Services?" *Humanitarian Affairs Review*, Summer 2004 issue <http://www.humanitarian-review.org/opload/pdf/singerEnglishFinal.pdf> (accessed 4 September 2004).

Singer, Peter. "Warriors for Hire in Iraq". *The Brookings Institution*, 15 April 2004 <http://www.brookings.edu/views/articles/fellows/singer20040415.htm> (accessed 25 August 2004).

Taulbee, J.L. "Mercenaries, Private Armies and Security Companies in Contemporary Policy". In *Global Society in Transition. An International Politics Reader*, edited by D.N. Nelson and L. Neack, pp. 85–109 (The Hague: Kluwer Law International, 2002).

Trillanes IV PN, Lt Antonio F. "Corruption in the Philippine Navy Procurement System". March 2002 <http://www.pcij.org/HotSeat/trillanes4.html> (accessed 20 September 2004).

"Twenty Percent Drop in Acts of Piracy in First Half of 2004". *Channelnewsasia.com*, 26 July 2004 <http://channelnewsasia.com/stories/afp_world_business/print/975631/1/.html> (accessed 7 August 2004).

United Kingdom Parliament, Select Committee on Foreign Affairs Minutes of Evidence, <http://www.publications.parliament.uk/pa/cm200102/cmselect/cmfaff/922/2061321.htm> (accessed 26 August 2004).

Vaknin, Sam. "On Maritime Piracy" <http://www.knowledgerush.com/kr/jsp/db/view.jsp?columnId=138&contentType=column> (accessed 26 August 2004).

Vreij, Hans de. "Privatising the Iraq War". *Radio Netherlands*, 14 May 2004 <http://www.rnw.nl/hostspots/html/irq040514.html> (accessed 15 August 2004).

Warren, James Francis. "A Tale of Two Centuries: The Globalisation of Maritime Raiding and Piracy in Southeast Asia at the End of Eighteenth and Twentieth Centuries". Paper presented at KITLV Jubilee Workshop, Leiden, 14–16 June 2001.

Yeoman, Barry. "Soldiers of Good Fortune". *Mother Jones*, May–June 2003 Issue <http://www.motherjones.com/news/feature/2003/05/ma_365_01.html> (accessed 24 August 2003).

Homepages

Aegis Defence Services Ltd homepage <http://www.aegisdef.com>. (Also accessible through <http://www.aegisworld.com>.

Australian National Security Service homepage <http://anss.com.au/Introduction-to-ANSS.htm>.

Control Risks Group homepage <http://www.crg.com>.

Enterprising Securities homepage <http://www.enterprisingsecurities.com/index.html>.

GMSSCO homepage <http://gmssco.com>.

Gray Page Limited homepage <http://www.graypagelimited.com>.

G.S. SEALS homepage <http://www.gsseals.com/profile.htm>.

MSG MarineServe homepage <http://www.marineserve.de>.

Pilgrim Elite Ltd homepage <http://pilgrimelite.com.uk>.

Securewest International homepage <http://www.securewest.com/home.ikml>.
Trident Group homepage <http://www.gotrident.com>.
Trident Maritime homepage <http://www.technosci.com/trident/index.php>.

Unpublished Interviews and Emails
Armstrong, Dominic. MD, AEGIS Research and Intelligence. Interview with author, 22 June 2004. 118 Piccadilly, London.
Chan Kok Leong, Captain. General Manager, GBLT Shipmanagement Pte Ltd. Interview by author, 13 February 2004. Beach Road, Singapore. And telephone conversation with the vessel's captain, 13 February 2004.
Choong, Noel. Regional Manager, IMB Piracy Reporting Centre. Interviews by author, 23 October 2002. Piracy Reporting Centre, Kuala Lumpur.
Corless, Joe. Operations Director, Gray Page Limited. Interview by author, 23 June 2004. Baltic Exchange, London.
Duperouzel, Alex. Managing Director, *Background Asia*. Interview by author, 3 September 2004. Six Battery Road, Singapore.
Mak Joon Num. Maritime security expert. Conversation with author, 1 September 2004. ISEAS, Singapore.
Morrison, Alex. Security Manager, GMSSCO. Interview by author, 20 May 2004. Alexandra Point, Singapore.
Mukundan, P., Captain. Director, IMB. Interview by author, 21 June 2004. Maritime House, Barking, Essex.
———. "Re: FW: Piracy Questions". Email to the author, 1 September 2004.

8

Unilateralism and Regionalism: Working Together and Alone in the Malacca Straits

J.N. Mak

Introduction

The leaders of the Association of Southeast Asian Nations (ASEAN) declared categorically in 2003 that, "maritime cooperation between and among ASEAN member countries shall contribute to the evolution of the ASEAN Security Community".[1] This perception of the key role that maritime cooperation would play in ASEAN security was re-emphasized by the association's foreign ministers in Jakarta in June 2004 when they reiterated, "maritime cooperation is vital to the evolution of the ASEAN Security Community" and agreed to explore the possibility of establishing a maritime forum.[2] However, if maritime cooperation is seen as the key to the establishment of the ASEAN Security Community, then the voyage will be a long and arduous one.

Maritime issues, more often than not, are given low priority in Southeast Asia, relegated to the realm of functional cooperation and low politics. More importantly, contending interests are likely to make cooperation over maritime issues problematic. In fact, the little maritime cooperation that has taken place in the past in the ASEAN region has been marked by contention, dissension and contestation. Nowhere is this more evident than in the Straits of Malacca and Singapore, which has witnessed more than sixteen years of contestation between littoral states and user states between 1965 and 1982, first over the nature of passage through the Straits and then over the regulation of maritime traffic. The Malacca Straits is currently witnessing a third "battle" over how best to safeguard the waterway against pirates and terrorists. One aim of this chapter is to analyse why the Straits of Malacca has been the subject of great controversy rather than cooperation, and to derive from it insights into how and under what circumstances cooperation takes place in the Malacca Straits, as well as the constraints and obstacles to cooperation.

There have been three initiatives to establish regimes to govern the use of the Malacca Straits and to ensure its safety.[3] Two of these initiatives were closely intertwined — the attempt to emplace a legal regime governing passage through the Straits, and the concomitant effort to establish a navigational safety regime. Both these international processes began in the late 1960s, and were largely completed and accepted by all parties involved by the late 1970s and early 1980s. The latest attempt at cooperation in the Straits of Malacca is the current initiative to secure the Straits against attacks by pirates and terrorists, a process which began at the end of 2003 and which is ongoing. As the present controversy over securing the Malacca Straits against possible terrorist attacks indicates, getting states to work towards what appears to be an obvious common good, or objective, is difficult. As for the past initiatives, major accommodations had to be made before an acceptable legal regime governing transit through the Straits as well as a feasible navigational safety regime was put in place, which involved years of negotiations and horse-trading.

Why is cooperation so difficult to achieve in the Straits of Malacca and Singapore? The primary and overarching problem was the clash of interests between the key littoral states of Malaysia and Indonesia, which are essentially coastal states with coastal interests on the one hand, and the international users of the Straits on the other hand, in particular the major maritime nations. Singapore occupies a unique position in Straits cooperation, being geographically a littoral state, but in terms of interests and perceptions, more inclined to adopt the worldview of a maritime state. These different perceptions of the utility of the seas and oceans, that is, the clash of interests between the coastal states and the maritime nations that use the Straits of Malacca, was the primary reason why the safety and security of the waterway became contentious issues. Moreover, the Malacca Straits was not the only concern of Indonesia and Malaysia, since they had other, much larger sea areas and maritime boundaries to worry about. The maritime users of the states, in contrast, looked on the Malacca Straits as one key link in the global sea lines of communications. From their perspective, the Straits' greatest, and perhaps only, utility is that of a maritime highway providing the optimal link between the Indian Ocean and the East Asian seas.

This chapter attempts to accomplish the following tasks. First, it describes the chief characteristics that distinguish coastal states from maritime nations, with the primary feature being that maritime states have global interests while coastal states have a more insular outlook. Second, it argues that these interests came into play during the rush by newly independent states in the 1960s to "fence off" the ocean when Malaysia and Indonesia unilaterally extended their maritime boundaries. Third, it explains the effect of these unilateral extensions in terms of the threat posed towards the customary regime of free passage through the Malacca Straits, which led to a diplomatic and legal battle between the maritime nations and Indonesia and Malaysia over the future nature of transit through the Straits. The issue of a mutually acceptable legal regime for Straits transit, which was closely intertwined with the attempts to put in place a navigational safety regime, is discussed in this same portion.

Fourth, the chapter then shows how these differing perceptions, interests and tensions have resurfaced in the current controversy over how the Straits of Malacca should be secured against attacks by pirates and terrorists. This section puts in perspective the attitudes of both Singapore and its tacit allies on the one hand, and that of Indonesia and Malaysia on the other, by underlining the importance of maritime sovereignty and what it means to the littoral states. The chapter concludes by arguing that Malaysia and Indonesia, believing that they failed to achieve complete sovereignty in the Straits of Malacca because of the existence of the transit passage regime which disallows them from impeding the freedom of navigation in the waterway, are consequently extremely touchy about any perceived attempt to further erode their sovereignty. Maritime sovereignty is important for both countries because it allows them rights over valuable offshore resources. However, it is the strategic and security dimension, which is paramount for Indonesia. The need to prevent any further erosion of maritime sovereignty for Malaysia, in contrast, is critical because its maritime zones, which it claimed in a map published in 1979, is still not accepted internationally. As such, this state of affairs will continue to bedevil Straits cooperation. Until a final political settlement is reached by convincing Malaysia and Indonesia that their maritime boundaries are sacrosanct, cooperation will always remain difficult and contentious.

Maritime Nation or Coastal State?

The use of the oceans and straits of the world today revolve around three sets of interests. The first is the use of the oceans for warfare, and for the projection of military power as rapidly and cheaply as possible across the globe. The second set of interests is commercial, that is, maritime trade, which requires the freedom of navigation and unimpeded access to all the ports of the world. The third is the direct economic exploitation of the sea, which demands not only access to the desired resources, but the ability to exclude others from exploiting it, that is, the ability to establish sovereignty or property rights.[4] Maritime nations are concerned with the first two sets of interests — the use of the ocean for power projection and for free trade — while the majority of coastal states are mainly interested in the economic exploitation aspect, and hence in extending their maritime jurisdiction and sovereignty. Coastal states, in general, see their adjacent seas as important sources of wealth, and equally important, as a buffer against foreign intrusions.

As such, at the end of World War II, the newly independent coastal states were all for extending their territorial sea claims from the traditional three-nautical-mile limit up to six, twelve and even 200 nautical miles. The seas were not important as lines of communications, but for the living and non-living resources they contained. Thus the extension of maritime sovereignty and jurisdiction was a priority for the coastal states. In contrast, the freedom of navigation was the primary concern of the maritime nations. All straits used for international navigation, in particular, were of special concern to the maritime powers, since "nations which depend on their merchant marine and navies for economic and national security…can be strangled by having access to oceans limited or delayed when passing through narrow international straits".[5]

Malaysia and Indonesia are basically coastal states, although they have often been labelled as maritime nations because of their large sea areas, their long coastlines, the contribution of living and non-living ocean resources to their national economies, and their seafaring histories. However, long coastlines and economic dependence on contiguous sea resources do not automatically turn a costal state into a maritime nation. Former Malaysian Prime Minister Mahathir Mohamad candidly admitted that Malaysia was by no means a maritime nation yet:

> A country cannot claims [sic] itself to be a maritime nation merely by virtue of attributes such as suitable geographical position, physical conformation or strength of population...A true maritime nation is one which has the capability to fully exploit its God given maritime endowments to enhance its socio-economic standing among the community of nations...though Malaysia has all the makings of a maritime nation, strategically located at the centre of shipping lane [sic] and a large sea area rich in fishery, oil and gas resources, it has yet to optimise all these attributes to qualify as a maritime nation in the true sense of the word.[6]

The chief characteristic of a maritime nation is therefore its global interests, reach and influence which must transcend its coasts and adjacent seas. Most maritime powers also possess highly developed maritime infrastructures, both "hard" and "soft". Soft maritime infrastructure would include a sound and predictable legal system, advanced research and development, and the provision of a comprehensive suite of maritime services including banking, insurance, and maritime financing. Most important, it would possess the right manpower resources and expertise. In addition, it would also have "hard" or physical infrastructure such as well-developed port systems, both domestic and offshore, an efficient, quality international shipping fleet, and modern shipbuilding and ship repair facilities, bunkering and logistics support. Other important attributes would be the capacity to project maritime power — either economic or military or both — over considerable distances from its shores. Its global reach is such that its actions and decisions will affect the global maritime environment. Finally, a maritime nation is also usually a focal point for the global maritime industry, able to attract maritime activities in all its myriad forms as well as extend its maritime interests offshore by investing in, and developing maritime industries overseas.

Coastal states by nature are more insular in outlook. Such states normally possess long coastlines, and depend on the sea for certain resources, some which may be critical for the country's wealth. These may include important coastal fisheries, offshore energy resources, and a well-developed but domestic shipping fleet. Most of all, however, coastal states invariably have little or no global reach and interests. Thus while maritime resources, especially offshore petroleum are important sources of wealth for Malaysia and Indonesia, they are still essentially coastal states. National attitudes towards the sea also define the difference between coastal and maritime states. Maritime states such as Norway look towards the sea for their long-term economic growth and prosperity, and hence are psychologically maritime-oriented. Coastal states, on the other had, have a more landward focus and are interested only in their immediate seas. As former Malaysian Prime Minister Mahathir Mohamad succinctly put it:

> Though we were once renowned seafarers...unfortunately we have somehow lost this trait. The long years under colonial rule have perhaps made us landlubbers with a distinct dislike for being away from home for any length of time.[7]

Using these criteria, Singapore may be said to possess the key characteristics of a maritime nation although it may be geographically a littoral state of the Malacca Straits. This is reflected in the maritime "reach" of Singapore today. Not merely does it attract maritime investments and economic activities to its shores, it has also gone offshore in a substantial way. Moreover, to use the terminology of the Law of the Sea, Singapore is a geographically disadvantaged shelf or zone-locked nation, that is, a nation locked by the maritime zones of its neighbours. Indeed, Singapore's territorial sea extends only three nautical miles, and its exclusive fishing zone is "within and beyond its territorial sea, as defined in treaties and practice".[8] Since Singapore had no hope at all of expanding its maritime zones, the question of extending its maritime jurisdiction and sovereignty was irrelevant. The critical issue, instead, was to ensure that land and sea access to the island would remain unimpeded. Thus its interests are very much that of a maritime state, which explains its preoccupation with freedom of navigation unlike its neighbours Indonesia and Malaysia. This had far-reaching results on Straits cooperation, which will be discussed in more detail later. The clash of interests was therefore not confined to littoral states and user states, but was also endemic among the littoral states.

Indeed, the importance of the Malacca Straits differed even between Indonesia and Malaysia. From the Indonesian point of view, the Straits are relatively unimportant as an economic lifeline because it runs alongside the under-developed eastern coast of Sumatra. Indonesian officials have, in fact, sometimes privately admitted that the closure of the Malacca Straits would not trouble Jakarta too much, since maritime traffic would then be forced to use either the Sunda or Lombok-Makassar Straits. Moreover, Indonesia would be least affected by any environmental disaster in the Straits of Malacca. However, the Malacca Straits are of critical strategic importance since it is the only maritime highway that pierces the Indonesian archipelagic border. Equally important, any erosion of Indonesian sovereignty and authority in the Malacca Straits would have serious ramifications for Indonesia's attempts to regulate traffic in its other straits used for international navigation.

The Malacca Straits, however, is seen as a critical economic artery by Malaysia. The Straits runs parallel to the industrial heartland of Malaysia, serving the so-called "Western Corridor" of Malaysia. Every major Malaysian port is located along the Malacca Straits, and this is reflected in the Malaysian effort to promote two Straits ports — Port Klang and the Port of Tanjung Pelepas — as international transhipment hubs for container traffic.

The roots of the coastal-maritime state conflict began during the decolonization process after the end of World War II, when the many newly independent states began to look to their adjacent seas as potential sources of wealth, and thus joined in the international move to extend their sea boundaries. The trend to enclose coastal seas also included straits used for international navigation, which included the Straits of Malacca. The Straits was considered by the maritime powers, especially the United States, as one of most critical straits in the world. Hence the Straits of Malacca became a centrepiece in the battle to establish a new oceans regime that finally culminated in the 1982 UN Convention on the Law of the Seas.

Historical Background: The Rush to Fence off the Ocean

The end of World War II saw two developments, the first political, and the second technical, that resulted in a fundamental shift from the classical regime of the high seas and freedom of navigation (the *mare liberum*) to that of the closed sea regime (*mare clausum*). The era of the open or high seas regime began in the eighteenth century and lasted for more than 200 years as a result of the mercantilist and colonizing policies of countries such as the Netherlands, Britain, and to a lesser extent France. Thus freedom of navigation was regarded as essential for trade between metropolitan countries and colonies. The only sea area under national jurisdiction then was the adjacent territorial sea, usually limited to a three-nautical-mile breadth.

Ironically, it was the United States, with its Truman Declaration of 1945 claiming jurisdiction over the resources of the continental shelf contiguous to the U.S. coast, that triggered off the race to extend coastal state jurisdiction beyond the three-nautical mile limit. The number of players in this race rose sharply in the 1960s, when decolonization created a slew of new coastal states stretching from the Caribbean, to Africa and Asia. Illustrative of the divide between the developed maritime nations and the newly independent coastal states was that of the 101 states that became members of the United Nations (UN) from 1946 to 1980, only three of them agreed to a three-nautical-mile territorial sea limit. The rest wanted at least twelve nautical miles, or even more. The second factor that accelerated the post-War race to fence off ocean space — in many instances, unilaterally — was the development of technology to exploit seabed resources, which had matured by the 1960s. For instance, between 1960 and 1968, offshore oil was being extracted from the seabeds of more than twenty countries, including Malaysia and Indonesia. This "raised hopes of offshore oil wealth in almost every coastal state".[9]

Malaysia and Indonesia's New Maritime Boundaries

Malaysia and Indonesia were not only caught up in this global trend to extend maritime boundaries, but Indonesia played a key role in extending maritime jurisdiction by pushing for international recognition of its archipelagic concept as a strategic device to unite the nation of almost 14,000 islands. The basic principle of this concept was that straight lines (baselines) would be drawn between the outermost islands of the archipelago, and all waters enclosed by the baselines would then be regarded as internal waters. Indonesia announced its Archipelago Act in 1960 (Act No. 4 of February 1960), which claimed straight baselines drawn between the outermost islands of the Indonesian archipelago. In addition, it extended its territorial sea from three to twelve nautical miles, to be measured from the archipelagic baselines. All waters within the straight baselines were considered to be the internal waters, which would enjoy the same status as land, where Indonesian law would apply. The Act increased Indonesian territory by 250 per cent, from more than 2 million square kilometres to nearly 5.2 million kilometres.[10]

Malaysia's extended its maritime boundaries incrementally in the 1960s and 1970s, and finally published a map showing the extent of all its maritime claims in December 1979. Popularly known as the *Peta Baru* or New Map, the 1979 map is characterized by the use of straight baselines, with the outer limits and turning point coordinates of its territorial sea and continental shelf derived from both treaty and unilateral declaration. Ten years before that date, it had by Emergency Ordinance, extended its territorial sea limit from three to twelve nautical miles in August 1969. At the same time, it adopted a system of straight baselines (despite the fact that Malaysia cannot be considered an archipelagic state to qualify for the use of straight baselines) to "ensure an equitable basis for negotiations on maritime issues with Indonesia".[11] Significantly, it was Indonesia that influenced Malaysia to extend its territorial sea limits, and the Malaysian enactment was carried out only after prior consultations with Jakarta.[12] Equally significantly, all these boundary extensions took place before the final 1982 UNCLOS, which set the limits of extension.

Both Malaysia and Indonesia saw the need to extend their maritime boundaries because of military, geo-strategic, navigational safety, and economic considerations. Extended maritime jurisdiction could provide a legal basis for keeping foreign powers from intruding into their national waters and air space. This was important at a time when Malaysia and Indonesia were officially attempting to keep aloof of the Cold War. In addition, as militarily weak states, both countries felt the need for a legal instrument which would help keep out foreign intruders. A more immediate consideration for Indonesia was its campaign to win West Irian from the Dutch, which finally ended in 1963. The Dutch were using the waters of the archipelago to transit to West Irian, and Jakarta was looking for ways to end this free passage. In addition, foreign vessels were also used to provide arms and equipment to the various regional rebellions, the most serious being in West Sumatra with the setting up of the Provisional Revolutionary Government of Indonesia in 1958. Evidence of U.S. complicity in the rebellion was confirmed when a U.S. Air Force major was captured after his B-26 bomber was shot down over Sulawesi in mid-1958.[13] Thus Indonesia saw the need for integrating the archipelago by declaring it as internal waters, and at the same time making foreign military intrusions illegal.

The Indonesian elite also believed that the fragmented nature of the Indonesian archipelago was an important cause of the various separatist and revolutionary movements in the 1950s and 1960s. As such, it introduced the Archipelagic Doctrine as a nationalist and legal tool to unite an otherwise fragmented Indonesia. This doctrine was internalized as the *Wawasan Nusantara* or Archipelagic Outlook in 1966 by President Suharto, with the internal waters of Indonesia uniting rather than dividing its people. The elite discourse in Indonesia also referred to the republic as being the crossroads of the region, located between two oceans and two continents. This *posisi-silang* rendered Indonesia vulnerable to intrusions from all directions. The straits used for international navigation therefore provided a "direct channel into and through the maritime approaches and interstices of the Indonesian state".[14] However, the Malacca Straits was considered to be the most dangerous arrow pointing at the Indonesian heartland, because it was the only strait that Indonesia shared with other littoral states and was therefore considered as "a frontline defence".[15]

Navigational safety was an especially important consideration for Malaysia with regard to the Malacca Straits. The increasing number of ships, and their burgeoning size, led to increasing congestion of the Straits and the possible danger of groundings, collisions and the attendant environmental impact. Another key reason for both Indonesia and Malaysia to unilaterally extend their maritime boundaries was that it would give them access to new economic resources, especially offshore oil and gas. The revenue earned from oil and gas added greatly to their state capacities. The legitimacy of both the Malaysian and Indonesian elites in the 1960s and 1970s depended a great deal on their ability to meet development objectives and to sustain economic growth, that is, performance legitimacy. The contributions of offshore oil and gas revenues were therefore critical at this point in time. Significantly, most of the gas and oil being exploited beginning in the 1960s came from the new maritime zones claimed by both countries.[16] Offshore petroleum exploration began off Sarawak in 1962, and off Trengganu in Malaysia in 1968, well before Malaysia published its 1979 *Peta Baru*.[17] The contribution of maritime resources to the building of state capacity and economic growth has been of considerable importance.

Thus, Malaysia and Indonesia are understandably jealous of, and sensitive to, any perceived erosion of their maritime sovereignty in any part of their maritime zones, including the Malacca Straits. Indonesia's preoccupation with sovereignty stems largely from strategic considerations, while Malaysia is more concerned with protecting its economic resources in its still contested maritime zones. The clash of interests between the coastal states of Malaysia and Indonesia, and the maritime states, including Singapore, with regard to passage through the Straits is clearly seen in the following case studies, the first two being the struggle to develop transit passage and navigational safety regimes for the Malacca Straits and the third being the attempt to protect the waterway against pirates and other non-state actors.

Sovereignty, Transit Passage and the Struggle for a Navigational Safety Regime, 1960–82

The Malacca Straits proved to be a key proving ground in the battle between maritime nations, which wanted to maintain the customary right of navigational freedom by insisting that the territorial sea remain three nautical miles wide, and the coastal states that wanted to extend their territorial jurisdiction to at least twelve nautical miles. The concept of "innocent passage" versus "transit passage" was central to this contest. Put very simply, "innocent passage" is the legal regime which applies when ships pass through the territorial waters of a state. Under the UN Convention on the Territorial Sea and the Contiguous Zone, 1958, "passage is innocent so long as it is not prejudicial to the peace, good order or security of the coastal State."[18] "Innocent passage" could therefore be suspended by the coastal state if it felt that its peace and security was being threatened. "Transit passage" was a novel regime *sui generis* designed to get round the problem of ships transiting the straits used for international navigation whose waters were overlapped by the territorial waters of adjoining states. Fundamentally, maritime nations using such straits demanded that a new regime be introduced where passage cannot be impeded by coastal states under any circumstances. This resulted in the introduction of the "transit passage regime" in the 1982 UN Convention on the Law of the Sea.

Transit passage became critical after Indonesia and Malaysia concluded a bilateral treaty demarcating their territorial sea boundary in the Straits of Malacca in March 1970. This move challenged in one stroke the customary status of the Malacca Straits as high seas, and as an international strait. This is because the Malacca Straits varies in width from 126 nautical miles towards its north-western entrance, narrowing down to a funnel shape south of the One-Fathom Bank to about 7.8 nautical miles in width near Kukup, in the Malaysian state of Johore. This meant that a substantial length of the Straits towards its southern end, where the width is less than 24 nautical miles, would fall within the claimed territorial seas of Indonesia and Malaysia. The primary reason given by Indonesia and Malaysia for their attempt to assert sovereignty in the Straits was the need to regulate the increasing volume of traffic in the waterway. Another reason was the belief in the 1970s that important deposits of oil could be found in the seabed of the Malacca Straits itself.[19]

The major users of the Straits, especially the United States, not surprisingly, challenged the Malaysian-Indonesian claims. They argued that under customary international law, the Malacca Straits was a strait used for international navigation and that the right of passage through such straits "cannot be suspended for security reasons even temporarily".[20] Freedom of navigation was to the advantage of maritime powers such as the United States, Great Britain and the then Soviet Union for two reasons. First, they wanted unhindered access through straits traditionally used for international navigation so that they could deploy naval forces as quickly and as expeditiously as possible from one theatre of operation to another. In this context, the Malacca Straits was important in America's "swing strategy" of the 1970s that involved moving naval carrier groups between the Pacific and Indian Oceans and the Middle East. It was noted at that time that naval mobility was a key plank of U.S. maritime security interests, of which "free transit" through international straits constituted the legal foundation.[21] Freedom of navigation was also important for the commercial interests of the maritime powers, since their aim was to minimize shipping costs by using the shortest sailing routes, and by loading vessels up to their maximum capacity. The Malacca Straits was thus critical for the maritime powers because it provided the fastest and cheapest route for their naval forces and commercial vessels between two key ocean regions.

Malaysia and Indonesia assured the Straits users that they had no intention of stopping maritime traffic from using the Straits of Malacca. However, passage through the Straits should be regarded as passage through their territorial waters, and therefore the legal regime of "innocent passage" should apply. As a counter, the United States and the Soviet Union, in a rare show of unity, submitted draft articles for a special regime of transit passage to cover straits used for international navigation to the UN Seabed Committee in July 1971.[22] The trade-off demanded by the United States was that it would only recognize any twelve-nautical mile territorial sea claim provided provision was made for a special transit passage regime to cover international straits.[23] In the end, the maritime states managed to get the transit passage regime accepted and incorporated in the 1982 UN Convention on the Law of the Sea (UNCLOS II). Under transit passage, "all ships and aircraft enjoy the right of transit passage, which shall not be impeded".[24] Indonesia refrained from pressing home its insistence on innocent passage for the Malacca Straits because international support for its archipelagic concept was more important, while Malaysia had far more to gain from international recognition of its newly declared twelve-nautical mile territorial sea limit because of its extensive coastlines in Peninsular Malaysia, Sabah and Sarawak.

Nevertheless, the point to note is that two legal regimes therefore exist in the Malacca Straits. The first is that of the territorial sea, where the regime of "innocent passage" would normally apply. The second regime is that of "transit passage", which however, takes precedence over the regime of "innocent passage". Thus, from the point of view of Indonesia and Malaysia, while they had established maritime sovereignty in the Straits of Malacca, that sovereignty was incomplete, and therefore has to be jealously guarded.

The battle between "innocent passage" and "transit passage" became inextricably intertwined with the attempt at establishing a navigational safety regime for the Straits of Malacca. The process of establishing first, the nature of transit for the Straits, and then a regime to enhance the navigational safety of the waterway, brought to light the inherent tensions between Singapore as a nascent maritime state, and its two littoral partners. Far from being a simple and straightforward technical exercise, the effort to emplace a navigational safety regime proved to be highly contentious and political.

The Hazards of Navigational Safety

There was increasing concern in the 1960s over navigational safety in the Malacca Straits for the following reasons. The increasing speeds, volume and density of maritime traffic increased the likelihood of collisions. In addition, larger and larger ships, especially tankers bound for Japan, began using the relatively narrow and shallow Straits. These large tankers, with their single screw and single rudder, were unwieldy with poor handling characteristics. Combined with their deep draught, this raised fears that the number of groundings and collisions would occur more often. Another problem was the increasing number of small craft, comprising barter boats, ferries, fishing vessels and leisure craft, criss-crossing the Malacca Straits. All these factors made navigational safety a critical issue. Both Malaysia and Singapore were especially aware of the danger of a major shipping disaster, since the two countries would be directly affected by any major oil spill. The main components of the proposed navigational safety regime would include surveying and marking the deep-water channels suitable for large ships using the Straits, and establishing a Traffic Separation Scheme for critical stretches. The first step was taken in 1967 when Japan proposed to the London-based Sub-Committee on the Safety of Navigation of the Inter-Governmental Maritime Consultative Organization (IMCO)[25] that sea lanes should be established in the Malacca and Singapore Straits.[26]

Japan had a direct interest in the safety of navigation since they depended on the Straits of Malacca as the primary conduit for their energy supplies. One estimate was that 90 per cent of Japan's oil supplies in the 1970s were shipped via the Straits.[27] Tokyo as a consequence played a key role in the establishment of the navigational safety regime for the Straits by funding the necessary hydrographic surveys and paying for the navigational aids needed to mark the designated deep-water channels.

The three littoral states gave permission for Japan to conduct a preliminary hydrographic survey of the Straits, and agreed that the survey should begin in 1969. After completing a successful preliminary survey by March 1969, Japan announced that it would embark on a full-scale survey in1970. This was when "sovereignty" asserted itself. Following the enactment of its 1969 Ordinance to extend its territorial sea to twelve nautical miles, Malaysia demanded that Japan recognize its new territorial sea limit as a pre-condition for Japan to conduct the full-scale hydrographic survey. The Japanese refused to do so, and the project was delayed a year until creative thinking solved the impasse. The survey was conducted using an Indonesian vessel.[28]

This incident was illustrative of the inherent tensions between coastal state interests and that of the maritime nations. Another indication that the three littoral states themselves did not view the Malacca Straits in the same light was the comment made by former Singapore Prime Minister Lee Kuan Yew in 1968 that "Singapore is ever willing and ready to help Japan maintain the safety and freedom of navigation of the high seas *which include the Straits of Malacca*".[29] The tension between sovereignty and navigational safety again came to the fore when the Japanese Ministry of Transport circulated at IMCO a draft proposal on Straits navigational safety suggesting, among other things, that a "Malacca-Singapore Straits Board" be set up to which the coastal states would have to submit annual reports.[30] Indonesia responded in no uncertain terms, its representative declaring at the 11th session of the IMCO Sub-Committee on Safety of Navigation in 1971 that Indonesia "cannot accept any idea that might lead to the internationalization of the strait, in the sense that among others the right to control and supervise the strait is taken away from the coastal states".[31] The significance of the Indonesian reaction is that even as early as 1971, there was already the deep-rooted conviction, at least on the part of Malaysia and Indonesia, that the management and safety of the Straits of Malacca was the sole prerogative of the littoral states. Any attempt at internationalizing the Straits was totally out of the question. Singapore, as we shall see later, had a more liberal view of the issue.

The perceived attempt by Japan to internationalize the Straits, as well as the U.S. submission to the UN Seabed Committee in July 1971 for a special regime to govern passage through straits used for international navigation, galvanized Indonesia into taking the lead to ensure that all three littoral states adopted a common policy stand over the Straits. Bilateral discussions were held between Singapore and Indonesia on 8 October 1971, followed by discussions between Indonesian and Malaysian ministers a week later. The result of these negotiations led to a joint statement released simultaneously in Jakarta, Kuala Lumpur and Singapore on 16 November 1971. This joint statement made it clear that the management of navigational safety in the Straits of Malacca and Singapore was the sole prerogative of the three littoral states, that tri-partite cooperation was necessary to ensure the safety of navigation, and third, that a coordinating body for the safety of navigation comprising only the three coastal states be set up as soon as possible.

The rest of the joint statement, however, showed the geo-political and policy divide between the coastal states of Malaysia and Indonesia and the maritime state of Singapore. The second half of the joint statement reads in full as follows:

(iv) The three Governments also agreed that the problem of the safety of navigation and the question of the internationalisation of the straits are two separate issues;

(v) The Governments of the Republic of Indonesia and of Malaysia agreed that the Straits of Malacca and Singapore are not international straits, while fully recognising their use for international shipping in accordance with the principle of innocent passage. The Government of Singapore takes note of the position of the Governments of the Republic of Indonesia and of Malaysia on this point.

(vi) On the basis of this understanding, the three Governments approved the continuation of the hydrographic survey.

The fact that Singapore refrained from endorsing the attempt to "de-internationalize" the Straits is highly significant. As mentioned before, Singapore's maritime interests were more in line with those of the maritime powers than its littoral neighbours. Singapore was by the 1970s, already a nascent maritime state because it realized that its economic and strategic survival would depend on unimpeded access to the island republic, and the ability to integrate itself with the global economy.[32] Singapore's aim as such was to develop its strength as the regional entrepôt even further, and its "policy is therefore ...to oppose any kind of extension of jurisdiction towards the high seas".[33] Singapore's then Foreign Minister S. Rajaratnam unequivocally declared before parliament in 1972 that Singapore stood "for the unimpeded passage of all ships of all nations through the straits".[34]

The bid by Malaysia and Indonesia to assert sovereign authority, on the other hand, was also due to their realization that as littoral states, they had to ensure the safety of navigation because they would be the first victims of any shipping disaster in the waterway. The user states, in this context, were viewed as "free riders". Thus Tengku Razaleigh Hamzah, who was later to become Finance Minister under the Mahathir administration, suggested in 1972 that a Malaysia-Indonesian corporation be set up to levy tolls on ships plying the Straits.[35] Singapore and the user states, however, were not in favour of the idea and in any case, the notion of a levy was disallowed by the 1982 transit passage regime since it was an impediment to free passage.

Nevertheless, although the 1971 Malaysia-Indonesia-Singapore joint declaration encapsulated the fundamental differences between the three littoral states, one clear message emerged — navigational safety would remain their exclusive purview. Any effort to put in place a navigational safety regime would therefore need the blessings of the three states. This message was not lost on Japan, which henceforth made no further attempts to internationalize the management of navigation in the Straits of Malacca. It thereafter worked closely together with the littoral states to complete the necessary hydrographic surveys without any more setbacks.

However, there was a final hurdle to clear before a formal agreement on a navigational safety regime could be initialled. That was the issue of under keel clearance (UKC) for large vessels using the Straits, an issue that pitted Singapore once more, against its two littoral neighbours. The Japanese and other hydrographic surveys had revealed that the Straits was not only relatively shallow with an average depth of twenty-three metres, but that shifting underwater sand waves could reduce the depth even more in unexpected places. Indonesia and Malaysia felt that as a precaution, tankers of more than 200,000 dead-weight tons (DWT) should be barred from using the Straits of Malacca and be re-routed through the Lombok-Makassar Straits. This was because a fully laden 200,000 DWT tanker would have a draught of about twenty metres, leaving just three metres between the bottom of the vessel and the seabed.[36] Singapore however, argued that an under keel clearance of 2.6 metres was adequate, whereas Indonesia demanded not less than 4.6 metres.[37] The argument over what constituted a safe minimum under keel clearance was grounded not merely on safety considerations, but on economics as well. Although Singapore did not possess offshore oil resources, it had become by the 1970s the world's third largest oil refining centre[38] and had built its oil terminal berths to take on Japanese tankers up to the size of 300,000 DWT.[39] Thus it saw the Indonesian demand for 4.6 metres of under keel clearance as a Indonesia-Malaysia plot to "weaken the economy of the island-state under the guise of promoting environmental control".[40] This perception was reinforced by suggestions at the time that bulk oil storage installations and mooring facilities be built in the Lombok Straits area.[41] Japan was inclined to support the Singapore stand for two reasons. The first was that it had built 230,000 DWT tankers with strengthened bottoms for a 2.6-metre under keel clearance, in other words, a tanker designed specifically for the Malacca Straits. Secondly, it was reluctant to use the Lombok-Makassar Straits because it involved not only a longer voyage but also because that meant using a strait claimed by Indonesia to be entirely under its control. The other solution, of course, was to load a tanker to less than its designed limit. For a 200,000 DWT tanker, to increase every metre of under keel clearance, the ship would have to carry 15,000 tons less of oil on average.[42]

The agreement over what constituted a safe under keel clearance limit was hastened by a series of collisions, groundings and oil spills involving tankers and other types of commercial vessels between 1975 and 1976.[43] The mood of compromise was also hastened by the Japanese hydrographic survey of the Lombok-Makassar Straits, undertaken at the invitation of Indonesia, which started in 1974 and was completed in August 1975.[44] This was an indication to Singapore that the Japanese were reconsidering the Lombok-Makassar Straits as a viable alternative route for their VLCCs. After a major accident in which the 52,000 DWT tanker *Diego Silang* collided with two other vessels off Batu Pahat, south of One-Fathom Bank in 1976, the stage was set for a compromise. By this time, Singapore indicated that it was willing to settle for a three-metre under keel clearance, while Indonesia and Malaysia brought the minimum under keel clearance to four metres. In the end, both sides agreed to compromise at 3.5 metres. Thus, at the 1977 ASEAN meeting in Manila, the foreign ministers of Malaysia, Indonesia and Singapore sat down to initial the Agreement on Safety of Navigation in the Straits of Malacca and Singapore.

Thus the basis of a navigational safety regime was finally put in place after years of negotiations, political angst, mutual suspicions and horse-trading. The issue of the legal nature of transit in the Malacca Straits was threshed out in another forum — the Third UN Conference on the Law of the Sea, which began in 1974 and ended with UNCLOS II in 1982. While Malaysia and Indonesia did not win complete sovereignty in the Straits, Indonesia at least had the satisfaction of its archipelagic claims officially recognized and incorporated under the regime for archipelagic states in the 1986 UN Convention.[45] Malaysia, together with many other coastal states of the world, had its twelve-nautical mile territorial sea limit legalized as well. However, its continental shelf claims, and its use of a single maritime boundary, which incorporates both its continental shelf and exclusive economic zone limits, have yet to be officially recognized and accepted by the international community. Thus for Malaysia, the issue of its maritime sovereignty, to its disquiet, remains unresolved. This accounts for why maritime sovereignty remains a particularly sensitive issue for Malaysia. And this awareness of the need to maintain its maritime claims and borders is why it is so insistent that no outside power should be included in the management of Malacca Straits security, and that only the littoral states have the sovereign right to patrol the Straits of Malacca.

Securing the Straits against Piracy and Terrorism

The latest saga with regard to Straits cooperation, at the time of writing, is the controversy over whether piracy and terrorism has become a major threat in the Straits of Malacca, and if so, how best to deal with the problem. Once again, the maritime states, especially Singapore, have taken a very different view from that of its coastal neighbours. Singapore is convinced that pirates and terrorists have joined forces to target the island republic's port and shipping facilities and that therefore there exists a piracy-terrorism nexus. Consequently, the island republic sounded the warning, beginning in December 2003, that a terrorist attack in the Straits of Malacca was real and imminent, and that it was not a question of if but when such an attack would occur. Singapore pointed out that the Malacca Straits would be a prime target, especially towards the southern end near the entrance to Singapore port, because of heavy traffic congestion, the very narrow channel, and the fact that the shipping route ran very close to Singapore Port. To compound the problem, the increasing number of piracy incidents in the southern end of the Straits made it is extremely difficult to distinguish criminal acts of piracy from *potential* acts of terrorism. No distinction should therefore be made between piracy and terrorism.[46]

Singapore's security discourse on the piracy-terrorism nexus initially did not evoke any response from either Malaysia or Indonesia, which viewed the problem very differently. For one thing, piracy was not high on the Indonesian list of security priorities, since it had limited resources to deal with a whole host of threats facing the state, especially the separatist movement in Aceh. Malaysia, too, was inclined to view piracy as nothing more than a criminal act until the members of the Abu Sayaf group kidnapped twenty-one Malaysians and foreign tourists from the resort island of Sipadan, off the east Coast of Sabah, in 2000. This incident was a watershed for Malaysia because it made the Malaysian Government appear incapable of safeguarding its sovereign territory from foreign intrusions. Thus its defence minister warned that henceforth, the kidnapping of Malaysians from within its borders would be considered a violation of Malaysian sovereignty.[47] Therefore, the issue of sovereignty was, once again, the primary concern. Malaysia was not worried about piracy and terrorism *per se* in the Straits of Malacca, but by the threat to its sovereignty posed by the intrusion of non-state actors. After the Sipadan kidnappings, it stepped up patrols in the Straits of Malacca and tightened security and was therefore confident it had the security situation under control. Besides, the Malaysian belief was that patrols at sea by themselves were inadequate, but the key to combating terrorism was "intelligence sharing and choking terrorists' financial and logistical networks".[48]

However, Indonesia and Malaysia suddenly took notice of the Singapore position on piracy and terrorism when an April 2004 *Agence France Presse* (AFP) report quoted the then U.S. Pacific Command Chief, Admiral Thomas Fargo, as saying that U.S. marines and Special Forces would help patrol the Straits of Malacca. Although the United States subsequently claimed that Admiral Fargo only referred to "several hypothetical options", Malaysia and Indonesia saw it as part of a plot to internationalize the security of the Malacca Straits. This was because following Admiral Fargo's remarks, Singapore's Defence Minister Teo Chee Hean said in a public speech that given the very large number of ships plying the Straits of Malacca and Singapore, it was beyond the capacity of any single state to safeguard the Straits. An international effort would therefore be needed.[49]

The response by Malaysia and Indonesia to what they saw as Singapore's unilateral initiative was to make it clear that no outside power should be involved in any attempt to protect the Straits of Malacca, and that only the littoral states had the right to protect the Straits. More than that, Malaysia pointedly stated that security should not be used as an excuse to compromise the country's sovereignty, and Malaysian Foreign Minister Syed Hamid warned Singapore against "going it alone" in engaging U.S. forces to patrol the Malacca Straits.[50] Significantly, Syed Hamid added that Singapore should not engage in public discourse on the subject and that Malaysia was "trying to avoid as much as possible any debate in the open that can create misunderstanding between our two countries".[51] The Malaysian position, as its Defence Minister and Deputy Prime Minister Najib Abdul Razak put it, was that the piracy and terrorist threat to the Straits had been exaggerated, and that Kuala Lumpur had the security situation in the Straits well in hand.[52]

'We may need a thousand ships, but not the Americans ...
These are our straits'

These words were attributed to a veteran of the Indonesian Coast Guard who was on patrol south of Singapore.[53] Although not part of the elite discourse, his feelings reflected those of the Indonesian Government in general, which was that any foreign military patrols in its waters would be inconsistent with international law, would harm Indonesia's national interests and would be against the country's non-alignment policy.[54] The then Indonesian Chief of Navy, Admiral Bernard Sondakh, went so far as to say that the piracy situation in the Malacca Straits had been deliberately exaggerated, and that it was part of an international ploy to justify foreign intervention in Indonesia by portraying the country as weak and incapable of looking after its own waters.[55] Similarly in June 2004, Mohamed Nazri Abdul Aziz, a Malaysian Minister in the Prime Minister's Department, remarked that if the Straits was not "guarded properly, foreign powers may be prone to intervene in its management, and this will pose a threat to the country's sovereignty."[56] The issue for Malaysia and Indonesia was that their sovereignty over the Malacca Straits must not be eroded, and any military use of the waterway must have the prior sanction of the two coastal states. Thus the fact that although Indian warships had escorted "high value American cargo" through the Malacca Straits for six months from July 2002 under a specific Washington-New Delhi arrangement, Jakarta and Kuala Lumpur did not raise any objections. This was because all three littoral states had been consulted before the announcement of the Indo-U.S. arrangement.[57] In an effort to convince Straits users that the waterway was safe, Malaysia went so far as to offer naval escorts at no cost for "high risk" vessels transiting the Straits.[58] In addition, it gave the impression that the primary role of its coast guard agency, the Malaysian Maritime Enforcement Agency (MMEA), scheduled to begin operations in 2005, would be to safeguard the Straits of Malacca although the agency's responsibilities covered all of Malaysia's vast maritime zones.[59] Nevertheless, despite all the Malaysian assertions that the security situation was not alarming, both Malaysia and Indonesia felt compelled to, at least, be seen to step up security in the Malacca Straits. Once again, it was the sense of "incomplete sovereignty" in the Malacca Straits and the fear that their maritime sovereignty could be further eroded that made Malaysia and Indonesia respond to the Singapore call for stepping up security in the Malacca Straits.

The Singapore discourse on Straits security implied that the situation was so potentially serious that unless the littoral states that claimed sovereignty over the waterway made the Malacca Straits safe, it was inevitable that foreign powers would eventually step in to secure the waterway. Malaysia and Indonesia in fact tried to argue that there was no evidence of any terrorist-piracy linkage. For instance, Malaysian Deputy Internal Security Minister Chia Kwang Chye said after opening an international meeting on piracy in Kuala Lumpur that there was no evidence of any link between terrorists and pirates in the Straits of Malacca.[60] Nevertheless, the possibility remained, however remote, that terrorists could still exploit piracy in some way. It was something that was difficult to prove conclusively one way or the other.

Both the Indonesian and Malaysian elites therefore decided to step up patrols in the Straits. This decision stemmed largely from the perception that the United States would intervene to secure its interests against terrorism. There were already indications that the Westphalian norm of sovereignty was being increasingly eroded by the U.S. initiatives to protect its global interests from attacks by non-state actors. The notion of non-interference in the internal affairs of another country had been one of ASEAN's key norms. This Westphalian concept, based on international recognition of the legal right of a country to exist without external interference in its domestic affairs, that is, the exclusion of external actors, was being increasingly eroded by new sovereignty concepts that see legal authority as quite distinct from the ability to exercise effective control. For example, the concept of domestic sovereignty is based on the ability of the authorities in power to exercise control in their sovereign territories.[61] The literature on weak and failing states reflect this preoccupation with domestic sovereignty, and the post-Cold War debate on the right of external powers to intervene in states that are unable to maintain domestic law and order and to uphold the peace also threatened to erode the ASEAN norm of sacrosanct territoriality.

The war against Iraq, and the U.S. global initiative against (and the hunt for) weapons of mass destruction further reinforced the view that the United States would not respect territorial sovereignty if it saw its global interests threatened.[62] For instance, an editorial opinion piece published in the *Jakarta Post* warned that any agreement on security cooperation in the Straits of Malacca must be effectively implemented by the littoral states otherwise it would "result in a renewed push by the United States to allow its forces to patrol the strait". Unless the littoral states could secure the

Straits, the United States could be provoked "into using its own forces in the waterway".[63]

Working Together: The MALSINDO Patrols

Given these perceptions of the potential threat posed to their sovereignty, *not by pirates and terrorists but by foreign powers intervening in the Straits*, Malaysia and Indonesia agreed in June 2004 to enhance security in the Malacca Straits by increasing naval patrols. Both littoral countries, however, laid down stringent pre-conditions for the patrols. Malaysia and Indonesia made it clear that these patrols would be confined only to the forces of the littoral states. Second, these would be coordinated patrols and not joint patrols, that is, the ships of each respective littoral state would keep strictly to their own waters. As the Malaysian Deputy Prime Minister and Defence Minsister Najib Abdul Razak succinctly put it: "[Y]ou don't enter others' territorial waters. No sharing of vessels, no hot pursuit. *We have to respect the cardinal principle of national sovereignty.*"[64] Malaysia, Indonesia and Singapore had already conducted coordinated patrols of the Malacca Straits, limited to four a year, since 1992. The new coordinated patrols, however, would involve year-round patrols with seventeen ships from the littoral states dedicated to the task force.[65] Thus the MALSINDO (Malaysia-Singapore-Indonesia) coordinated patrols in the Malacca Straits were launched on 20 July 2004, amidst much pomp and ceremony aboard an Indonesian navy ship with all the top military brass of the three littoral states present.

However, the efficacy of the MALSINDO patrols to curb piracy and terrorism came under criticism right from the start. The original coordinated patrols, begun in 1992, had apparently become "ineffective" by 1995 to the extent that insurance companies began levying "war risk" insurance rates for ships using some Indonesian ports.[66] A senior Indonesian navy officer also described the concept of coordinated patrols as a serious policy shortcoming, and "a potential cause for confusion, inefficiency and misallocation of resources".[67] The International Maritime Bureau in fact described the system as "ridiculous" because law enforcement agencies could not cross territorial sea boundaries while pursuing pirates.[68] Moreover, while Malaysia and Singapore had done a great deal to secure the Straits, Indonesia was the weak link in the system of coordinated patrols. Not only were the majority of piracy incidents taking place in Indonesian waters, but Jakarta's maritime enforcement capability was currently severely overstretched with the Indonesian Navy "desperately" needing more money and equipment.[69] Therefore if the littoral states were really serious about using maritime patrols to curb piracy and terrorism, it would address this key jurisdictional problem, thus allowing Malaysian and Singaporean vessels to help patrol Indonesian waters.

However, because of sovereignty sensitivities, both Malaysia and Indonesia are obviously not prepared to implement any system of joint patrols. It appears therefore that the primary aim of MALSINDO was not so much to curb piracy and terrorism, but to forestall possible foreign intervention in the Malacca Straits. This was because there was no attempt to introduce the strategic and policy underpinnings that would make naval patrols in the Malacca Straits really effective against pirates and terrorists. Moreover, the Director of the Indonesian State Intelligence Agency admitted that besides a lack of resources, "security along the strait has been sorely lacking" because of the jurisdictional problem, which complicated naval coordination.[70] It can therefore be argued that the MALSINDO initiative was essentially a Malaysia-Indonesia public relations exercise to show to the world that the two littoral states were taking Straits security seriously and were doing something about it so as to forestall possible foreign military intervention in the waterway.

Conclusion

From the three case studies, it would appear that cooperation in the Straits of Malacca is not a straightforward technical issue. Although the three littoral states might face common problems, such as ensuring safe navigation, fighting piracy and preventing any possible terrorist attacks in the Straits, their responses have been tempered by their individual perceptions of their national interests, their varying degrees of concern over maritime sovereignty, and by their capacity to deal with the problems facing them. In short, a state's hierarchy of interests and its attendant state capacity are important variables in inter-state cooperation. The convoluted attempts to put in place a regime governing the use of the Malacca Straits together with a navigational safety regime illustrate the differing interests, priorities and perceptions between not only user states and coastal states, but among the littoral states themselves. The primary aim of Malaysia and Indonesia then was to make sure that they had as complete a control over the Straits of Malacca as possible. Thus they worked hand-in-hand to extend their authority over the waterway by bilaterally demarcating and extending their territorial sea and continental shelf boundaries in the Straits, and by insisting that the regime of innocent passage should apply to all vessels using the Straits of Malacca. Singapore, limited to only a three-nautical-mile territorial sea zone, saw the attempt by its two neighbours to enclose the Malacca Straits as a threat to its sovereignty and prosperity as an international maritime centre. Not surprisingly, Singapore refused to endorse the Malaysia-Indonesia stand in 1971 that the Straits of Malacca was not an international strait. Nevertheless, as a littoral state, it was as equally concerned as its neighbours over ensuring the safety of navigation. Even then, there was considerable disagreement over the issue of under keel clearance for tankers, with Singapore pressing for minimal clearance because it wanted Japanese oil tankers to have direct access to its petroleum refineries. Singapore also implicitly allied itself with the international users of the Malacca Straits, in particular with the United States. It saw the value of a U.S. presence not merely in commercial terms, but also as a military counterweight to maintain "stability and peace in the Asia-Pacific region".[71] This is reflected in the building of Changi Naval Base with its docking facilities specially designed for U.S. nuclear aircraft carriers.[72]

Cooperation therefore depends not only on political will, but a state's hierarchy of interests and its capacity are also critical. A good example is that of Indonesia. It has, in the past, paid relatively little attention to the problem of maritime piracy and terrorism simply because it had other more pressing priorities on land to attend to. The bomb attacks in Bali in October 2002 and Jakarta in August 2003 attributed to the Jemaah Islamiyah, the problem of separatist movements in Papua and Aceh, inter-religious strife in Ambon and its economic problems, have occupied the attention of the Indonesian elite. Similarly, Malaysia's maritime concerns are not limited to pirates and terrorists. It sees its maritime problems in more macro dimensions, which involves preserving its maritime borders from being penetrated by all manner of non-state actors, including illegal migrants, fish poachers, drug smugglers and potential terrorists.[73] Indonesia and Malaysia, in contrast to Singapore, have much larger maritime zones to protect and a whole slew of maritime concerns and problems to attend to. The offshore maritime zones of Malaysia and Indonesia are not only strategic and extensive, but they also contain valuable living and non-living resources. Malaysia's maritime boundaries in particular, are still not universally recognized and accepted by the international community. Thus maritime sovereignty in the Malacca Straits is important for Indonesia and Malaysia not merely because the Straits is a strategic waterway for them, but because any change in their authority over, and management of, the waterway would have ramifications for their extensive maritime boundaries and zones beyond the Straits.

Singapore, because of its limited maritime zone, central location in the regional seas, and its wealth, is able to focus exclusively on the Malacca Straits. It strong concern over the inadequacies in current security measures in the waterway stems from its strategic and economic priorities as a maritime state, which is to ensure that the sea lines of communications are kept open, and that Straits traffic should not be put in harm's way. The Singapore conviction that an alliance of pirates and terrorists posed an imminent threat to the safety of the Malacca Straits put pressure on Malaysia and Indonesia to increase naval patrols in the waterway not because they shared Singapore's threat perceptions, but because they saw that Singapore's security discourse had the effect, intentional or otherwise, of internationalizing Straits security by giving external powers the potential political space to manage the waterway. It is significant that the Singapore strategy in the Straits has been that of close-in defence, that is, using maritime patrols to stop direct terrorist attacks in the Straits of Malacca. Nowhere in the Singapore discourse has any mention been made of tackling the piracy and terrorism problem at source, that is, in Indonesia. However, there are signs that Singapore, of late, has become increasingly aware of, and sensitive to, the importance that its two littoral neighbours attach to their maritime sovereignty. In late August 2004, the Singapore Deputy Prime Minister and Coordinating Minister for Defence and Security, Dr. Tony Tan, said that while Singapore would cooperate with all parties with regard to Straits security, "what is important to remember is that all of these efforts must take into account the sovereignty and territorial integrity of the littoral states. So, we will not do anything which will infringe on this sovereignty."[74]

As for Indonesia, the loss of the island of Sipadan in the Celebes Sea, awarded by the International Court of Justice to Malaysia in 2002, has been a reminder that its maritime sovereignty can be eroded, and it has therefore to work to maintain the integrity of its *Wawasan Nusantara* or the archipelagic underpinnings of a unitary Indonesia. On balance, therefore, maritime cooperation involving regional states cannot be seen as a technical issue to be left to experts to resolve and implement. Cooperation is highly politicized because the issue of maritime sovereignty, the demarcation of maritime boundaries and rights over the exploitation of living and non-living resources have yet to be completely resolved in the region. Until and unless the issue of maritime sovereignty is settled to the satisfaction of all parties, cooperation in the Straits of Malacca, and in the other regional seas and waters of Southeast Asia, will remain difficult — if not impossible.

Notes

1   Paragraph 5, Section A, Declaration of ASEAN Concord II (Bali Concord II), 2003.
2   "Indonesian Presses Asean to Pursue Security Bloc", *Reuters* report, *International Herald Tribune*, 30 June 2004.
3   Regimes can be defined, for the purposes of this chapter, as formal or informal institutions to facilitate cooperation by reducing transaction costs and reducing conflicts in a given issue area.
4   Daniel Moran, "The International Law of the Sea in a Globalized World", in *Globalization and Maritime Power*, edited by Sam J. Tangredi (Washington: Institute for National Strategic Studies, National Defense University, 2002).
5   Leigh S. Ratiner, "United States Oceans Policy: An Analysis", *Journal of Maritime Law and Commerce* II, no. 2 (January 1971): 226. Ratiner was the then chairman of the U.S. Department of Defense Advisory Group on the Law of the Sea.
6   Mahathir Mohamad, Keynote address, *Malaysia's First International Maritime Conference*, Langkawi, 4 December 1997.
7   Ibid.
8   <http://www.cia.gov/cia/publications/factbook/geos/sn.html#Geo>.
9   Barry Buzan, *Seabed Politics* (New York: Prager, 1976).
10   Dino Patti Djalal, *The Geopolitics of Indonesia's Maritime Territorial Policy* (Jakarta: Centre for Strategic and International Studies (CSIS), 1996), p. 40.
11   Michael Leifer, *International traits of the World: Malacca, Singapore, and Indonesia* (Alphen aan den Rijn, the Netherlands: Sijthoff and Noordhoff, 1978), p. 30.
12   Leifer, op. cit., p. 30.
13   Djalal, op. cit., pp. 31–33.
14   Leifer, op. cit., p. 27.
15   Djalal, op. cit., p. 116.
16   The most productive Indonesian fields, for example, were to be found within the Indonesian Archipelagic baselines. An idea of the importance of offshore oil to the Indonesian economy may be seen from the increase in oil corporation tax collection from US$2 million in 1966 to US$2,345 million in the 1974/75 fiscal year. Dino Patti Djalal, op. cit., p. 82. Chapter 4 (pp. 76–96) gives a comprehensive account of the contribution of offshore resources to economic development programme of Suharto's New Order government.
17   Wan Leong Fee, *The Economic Prospects of Malaysia's Petroleum Economy* (Kuala Lumpur: MIMA Issue Paper, Maritime Institute of Malaysia, 1994), p. 1. The contribution of petroleum to the Malaysian federal revenue grew from 3 per cent in 1974 to a peak of 22.6 per cent in 1985, dropping to 10.9 per cent in 1993.

As a percentage of GNP, the figure rose from 1.8 per cent to 13.4 per cent in 1980, declining to 10.9 per cent in 1993. Wong Leong Fee, op. cit., pp. 18–21.

[18] International Law Commission, UN Convention on the Territorial Sea and the Contiguous Zone, 1958, Article 14 (4), <http://www.un.org/law/ilc/texts/terrsea.htm>.

[19] Murgugesu Pathmanathan, "The Straits of Malacca: A Basis for Conflict or Co-operation", *Readings in Malaysian Foreign Policy*, mimeographed (Kuala Lumpur, 1976), pp. 44–45.

[20] Koh, *Straits In International Navigation: Contemporary Issues* (New York: Oceana Publications, Inc., 1982), p. 35.

[21] Ann L. Hollick and Robert E. Osgood, *New Era of Ocean Politics* (Baltimore: The John Hopkins University Press, 1974), p. 78.

[22] Koh, op. cit., pp. 21–22.

[23] John E. Lawyer, Jr, "International Straits and the Law of the Sea Conference", *Air University Review* (September–October 1974), <http://www.airpower.maxwell.af.mil/airchronicles/aureview/1974/sep-oct/Lawyer.html>.

[24] 1982 UN Convention on the Law of the Sea, Part III, Article 38, Right of Transit Passage.

[25] This UN organization is today known as the International Maritime Organization (IMO).

[26] Leifer, op. cit., p. 37.

[27] Pathmanathan, op. cit., p. 42.

[28] Leifer, op. cit., pp. 43–44.

[29] *Japan Times*, 30 August 1968. [Author's emphasis].

[30] Leifer, op. cit., p. 46.

[31] Ibid.

[32] Singapore's natural resources are described in the U.S. CIA's *The World Factbook* as fish and deepwater ports. <http://www.cia.gov/cia/publications/factbook/geos/sn.html#Geo>.

[33] Phiphat Tangsubkul, *ASEAN and the Law of the Sea* (Singapore: Institute of Southeast Asian Studies, 1982) p. 15.

[34] Parliamentary Debates, Singapore, 17 March 1972, cited in Leifer, op. cit., p. 34.

[35] Singapore International Chamber of Commerce *Economic Bulletin* 19 (31 March, 1972), cited in Koh, op. cit., p. 61.

[36] Koh, op. cit., p. 77.

[37] Leifer, op. cit., p. 68. For a technical discussion of how under keel clearance is calculated, see Koh, op. cit., pp. 84–86.

[38] Phiphat Tangsubkul, op. cit., p. 89.

[39] Leifer, op. cit., p. 67.

[40] Ibid., p. 64.

[41] Koh, op. cit., p. 85.

[42] Leifer, op. cit., p. 71.

43   For details of these ship incidents and oil spills, see Koh, op. cit.,
     pp. 77–80.
44   Leifer, op. cit., p. 68.
45   United Nations Convention on the Law of the Sea, 1982, Part IV, Archipelagic
     States.
46   "Piracy equals terrorism on troubled waters: Minister", *Agence France Presse*,
     21 Dec 2003. <http://www.singapore-window.org/sw03/031221af.htm>.
47   "Troops on Isles. Najib: Soldiers to be Deployed on All Islands along Sabah's
     East Coast", *The Star*, 15 September 2000.
48   "Malaysia Pledges to Wipe out Maritime Piracy, Work with US against Terror",
     Agence France Presse, 6 June 2004.
49   Minister for Defence Teo Chee Hean, keynote address at the opening of the
     2nd Western Pacific Mine Countermeasures and Diving Exercises, Singapore,
     21 April 2004.
50   "Don't Act Alone, Singapore Told", *New Straits Times*, 7 April 2004.
51   "Malaysia Rejects US Patrols in Malacca Straits, Raps Singapore", *Agence France
     Presse*, Kuala Lumpur, 27 April 2004, <http://www.singapore-window.org/
     sw04/040427af.htm>; "No Public Debate Please, says FM", *The Star*, 28 April
     2004.
52   "Malaysia Says has Malacca Security in Hand", *Reuters*, 27 April 2004.
53   "Terror Malacca Straits", *Associated Press*, 2 June 2004.
54   Nugroho Wisnumurti, Former Director General for Political Affairs, Ministry
     of Foreign Affairs, Jakarta, *Jakarta Post*, Opinion and Editorial, 12 April 2004.
55   "Indonesian Navy Chief Sees Foreign Interests behind Sea Piracy Accusations",
     Agence France Presse, Jakarta, 19 July 2004. It is significant that these remarks
     were published just one day before the official launch of the MALSINDO
     Malacca Straits Coordinated Patrols aboard an Indonesian Navy vessel.
56   *Asia Times Online*, 16 June 2004, <http://www.atimes.com/atimes/
     Southeast_Asia/FF16Ae01.html>.
57   "India to be Sounded on Malacca Straits Security", *The Hindu*, Singapore,
     29 August 2004; "Marines and Malacca Straits", *Frontline* 21, no. 11 (22 May–
     4 June 2004).
58   "Malaysia Offers Navy Escorts through Malacca Straits", *Straits Times*, 18 April
     2004.
59   "Local Coast Guards to Begin Early Next Year", *The Star Maritime*, 9 August
     2004. The idea of establishing the Malaysian Coast Guard or the Malaysian
     Maritime Enforcement Agency (MMEA) was mooted years ago, well before
     2001. In any event, the decision to set up the MMEA was formally announced
     in 2002.
60   "No Evidence of Terror Threats in Malacca Straits, Experts Said", *Kyodo News
     Agency*, Kuala Lumpur, 29 July 2004.
61   See Stephen D. Krasner, *Sovereignty: Organized Hypocrisy* (Princeton: Princeton
     University Press, 1999).

[62]   A Malaysian Chinese language daily, *Nanyang Siangpao*, owned by the Malaysian Chinese association (MCA) went so far as to say that that "the US military is capable of interfering in the defense matters of other countries and can even forcefully invade another's land. Therefore there is reason why Malaysia distrusts the US. The farmer has the responsibility to protect his animals, but he cannot accept the suggestion that a weasel will help guard his farm." *Radio Singapore International: Regional Press Review*, <http://www.rsi.com.sg/english/regionalpressreview/view/20040408172245/1/.html>.

[63]   "U.S. Interests in Malacca Straits", *Jakarta Post*, 7 July 2004.

[64]   Author's emphasis. "Malaysia, Indonesia Rule out Joint Patrols in Malacca Straits", *Channel NewsAsia*, 1 July 2004.

[65]   "Indonesia, Malaysia, Singapore Agree on Joint Malacca Straits Patrols", *Channel NewsAsia*, 20 June 2004.

[66]   Dana Dillon and Lucia Selvaggi, "Stopping an Al Qaeda Attack in the Malacca Straits", *Wall Street Journal*, 28 January 2004.

[67]   Ioannis Gatsiounis, "Strait: Target for Terror", *Asia Times Online*, July 2004.

[68]   "Malaysia, Indonesia Rule out Joint Patrols in Malacca Straits", *Channel NewsAsia*, 1 July 2004.

[69]   "Concerns over Straits of Malacca", *The Jakarta Post*, Editorial, 9 June 2004; "International maritime experts cheer joint patrols in Malacca Straits", *Channel NewsAsia*, 29 June 2004.

[70]   "Jakarta-S'pore Ties: Time Right for Fresh Start", *Jakarta Post* comment by Hendropriyono, Director of the State Intelligence Agency, Indonesia, reprinted in *Straits Times*, 26 August 2004.

[71]   Transcript of Joint Press Conference chaired by the Deputy Prime Minister and Minister for Defence, Dr. Tony Tan and Admiral Blair, Singapore, MINDEF, 29 January 2002. See also Amitav Acharya, "Asian Security After September 11: A View from Southeast Asia", paper prepared for the *Asia Pacific Foundation of Canada's Roundtable on the Foreign Policy Dialogue and Canada-Asia Relations*, 27 March 2003, Nanyang Technological University and York University, p. 5.

[72]   "Singapore Changi Naval Base", <http://www.globalsecurity.og/military/singapore.htm>.

[73]   J.N. Mak, "Securitising Piracy in Southeast Asia: Malaysia, the International Maritime Bureau & Singapore", paper presented at the *IDSS-Ford Foundation Programme on Non-Traditional Security Issues*, Singapore, 3–4 September 2004.

[74]   "India to be Sounded on Malacca Straits Security", *The Hindu*, Singapore, 29 August 2004, <http://www.hindu.com/2004/08/29/stories/2004082901630900.htm>.

9

Maritime Piracy in Southeast Asia: The Evolution and Progress of Intra-ASEAN Cooperation

Tamara Renee Shie

Introduction

Although maritime piracy is not a new phenomenon, it is one that has, over the last two decades, received increasing amounts of both media and political attention. This has been in part due to the transformation of security issues at the closing end of the Cold War and the spectacular rise in piracy attacks during the same time period. The 11 September 2001 terrorist attacks brought further attention to the issue, as concerns over the mounting vulnerability of the international maritime transportation sector to piracy exposed an area ripe for terrorist exploitation.

Piracy is considered to be one of the many new or non-traditional security issues to have emerged in the post-Cold War era. These issues "arise from factors or actors which are sub-state or trans-state in character, are diffuse, are multi-dimensional and multi-directional, cannot necessarily be managed by traditional military means, and often threatening to something besides the state."[1] This is very different from the traditional view of security, which focuses mainly on the external threats to a states' security. Due to the transnational nature of crimes like piracy, the actions of a single state or even a limited number of states are often inadequate to combat the problem. Non-traditional security issues require more than occasional bilateral security agreements; they often require consistent and comprehensive multilateral cooperation.

For several reasons, Southeast Asia has emerged at the centre of the piracy maelstrom. First, the region hosts more piracy attacks than any other. In the 1994 International Maritime Bureau (IMB) Annual Report reported piracy attacks[2] worldwide totalled ninety; with more than fifty per cent of those attacks in Southeast Asia. Since then piracy attacks have increased almost five-fold, reaching a worldwide peak of 469 in 2000, with a majority of attacks occurring in Southeast Asian territory: the South China Sea, the Straits of Malacca and Singapore, and in the ports and waters of Malaysia, the Philippines, and Indonesia. Second, by virtue of their geographical location and relative efficiency, Southeast Asia's ports and waterways are essential to international maritime trade. Six of the world's top twenty-five container ports are located in Southeast Asia: Singapore, Port Kelang (Malaysia), Tanjung Priok (Indonesia), Tanjung Pelepas (Malaysia), Laem Chabang (Thailand), and Manila (the Philippines). Singapore currently ranks as the world's busiest port, the second largest container port, and the third largest port when considered in terms of global cargo percentage. It is also the location of the third largest oil refinery industry in the world. Over 135,000 maritime vessels were reported to have docked at Singapore in 2003. Therefore, the seas of Southeast Asia are some of the most heavily traversed in the world, conveying goods between the markets of Europe, the Middle East, East Asia and North America. One quarter of the world's commerce passes through the Straits of Malacca and Singapore. Third, despite both national and multinational attempts, international stakeholders have become increasingly concerned over the failure to bring piracy in the region under control.

Much of the past research on Southeast Asian piracy has more heavily acknowledged the anti-piracy efforts of extra-regional stakeholders, such as shipping companies or concerned nations like Japan and the United States over intra-regional unilateral, bilateral, or multilateral actions.[3] Indigenous approaches, although mentioned, are implicitly regarded as inadequate and ineffective. Therefore, proposed solutions have often placed greater emphasis on the involvement of outside parties.[4] This may be representative of a tacit consensus within the international community that because individual countries in the region and the regional

TABLE 9.1
Southeast Asia Reported Piracy Attacks by Location 1991–2004[5]

	1991	1992	1993	1994	1995	1996	1997	1998	1999	2000	2001	2002	2003	2004
Cambodia	0	0	1	1	1	1	1	0	0	0	0	0	0	0
Indonesia	55	49	10	22	33	57	47	60	115	119	91	103	121	93
Malacca Straits	32	7	5	3	2	3	0	1	2	75	17	16	28	37
Malaysia	1	2	0	4	5	5	4	10	18	21	19	14	5	9
Myanmar	0	0	0	0	0	1	2	0	1	5	3	0	0	1
Philippines	0	5	0	5	24	39	16	15	6	9	8	10	12	4
Singapore Strait	0	0	0	3	2	2	5	1	14	5	7	5	2	8
Thailand	0	0	0	0	4	16	17	2	5	8	8	5	2	4
South China Sea	14	6	31	6	3	2	6	5	3	9	4	0	2	8
Vietnam	0	0	0	2	4	0	4	0	2	6	8	12	15	4
Total	102	69	47	46	78	126	102	94	166	257	165	165	187	168

TABLE 9.2
Worldwide Reported Piracy Attacks by Region 1991–2004[6]

	1991	1992	1993	1994	1995	1996	1997	1998	1999	2000	2001	2002	2003	2004
Southeast Asia*	102	69	47	46	78	126	102	94	166	257	165	165	187	168
Far East	0	1	38	24	40	15	9	5	1	5	5	5	2	3
Indian-Subcontinent	0	5	3	3	16	24	37	22	45	95	53	52	87	32
Africa	0	0	7	6	20	25	46	41	55	68	86	78	93	72
Americas	0	0	6	11	21	32	37	35	28	39	21	65	72	44
Rest of World	0	0	0	0	12	6	17	4	5	7	4	5	4	6
Location Unavailable	5	31	2	0	1	0	0	1	0	0	1	0	0	0
Total	107	106	103	90	188	228	248	202	300	469	335	370	445	325
Southeast Asia as % of total	95%	65%	46%	51%	41%	55%	41%	47%	55%	55%	49%	45%	42%	52%

organization, the Association of Southeast Asian Nations (ASEAN), have been thus far unsuccessful in stemming piracy they are unable or even unwilling to do so. This perception has changed little since the early 1990s. Although available statistics indicate piracy has been rising significantly in Southeast Asia even as countries in the region have increasingly turned their attention toward combating non-traditional security threats such as piracy, this in and of itself provides neither clarification of the problem nor solutions. This trend deserves a more thorough examination beyond simply branding regional initiatives as ineffectual.

The intention of this chapter is not to negate the necessity of combined efforts to tackle a transnational issue such as piracy nor to devalue the measures taken by other stakeholders with an interest to reducing pirate attacks in the region, but instead to give Southeast Asian efforts a more central focus. One danger with writing off ASEAN as a major actor in reducing and controlling piracy is it can have the effect of relieving Southeast Asian nations from their responsibilities in addressing the problem. It also gives little regard to the leading role Southeast Asian nations should undertake in regional anti-piracy measures. Without their support, such measures are likely to fail. Neglecting ASEAN's attempts — both successful and unsuccessful — in the policy calculus also overlooks the value in studying the factors steering regional responses to piracy. Such an approach further dismisses the evolution and progress of ASEAN regional maritime security strategies. Not only has ASEAN developed as an organization since its inception in 1967, but the political and strategic environment at both the regional and international levels has transformed as well. Around the world the end of the Cold War ushered in profound changes in the international security paradigm, challenging conventional approaches to national security and broadening the scope of potential sources of state insecurity. The shift from a bipolar to a multipolar international system, coupled with the forces of globalization and increased economic and political inter-dependence, are generally thought to be behind nations recognizing the necessity of working together on common security issues. Regionally, Southeast Asian countries have emerged from the Cold War politically and economically stronger. ASEAN has doubled its membership and furthered cooperation on a greater number of issues. The region's approach to piracy has transitioned with these changes.

This chapter focuses on the development of Southeast Asian cooperation on maritime piracy through the examination of some situations and factors, which may have affected regional efforts towards piracy suppression during different chapters of the organization's existence. By closely examining some of the internal and external factors that have affected ASEAN's counter-piracy strategies at different points in time, future researchers and policy-makers can better understand the obstacles the region has and still must overcome to work together to combat piracy. For purposes of the analysis, ASEAN's development as an organization can be divided into three phases: Early ASEAN, ASEAN expansion, and ASEAN in the new millennium. Each section will present the major factors influencing regional cooperation — including the successes and failures of regional piracy strategies — the regional response to piracy, and the corresponding effect this response has had on the incidence of piracy.

Factors, Responses, and Piracy

In an article analysing ASEAN's significance at the dawn of the new millennium, Southeast Asian researchers Simon Tay and Jesus Estanislao chose to classify its organizational cooperation into three distinct periods.[7] In the first period from the Association's formation in 1967 until 1976, ASEAN was characterized by a "loose and highly decentralized structure" in which policies were presented and in turn implemented by the member governments, not by the organization as a whole. Although the second period from 1976 to 1992 was marked by increased political interactivity, the group remained decentralized. The third period begins in 1992 and ends in 2000, a period defined by increasing coordination and cooperation among member states. In terms of ASEAN responses to piracy however, it can be argued that the first two periods do not significantly differ. Therefore in this chapter, they will be placed within the same phase of "early ASEAN". The period from 1992 until 2001 is termed "ASEAN expansion" here. In addition to the extension of regional objectives to include cooperation on security issues as observed by Tay and Estanislao, this period also witnessed the enlargement of the organization's membership and maritime space. As a phase of accelerated economic, political, cultural and security cooperation, the period from 2001 to the time of writing is entitled "ASEAN in the new millennium".

Early ASEAN (1976–92)

The early years of ASEAN cooperation were characteristic of the political environment in which the organization was founded. Amidst the overriding regional dynamics of post-colonial ambiguity and the Cold

War milieu, the governments of Southeast Asia were particularly concerned with protecting their national integrity and interests from outside influences. In response to this environment, ASEAN's five founding members — Singapore, Malaysia, Indonesia, Philippines and Thailand — established organizational norms to maintain their respective autonomy during periods of cooperation.

Trademarks of ASEAN's cooperation strategy are its decision making process termed the "ASEAN Way" and the principal of "non-interference". The ASEAN Way is the distinctive and informal style of diplomacy developed for intra-ASEAN relations. It is characterized by the dual Malay terms of *musyawarah* (consultation) and *mufakat* (consensus), and a step-by-step process of dialogue over issues designed to build confidence and avoid conflict between members. An integral part of the ASEAN Way is the tenet of non-interference in the internal affairs of member states.

The principles of the ASEAN Way and non-interference were enshrined early in ASEAN's establishment. The founding Bangkok Declaration of 8 August 1967, reaffirmed the aims of the United Nations charter to protect nations from external interference. This was further supported by the 1971 Zone of Peace, Freedom and Neutrality (ZOPFAN) Declaration.[8] Finally conditions for institutional cooperation were laid out most specifically in the Treaty of Amity and Cooperation in Southeast Asia (TAC) signed in Bali, on 24 February 1976.[9] Among other things, the preamble states that "[t]he High Contracting Parties...convinced that the settlement of differences or disputes between their countries should be regulated by rational, effective and sufficiently flexible procedures, avoiding negative attitudes which might endanger or hinder cooperation"; hence formalizing the principle underpinning the ASEAN Way. Article 2 of the TAC also maintains that:

> In their relations with one another, the High Contracting Parties shall be guided by the following fundamental principles:
>
> a. Mutual respect for the independence, sovereignty, equality, territorial integrity and national identity of all nations;
> b. The right of every State to lead its national existence free from external interference, subversion or coercion;
> c. Non-interference in the internal affairs of one another;
> d. Settlement of differences or disputes by peaceful means;
> e. Renunciation of the threat or use of force;
> f. Effective cooperation among themselves.

Throughout the organization's existence member states have consistently reaffirmed these norms through ASEAN declarations as well as statements and agreements on a myriad of issues from combating the spread of infectious disease to improving the environment. Another way in which they are manifested is in the Association's preference for informal, voluntary, non-binding agreements.[10]

Despite the promise to effectively cooperate with one another, ASEAN was first and foremost established to foster regional economic, social and cultural development, not to deal with common security issues. Therefore, on issues of security, the ASEAN Way and the principle of non-interference have often led to the practice of *ad hoc* multilateralism.[11] This was endorsed in the Manila Declaration of 1987: "while each Member State shall be responsible for its own security, cooperation on a non-ASEAN basis among the Member States in security matters shall continue in accordance to their mutual needs and interests."[12] Generally, this means only the nations with a strong interest in resolving a matter become involved and they "act in response to their short-term coincidence of interests."[13] Otherwise, the matter might not be tackled at all, as many contentious issues are often dropped from the ASEAN agenda.

Of key significance to this chapter, piracy was very much alive in Southeast Asia during this first phase of ASEAN, although the naval presence of the United States, the Soviet Union, the United Kingdom and other major powers in the waters of the Asia-Pacific partially served to keep piracy in check during the 1960s and 1970s. In the late-1970s and 1980s, there were numerous attacks on Vietnamese "boat people" — boatloads of refugees fleeing the country especially after 1978 — in the Gulf of Thailand.[14] However, in the early 1980s, the International Maritime Organization (IMO) became increasingly concerned over the number of attacks also occurring in and around Singapore territorial waters.[15] Between 1981 to 1987, one source estimates there were 292 piracy attacks in Southeast Asian waters, excluding those against the Vietnamese boat people, averaging forty-two a year.[16] However it is likely the figures were much higher. In 1983 the IMO General Assembly adopted several resolutions to persuade member states to take firmer action to contain piracy and report incidents in their waters or involving their vessels.[17] Piracy control however remained very much a responsibility for individual nations.

By the early 1990s Southeast Asian nations collectively began to pay attention to the growing number of piracy attacks in the region. At certain regional workshops dealing with the management of potential conflicts in the South China Sea in the early 1990s, participating government officials and maritime experts began to raise the issue of piracy and began preliminary discussions on how to address it in a cooperative manner.[18]

ASEAN Expansion (1992–2001)

This period after the end of the Cold War era represented a major watershed in Southeast Asia as it ushered in new outlooks and responsibilities in areas of security. In the 1992 Singapore Declaration, ASEAN acknowledged the necessity of regional security cooperation for the first time and, in light of "the profound international political and economic changes that have occurred since the end of the Cold War", indicated its intention to "seek avenues to engage Member States in new areas of cooperation in security matters."[19] Indeed the end of the Cold War has brought a number of changes to Southeast Asia, not least of which was the withdrawal of the American and Soviet naval presence in the region. The closing of the last U.S. bases in Southeast Asia — Clark Air Force Base and Subic Bay Naval Station in the Philippines in 1991 and 1992 respectively — brought a chapter of Southeast Asian history to a close. The region was left, perhaps for the first time in decades, without the overt presence of great powers. Regional security had become the responsibility of regional actors, not just as a matter of principle.

Areas of non-traditional security also began to move into the spotlight at this time. Prior to 1992, drug trafficking was the only such issue on the ASEAN agenda.[20] In the Singapore Declaration however, member nations pledged not only to continue cooperation on drug trafficking but also to coordinate efforts on transboundary pollution and the spread of the AIDS virus. In response to the growing alarm over pirate attacks in the region, Southeast Asian countries welcomed the establishment of the International Maritime Bureau's Piracy Reporting Centre in Kuala Lumpur in October 1992. By 1996, ASEAN began discussing regional action on transnational crimes and agreed to hold their first Conference on Transnational Crime the following year. For the first time, ASEAN identified piracy as a regional problem, later embellished in the 1997 ASEAN Declaration on Transnational Crime.[21]

Although the 1992 Singapore Declaration indicated a strengthening of regional cooperation on security issues, it was only the littoral states of Indonesia, Singapore, and Malaysia which implemented bilateral strategies against piracy that year. Indonesia and Singapore agreed to coordinate their patrols and to authorize "hot pursuit" in the Singapore Strait and Philip Channel. Malaysia and Indonesia also set up a Maritime Operation Planning Team in December 1992 to coordinate patrols in the Straits of Malacca.[22] Later in 1994, Malaysia and the Philippines also established a Border Patrol Coordinating Group in order to prevent piracy and armed robbery in the maritime area between Malaysian Borneo and the southern islands of the Philippines.[23] However, at the same time, the reduction in foreign naval presence appeared to have brought about a diminished deterrent to piracy.[24]

Despite organizational moves toward greater cooperation, several events throughout the decade compromised the ability of ASEAN nations to jointly combat piracy. These include the enlargement of ASEAN's membership from 1991 to 2000, the entering into force of the United Nations Convention on the Law of the Sea (UNCLOS) in 1994, and the Asian Financial Crisis of 1997–98.

In the 1990s, the extent of the seas under Southeast Asian control increased significantly. The 1982 United Nations Convention on the Law of the Sea entered into force in accordance with its Article 308 on 16 November 1994 (twelve months after the date of deposit of the sixtieth instrument of ratification or accession), after it was first opened for signature in 1982.[25] The UNCLOS not only had the effect of changing the perception and value of maritime space in Southeast Asia, but also placed more maritime space under regional jurisdiction than land territory. A state's territorial seas were extended from three nautical miles from the coast to twelve nautical miles. Indonesia and the Philippines had been particularly strong proponents of the new convention as it afforded them special archipelagic status, in which the territorial sea of twelve nautical miles is drawn from the outermost points of their outermost islands, with all waters between these islands declared as archipelagic waters under their jurisdiction.[26] The convention also extended state jurisdiction beyond the twelve nautical mile zone into the exclusive economic zone (EEZ) 200 nautical miles from shore. Indonesia was a major beneficiary of the EEZ regime.

Although the expansion of the region's maritime territory was initially seen as a boon to economic and political control, in practice, patrolling these new waters proved problematic. The extension of maritime jurisdiction provided by UNCLOS necessitated an increase in Southeast Asia's maritime policing and enforcement capabilities. As the majority of pirate attacks tend to occur within the twelve-nautical mile range,[27] the region's coastal states have had an even greater responsibility to protect these waters. However, most regional naval forces have proved to be woefully inadequate to patrol and deter threats even in national waters, much less be prepared to take on further duties. In mid-2002, the Indonesian Navy publicly admitted none of its vessels were combat ready, and that more than ninety per cent of the fleet was over a decade old.[28]

The acceptance of four additional members into ASEAN may have also played a role in compromising the region's capability to suppress piracy. Notwithstanding the addition of Brunei in 1984, for much of the first twenty-eight years of ASEAN existence, its membership essentially remained unchanged. Only in the later half of the 1990s did ASEAN realize its goal of incorporating all the countries of the conceived geo-political region of Southeast Asia — Vietnam in 1995; Myanmar and Laos in 1997; and Cambodia in 1999. However, the integration of the region's continental states challenged a united Southeast Asian approach towards transnational crimes like piracy.[29] Notwithstanding the shared economic reliance on maritime endeavors and resources found in Southeast Asia — only Laos is land-locked — there are fundamentally different means of interaction between continental and archipelagic/peninsular states.[30] The boundaries of continental states are easier to cross and control and therefore interaction with neighbouring states are more frequent. Maritime states rely more heavily on the sea for the transportation of goods and people and are generally more insulated from interacting with other states. For that reason, the control of the maritime realm is more necessary to the security of archipelagic states than it is for their continental variants. Although "ASEAN is predominantly and uniquely maritime in nature",[31] in the decade leading up to the new millennium, its members did not adopt a regional maritime security agenda, as one might have expected.

For one thing, security measures have been more difficult to address in the larger ASEAN forum than economic and cultural interests. The enlargement of the organization to include countries not previously engaged with the first six members in cooperative strategies may have further undermined ASEAN's ability to reach an agreement on transnational security matters. The consensus agreement required of the ASEAN Way and the principle of non-interference were further tested with the addition of its Indochinese members. Consensus requires common interests, and in terms of piracy the national interests among ASEAN's members have varied considerably.[32]

Another possible contributing factor to the rise in piracy attacks in the late 1990s was the Asian Financial Crisis of 1997–98. The crisis exacerbated two of the root causes of piracy attacks — endemic poverty and low government expenditure on maritime security.[33] During the crisis, affected countries experienced soaring unemployment and under-employment rates, a decline in real wages and earnings, and an increase in the percentage of population below the poverty line, particularly in Indonesia and Thailand

— two of the countries most affected.[34] Additionally it follows that countries with better trained and higher paid maritime security forces tend to have significantly lower incidents of piracy.[35] Several countries in Southeast Asia already had low average salaries in general, particularly for marine security forces and port personnel. With the Asian Financial Crisis severely reducing GDP, government spending contracted. Between 1997 and 1998 for example, Indonesia's defence budget was reduced by 65 per cent, severely hampering the ability of its maritime forces to deter piracy.[36]

Table 9.3 illustrates how these factors may have affected the incidence of piracy in the region. Between 1991 and 1992, ASEAN's new approaches towards security and piracy coincided with a 33 per cent reduction in the number of pirate attacks in the region. The coordinated bilateral patrols of 1992 and 1993 may help to explain the reduction in the the number of reported attacks in Indonesia, Malaysia and the Straits of Malacca during that time. From 1992 to 1993, the number of reported pirate attacks in Southeast Asia further decreased from 69 to 47; a drop of about 32 per cent. The following year they were down to 46 reported incidents, a further 2 per cent drop. However by 1995, the total had again climbed to 78 reported incidents — a 70 per cent rise over the previous year —

TABLE 9.3
Possible Effect of Certain Factors on Piracy Incidence Levels in Southeast Asia 1991–2000

	1991	1992	1993	1994	1995	1996	1997	1998	1999	2000
Cambodia	0	0	1	1	1	1	1	0	0	0
Indonesia	55			22	33	57	47	60	115	119
Malacca Straits	32	7	5	3	2	3	0	1	2	75
Malaysia	1	2	0	4	5	5	4	10	18	21
Myanmar	0	0	0	0	0	1	2	0	1	5
Philippines	0	5	0	5	24	39	16	15	6	9
Singapore Strait	0	0	0	3	2	2	5	1	14	5
Thailand	0	0	0	0	4	16	17	2	5	8
South China Sea	14	6	31	6	3	2	6	5	3	9
Vietnam	0	0	0	2	4	0	4	0	2	6
Total	102	69	47	46	78	126	102	94	166	257

End of Cold War   UNCLOS   Expansion   Asian Financial Crisis   Other though the majority of this increase can be attributed to a rise in attacks in Philippine waters, many off the coast of the main island of Luzon. Interestingly, during the same time period of the decrease in attacks in Southeast Asia, there was an increase in reported attacks in the Far East. Also, although the incidence of piracy in and around the Straits of Malacca declined significantly during the patrols and remained low until the year 2000, there were upsurges in piratical activity elsewhere in the region. In 1997 and 1998 however, total incidence levels in the region appeared to drop, largely due to a significant decrease in reported attacks in Philippine and Indonesian waters in 1997 and in Thai, Singaporean, and Vietnamese waters in 1998.

The advent of UNCLOS in 1994 also coincided with a steady rise in pirate attacks to levels far beyond that year's decade low. In particular, the waters off Indonesia and the Philippines have experienced large increases in attacks after 1994. In the years 1995 and 1999, when Vietnam and Cambodia joined ASEAN, the total number of reported piracy attacks increased after two or three years of previous decline. However, pirate attacks did drop in 1997 with the addition of Laos and Myanmar, which could be attributed to regional moves on transnational crimes. Around this same time period, the aftermath of the Asian Financial Crisis was beginning to be felt in the region and elsewhere , including the rise in transnational crimes such as piracy. In 1996 and 1997, Thailand, a country with previously very few pirate attacks, experienced a leap in the number of incidents from 4 in 1995 to 16 and 17 these two respective years. The number of pirate attacks in Indonesia, which saw not only its economy crumble, but also underwent political instability following the overthrow of its long-time President Suharto in 1998, continued to climb. By 2000, pirate attacks worldwide and in Southeast Asia had hit an all-time high.

ASEAN New Millennium (2001–Present)

The 11 September 2001 terrorist attacks on the United States further elevated the significance of non-traditional security threats, perpetrated increasingly by non-state or transnational actors, in the global arena. Consequently, a primary factor driving Southeast Asian measures on security in the new millennium has been terrorism — the U.S. war on terror, the re-emergence of U.S. security interests in the region, and the alleged relationship between piracy and maritime terrorism.

After the invasion of Afghanistan in late 2001, the United States looked to other areas where the perceived threat of terrorism was high. Southeast

Asia, with its large Muslim population and known Islamic separatist and terrorist groups, naturally became a focal point of U.S. counter-terrorism policy. That the majority of the region's Muslim population live in maritime Southeast Asia — comprising Singapore, Indonesia, Philippines, Brunei, Malaysia and southern Thailand — only heightened U.S. concern over the possibility of terrorists attacking maritime-related targets. In 2002, India and the United States signed an agreement to jointly patrol the Straits of Malacca.[37] However preliminary discussions in April 2004 between Singapore and the United States to bring in U.S. Marines to assist in patrolling the same Straits against terrorists met with strong opposition in Malaysia and Indonesia.[38]

Eventually after the 9/11 attacks, the increasing levels and violence of piracy in Southeast Asia led the media to draw an association between piracy and maritime terrorism. Though no direct link has been substantiated and the two pursue vastly different agendas, this has not stalled the plethora of political and academic commentaries both inside and outside the region on the possibilities of pirate and terrorist cooperation.[39] To be sure, the high incident levels of piracy in and around major shipping lanes and ports indicate areas vulnerable to terrorist attack.[40]

Whether the threat is real or not, most of the recent communiqués on the ASEAN website concerning transnational crime have been related to terrorism. However the spotlight on terrorism has also led to a positive spin-off against other transnational crimes such as piracy. In 2001, ASEAN established the Special Projects division on Transnational Crime at the Secretariat in the Indonesian capital of Jakarta. Currently the division deals with eight types of transnational crime: Terrorism, trafficking in drugs, trafficking in persons, piracy, arms smuggling, money laundering, commercial crime and cyber-crime. At the Senior Officials Meeting on Transnational Crime (SOMTC) in Kuala Lumpur in May 2002, officials decided piracy would be dealt with exclusively by SOMTC.[41] At the same SOMTC, officials also approved a comprehensive Plan of Action to Combat Transnational Crime. What makes this plan different from previous undertakings is the introduction of an action plan, including some deadlines, for each work programme. As regard to piracy, the initiatives — which the ASEAN Secretariat planned to implement these in 2005 — include:

- Establishing a compilation of national laws and regulations of ASEAN Member Countries pertaining to piracy and armed robbery at sea;

- Compilation of national studies to determine trends and "modus operandi" of piracy in Southeast Asian waters;
- Consider the feasibility of developing multilateral or bilateral legal arrangements to facilitate apprehension, investigation, hot pursuit, prosecution and extradition, exchange of witnesses, sharing of evidence, inquiry, seizure and forfeiture of proceeds of a crime in order to enhance mutual legal and administrative assistance among ASEAN members;
- Enhance cooperation and coordination in law enforcement and intelligence sharing of piracy and armed robbery at sea activities.[42]

Regional discussions on collaboration towards reducing transnational criminal activities at sea have continued. In November of 2002, ASEAN and China signed the Declaration on the Code of Conduct in the South China Sea, which included a statement of the desire among parties "to explore or undertake cooperative activities" in "combating transnational crime, including but not limited to trafficking in illicit drugs, piracy and armed robbery at sea, and illegal traffic in arms". Seven months later, Southeast Asian nations along with their Asia-Pacific counterparts in the ASEAN Regional Forum (ARF) signed a Statement on Cooperation Against Piracy and Other Threats to Maritime Security acknowledging the need for regional cooperation and coordination in tackling maritime-related crime.[43] In another move recognizant of the growing international concern over the region's transnational crime and maritime issues, Southeast Asian leaders signified their intent to focus more on maritime security at the ninth ASEAN Summit held on 7 October 2003. The resulting Declaration of ASEAN Concord II indicates that the organization will construct an ASEAN Security Community (ASC) in which "maritime cooperation between and among ASEAN member countries shall contribute to the evolution" of that community.

In an unprecedented move toward greater maritime cooperation, Brunei, Myanmar, Singapore and the Philippines signed the 1988 United Nations Convention for the Suppression of Unlawful Acts against the Safety of Maritime Navigation (SUA), joining Vietnam, which acceded in October 2002, to bring half of ASEAN under the convention.[44] In October 1985 four armed Palestine Liberation Front members hijacked the Italian cruise ship the *Achille Lauro* in Egyptian waters, killing one American. In response, the IMO began to consider preparing a new international convention to cover such incidents. On 10 March 1988, the IMO adopted the SUA Convention, which entered into force 1 March 1992.[45] Although the SUA Convention was developed in response to an act of maritime terrorism, it neither names terrorism or piracy *per se* but applies to all criminal and intentional acts against maritime vessels or cargo and crew upon those vessels whether they are at port, in territorial, archipelagic, the EEZ or international waters. The SUA provides a comprehensive international legal framework for dealing with most acts of piracy in Southeast Asia.[46] Among several important provisions, the SUA sanctions the pursuance of vessels into another nation's territory during what it defines as "hot pursuit"[47] and establishes guidelines for extradition and prosecution of maritime criminals. With the exception of China, which acceded to the SUA in 1992, Asian countries were slow to join. By the end of 2000, China, Japan, India, Pakistan, and Sri Lanka had ratified the convention, although Southeast Asian nations remained reluctant to sign the SUA due to sovereignty concerns. The June 2003 ARF Statement on Cooperation Against Piracy called on all members to express their commitment to become parties to the SUA "as soon as possible, if they have not done so yet". Although Indonesia and Malaysia remain off its register, the accession of five ASEAN countries to the SUA represents a major step toward maritime cooperation against piracy.

Additionally, some Southeast Asian nations have undertaken further unilateral and bilateral ventures against piracy. In 2001 the littoral nations of the Straits of Malacca increased their individual patrols after the shockingly high number of attacks — seventy-five — committed in the Malacca Straits the year before. In February of 2002, Indonesia sent six warships to patrol the Straits to prevent arms smuggling and piracy in the area.[48] In 2002, the navies of Malaysia and the Philippines conducted a six-day joint military exercise. In addition Indonesia, Malaysia and the Philippines signed a trilateral security pact to bolster cooperation in transnational crime issues.[49] In February 2003, Indonesia and the Philippines conducted anti-piracy drills with Japan similar to those held between Malaysia and the Philippines.[50]

By early 2004, U.S. pressure was mounting on Indonesia and Malaysia to boost surveillance in the Straits of Malacca to guard against possible terrorist attacks. This included the U.S.-proposed Regional Maritime Security Initiative (RMSI)[51] and rumours spread over the possibility of U.S. marine forces being sent to the Straits. In response, the two countries emphasized only U.S. intelligence and financial support, not forces, would be welcome. On 18 June, Indonesia, Malaysia, and Singapore agreed to the formation of a joint task force on maritime security. This led to the announcement on the 29 of June that the three countries would carry out year-round joint naval patrols. However due to concerns over sovereignty, the three countries later concluded the patrols would not be joint, but instead "coordinated" — meaning no pursuit into neighbouring territorial waters.[52] The drills, including simulated pursuits of pirates, began in late July. This represented the first time a trilateral agreement, as opposed to a triangle of bilateral ones, has been formed to enforce security in the Malacca Straits. Furthermore, the three countries were reported to be discussing the expansion of the patrols to include countries such as India on top of Thailand which agreed to join in August 2004.[53]

Through the end of 2004 and early 2005, several countries announced additional piracy counter-measures. Some of the measures include: Vietnam decided to step up maritime security cooperation between the Ministry of Foreign Affairs, the Ministry of Defence, the Ministry of Public Security and the Ministry of Transport in late 2004.[54] Thailand and Malaysia conducted joint marine police patrols.[55] Sixteen Asian countries met in Tokyo in November and adopted the Regional Cooperation Agreement on Combating Piracy and Armed Robbery Against Ships in Asia (ReCAAP).[56] The participants selected Singapore to base their piracy Information Sharing Centre (ISC). In March 2005, Malaysia announced it would establish a 24-hour radar system to monitor security in the Straits of Malacca as well as have a new special team known as the Maritime Enforcement Agency in place by the end of 2005.[57]

Judging from press reports, the 2001 patrols in the Straits of Malacca could be said to have led to a significant reduction in the number of reported attacks between 2000 and 2001.[58] The number of reported pirate attacks in Southeast Asia between 2001 and 2002 remained the same, although attacks in the Straits of Malacca decreased slightly from seventeen to sixteen incidents. However between 2002 and 2003, the incidence of attacks rose again with more attacks reported off the coast of Vietnam, in the Straits of Malacca, and in Indonesian and Philippines waters as compared to the period from 2001 to 2002. Yet in 2004 regional attacks decreased by 10 per cent, particularly in Indonesian, Philippine, and Vietnames waters. Counter-intiuitive to the international attention on the Straits of Malacca, attacks rose by 24 per cent to thirty-seven there, the highest since the year 2000. Although this might indicate that the coordinated patrols in the Malacca Straits failed to stem piracy, Table 9.4 shows that reported attacks did decrease slightly in the Straits in the second half of the year after the patrols began. Indeed reported attacks decreased across the board throughout the region, indicating that even greater regional awareness and vigilance may serve as a deterrent to pirates.

TABLE 9.4
Southeast Asia Piracy Attacks for
First and Second Halves of 2004[59]

	1st Half	2nd Half
Cambodia	0	0
Indonesia	50	43
Malacca Straits	20	17
Malaysia	5	4
Myanmar	1	0
Philippines	3	1
Singapore Strait	7	1
Thailand	3	1
South China Sea	7	1
Vietnam	3	1
Total	99	69

Conclusion and Final Observations

There is indeed room for optimism. The promise of an ASC which places greater emphasis on non-traditional security and maritime issues is certainly a step in the right direction. As a region, ASEAN members have recognized the importance of the maritime domain to Asia-Pacific economic and political security, and both ASEAN and the ARF have identified piracy as a barrier to this security. The two organizations have outlined strategies aimed at enhancing regional and international cooperation on piracy. Having five ASEAN members sign the SUA Convention represents a major step toward strengthening regional capabilities in jointly pursuing and prosecuting pirates in territorial waters. Even regional unilateral measures against piracy appear aimed at strengthening domestic maritime security capacity and supporting more efficient cooperation on piracy. The coordinated patrols in the Straits of Malacca involving not only a trilateral agreement between the littoral states, but also Thailand's participation, have demonstrated how Southeast Asian nations can combine forces against piracy.

Regional cooperation on piracy is not without its shortcomings. The coordinated patrols also highlight three enduring problems with regional cooperation in tackling piracy: The issue of territorial sovereignty, the tendency toward *ad-hoc* multilateralism, and the focus on the Straits of

Malacca. The protection of national integrity and the fear of external interference continue to stand in the way of more robust and effective regional security cooperation. The proposed joint naval patrols in the Malacca Straits were abandoned in favour of the more politically cautious coordinated patrols in order to "respect the cardinal rule of national sovereignty". As a result law enforcement vessels will not possess the right of hot pursuit, but instead stop chase at territorial boundaries and notify their respective counterparts to continue where they left off, potentially losing the quarry in the process.

Not surprisingly, ASEAN members continue to prefer non-binding and ambiguous measures that first and foremost protect national interests. Coordination to suppress piracy therefore continues on a predominantly limited, *ad-hoc* basis. Without a cohesive and united regional response to piracy, such agreements have proven only marginally effective, with attacks simply moving to waters under less surveillance and returning when vigilance wanes. Although the current patrols are more extensive than those in the past, it is too soon to tell how effective they may be in the long term. The focus on protecting the Straits of Malacca loses sight of the bigger picture of piracy in the region. Although when piracy hit its peak in 2000, the reported attacks in the Straits accounted for only 29 per cent of the total for Southeast Asia despite being the highest percentage since 1991. Typically, reported attacks in the Straits have comprised less than 10 per cent of the total. In recent years it appears that attacks have increased in the area in spite of the patrols. Moreover, as various navies have redoubled their watch over the Malacca Straits, the number of piracy attacks reported in other parts of the region has risen — Indonesia, Philippines, and Vietnam as well as the Indian Sub-continent around India and Bangladesh in 2003; and Myanmar, the Singapore Straits, Thailand, the South China Sea and Malaysia in 2004. This trend is similar to that seen in 1993 and 1994 when attacks appeared to have shifted away from a more guarded Straits and deserves serious investigation.

There remain many challenges to successful piracy deterrence in Southeast Asia. Improved collection and analysis of piracy statistics that include a broader definition (including piracy, armed robbery at sea, and other acts of maritime violence as well as attacks on non-commercial vessels) will go a long way toward crafting and implementing more effective measures. The ARF-ISC should facilitate this.[60] ASEAN should also continue to re-evaluate its cooperation strategies and norms in order to improve its ability to collaborate on issues such as piracy. There have been moves by some members to expand the meaning of non-interference to "flexible engagement" on certain issues, though these have yet to be met with much support.[61] Patrols should be expanded in both participation and range, to more countries in and around the region and beyond the Straits of Malacca. The region should view piracy control in the context of an inter-related web of transnational crimes — many of which relate to the maritime realm in Southeast Asia — and as part of a broader range of maritime security issues from illegal fishing, people smuggling, to marine pollution. When seen in this light, maritime law enforcement patrols and government cooperation on maritime issues benefit the region as a whole, not only the nations bordering the Straits of Malacca. Additionally, paramilitary maritime agencies should replace regional naval forces in cooperative patrols and training exercises so as to reduce sovereignty issues.[62] Finally, stronger legislation needs to be introduced to support the patrols. To this end ASEAN could fulfil its promises in the Plan of Action to Combat Transnational Crime and the ARF Statement on Cooperation Against Piracy. In order to reinforce these commitments ASEAN might consider developing a regional code of conduct for territorial seas that may persuade the remaining five members, particularly Indonesia and Malaysia, to join in cooperation. A regional agreement similar to the SUA may be more palatable than a binding international one for nations still concerned over sovereignty and territorial issues.

Maritime piracy is a complex, multi-dimensional problem linked to such issues as law enforcement, organized crime, geography, good governance, conflict, poverty, unemployment, globalization, and other transnational crimes. This chapter is a preliminary attempt to evaluate some of the factors affecting the incidence of piracy in Southeast Asia and the capacity and effectiveness of the regional response. Further research is required to investigate parallels between historical and contemporary piracy and patterns in incidence levels in both the regional and global contexts. Additional studies into the inter-relationship between political, social, cultural, geographical, and economic factors and piracy are also needed. The escalation in piracy when thousands of Vietnamese fled their country in boats across the Gulf of Thailand in the late 1970s and early 1980s and the lull in piratical activity following the December 2004 Indian Ocean tsunami are two examples which necessitate deeper inquiry.

Around the world and within Southeast Asia there have been erratic rises and falls in piracy levels over the past several decades that cannot be attributed to any one cause and effect relationship. This is not to say that more cannot be done to produce more effective piracy counter-measures, but to emphasize that any failure to reduce piracy attacks in Southeast

Asia does not rest entirely with countries in the region or ASEAN. Interplay between internal and external forces has affected both the factors that contribute to pirate activity and the region's ability to effectively cooperate in piracy suppression. Due to prevailing political sentiments at the time, early ASEAN members considered piracy very much a domestic internal issue and it was handled accordingly. During the same period, piracy levels remained relatively low, perhaps partly a result of the presence of foreign naval powers. In the period of ASEAN expansion there was at the very least a rhetorical manifestation of ASEAN's willingness to cooperate more on regional security issues that coincided with major shifts in the international system. This was evident in the initial short-term bilateral and multilateral cooperative actions on piracy that for a time appeared to significantly reduce the number of attacks. However such obstacles as dealing with a larger and more diverse ASEAN membership, the increase in maritime territory and responsibility over that area with UNCLOS, and severe economic hardship as a result of the Asian Financial Crisis complicated further regional responses. With economic recovery and a solidified membership, ASEAN has been able to revive collective measures to combat piracy in the new millennium. Renewed U.S. security interests in the region and the global focus on terrorism have likely been a factor in accelerating regional initiatives. Although recently introduced port and maritime counter-terrorism initiatives[63] may reduce piracy in some areas or for a period of time, they neither address the underlying causes contributing to its occurrence, nor are they driven by Southeast Asian interests. Southeast Asia deserves some recognition and support for its continued progress on maritime security strategies. Extra-regional interests will wax and wane, but only firm and enduring regional dedication in collaboration with other stakeholders will diminish the causes and prevalence of piracy in Southeast Asian waters.

Notes

[1]   Terry Terriff, Stuart Croft, Lucy James and Patrick M. Morgan, *Security Studies Today* (Cambridge: Polity Press, 1999), p. 135.

[2]   A note about the definition of piracy and the statistics used in this article: In layman's terms "piracy" has come to encompass a broad range of maritime criminal activities from conventional piracy, maritime violence, armed robbery at sea, and the hijacking and ransoming of shipping vessels and crew. However in legal terms defining piracy has been far more complex. The IMB definition of piracy has always included acts of violence and crime against any ship either in international or territorial waters; however, until late 2000 the

International Maritime Organization (IMO) only defined piracy as that occurring in international waters. At the 74th Meeting of the IMO Maritime Safety Committee (MSC) the IMO addressed this matter, drafting a code to define "armed robbery against ships" as unlawful acts of violence and crime directed against a ship within a State's jurisdiction. See MSC/Circ.984 article 2.2 <http://www.imo.org/includes/blastDataOnly.asp/data_id%3D1880/ 984.pdf>. In this chapter the term "piracy" is used to refer to both piracy and armed robbery against ships. Unless otherwise stated, the statistics used in this article are from the IMB's Annual Reports. The numbers given for total pirate attacks refer to both actual and attempted piracy attacks, including those that happen while the vessel is at port or berthed. The statistics are not definitive — they reflect only those attacks *reported* to the IMB, and as the IMB is a division of the International Chamber of Commerce, most ships reporting are commercial vessels. Therefore, in all likelihood these piracy statistics under-represent the total number of pirate attacks. However, that noted, the data available can still reveal some trends in piracy.

3   See Robert C. Beckman, Carl Grundy-Warr and Vivian L. Forbes, "Acts of Piracy in the Malacca and Singapore Straits", *IBRU Maritime Briefing* 1, no. 4 (1994); Peter Chalk, "Contemporary Maritime Piracy in Southeast Asia", *Studies in Conflict and Terrorism* 21 (1998): 87–112; Zou Keyuan, "Enforcing the Law of Piracy in the South China Sea", *EAI Background Brief* no. 19 (24 August 1998); Mark J. Valencia, "International Cooperation in Anti-Piracy Efforts in Asia: Some Considerations" (20 February 2001) <http://www.glocomnet.or.jp/ okazaki-inst/ doc/0313ValenciaPaper.doc> [5 February 2003]; Adam J. Young and Mark J. Valencia, "Conflation of Piracy and Terrorism in Southeast Asia: Rectitude and Utility", *Contemporary Southeast Asia* 25, no. 2 (2003): 269–83; John J. Bradford, "Japanese Anti-Piracy Initiatives in Southeast Asia: Policy Formulation and the Coastal State Responses", *Contemporary Southeast Asia* 26, no. 3 (2004): 480–505.

4   With the exception of Robert Beckman's excellent article "Combatting Piracy and Armed Robbery Against Ships in Southeast Asia: The Way Forward", *Ocean Development and International Law* 33 (2002): 317–41, which focuses almost exclusively on enhancing Southeast Asian cooperation amongst regional states and with international laws and institutions.

5   1991 data from Jayant Abhyankar, "Piracy as a Growing Menace"; 1992–2003 data from ICC-International Maritime Bureau, *Piracy and Armed Robbery Against Ships Annual Report 2003*, p. 5; 2004 data from *Piracy and Armed Robbery Against Ships Annual Report 2004*, p. 4.

6   1991 data from Jayant Abhyankar, "Piracy as a Growing Menace"; 1992–2004 data from ICC-International Maritime Bureau, *Piracy and Armed Robbery Against Ships Annual Report 2003 and 2004*. *In the IMB reports Vietnam and South China Sea incidents are included in the Far East rather than Southeast Asia data; however, in this table the statistics have been re-adjusted to include those attacks in Southeast Asia.

7   Simon S. C. Tay and Jesus Estanislao, "The Relevance of ASEAN: Crisis and Change", in *A New ASEAN in a New Millennium*, edited by Simon S.C. Tay, Jesus Estanislao and Hadi Soesastro (Jakarta: Centre for Strategic and International Studies, 2000), pp. 10–11.

8   "Inspired by the worthy aims and objectives of the United Nations, *in particular by the principles of respect for the sovereignty and territorial integrity of all states...*[R]ecognising the right of every state, large or small, to lead its national existence free from outside interference in its internal affairs as this interference will adversely affect its freedom independence and integrity" (my italics). The full text of the Zone of Peace, Freedom and Neutrality Declaration is available on the ASEAN Secretariat website at <http://www.aseansec.org/1215.htm>.

9   The full text of the Treaty of Amity and Cooperation in Southeast Asia is available on the ASEAN Secretariat website at <http://www.aseansec.org/1217.htm>.

10 For more on the "ASEAN Way" see David Capie and Paul Evans, *The Asia Pacific Security Lexicon* (Singapore: Institute of Southeast Asian Studies, 2002), pp. 14–27.

11 For a examination of the Asia Pacific concept and use of "ad-hoc multilaterialism" see Capie and Evans, *The Asia Pacific Security Lexicon*, pp. 11–13. Alternatively, ASEAN members also engage in what is termed "concerted unilateralism" whereby states together identify issues of common interest but pursue policies toward those objectives unilaterally. Capie and Evans, *The Asia Pacific Security Lexicon*, pp. 82–83.

12 The full text of the Manila Declaration is available on the ASEAN Secretariat website at <http://www.aseansec.org/5117.htm>.

13 Capie and Evans, *The Asia Pacific Security Lexicon*, p. 17.

14 For example, in 1981, 15,598 Vietnamese emigrated to Thailand by boat, 77 per cent of the boats were attacked; in 1982, 5,913 refugees emigrated, 65 per cent of their boats were attacked; and in 1983, 3,383 refugees emigrated with 56 per cent of their boats being attacked. See Roger Villar, *Piracy Today: Robbery and Violence at Sea since 1980* (London: Conway Maritime Press, 1985), p. 131. For more on piracy attacks on Vietnamese boat people see, Villar, *Piracy Today*, pp. 33–36; and Eric Ellen, *Piracy at Sea* (Paris: ICC-International Maritime Bureau, 1989), pp. 83–119.

15 Villar, *Piracy Today*, p. 62. According to the figures in this book, the Singapore area experienced just one attack in 1980, 42 attacks in 1981, 54 attacks in 1982, and 48 such incidences in 1983. In 1984, the "number of piracy incidents ha[d] increased in the last few months [of that year]. The pirates appear to have resumed their operations after a prolonged period of inactivity," pp. 118–30.

16 A chronology of pirate attacks on merchant vessels during 1981 to 1987 can be found in Ellen, *Piracy at Sea*, pp. 241–71. However, it is assumed the chronology is incomplete for a number of reasons such as the infrequency and incompleteness of reporting. In addition, documented attacks during this period were only recorded for merchant vessels, with succeeding years being

even more incomplete due to delayed late reportage to the IMO. See Villar, *Piracy Today*, pp. 5–6.

17 Villar, *Piracy Today*, p. 62.
18 Hasjim Djalal, "Piracy and the Challenges of Cooperative Security and Enforcement Policy", *Indonesian Quarterly* 30, no. 2 (Second Quarter, 2002): 110.
19 The full text of the Manila Declaration is available on the ASEAN Secretariat website at <http://www.aseansec.org/5120.htm>.
20 See Ralf Emmers, "The Securitization of Transnational Crime in ASEAN", *Singapore Institute of Defence and Strategic Studies Working Paper, No. 39* (November 2002). <http://www.ntu.edu.sg/idss/WorkingPapers/WP39.pdf>.
21 The Declaration is available on the ASEAN Secretariate website at <http://www.aseansec.org/5640.htm>.
22 Djalal, "Piracy and the Challenges of Cooperative Security and Enforcement Policy", p. 109; Beckman, Grundy-Warr, and Forbes, "Acts of Piracy in the Malacca and Singapore Straits", p. 15.
23 Djalal, "Piracy and the Challenges ...", p. 109. Chalk, "Contemporary Maritime Piracy in Southeast Asia", p. 99.
24 Jayant Abhyankar, "Piracy — A Growing Menace", paper presented at the International Maritime Bureau conference on Combatting Piracy and Armed Robbery at Sea, Bangkok, 24–25 March 2001, <http://www.okazaki-inst.jp/doc/0319Abhyankar.DOC> (accessed 9 September 2004).
25 The full text of UNCLOS is available on the United Nations Division for Ocean Affairs and the Law of the Sea website: <http://www.un.org/Depts/los/convention_agreements/texts/unclos/unclos_e.pdf>. At the time the Convention came into force only the Philippines, Indonesia, and Vietnam were signatories. Singapore joined 17 November 1994, Myanmar on 21 May 1996, Malaysia on 14 October 1996, Brunei Darussalam on 5 November 1996 and Laos on 5 June 1998. As of 9 April 2005 Thailand and Cambodia are not party to the Convention although they still claim territorial waters and an Exclusive Economic Zone pursuant to the Convention.
26 The Philippines and Indonesia signed UNCLOS on 8 May 1984 and 3 February 1986. As of May 2004, all the members of ASEAN had ratified, accepted, approved or acceded to the Convention with the exception of Thailand and Cambodia who have signed on but not yet ratified.
27 Zou, *Enforcing the Law of Piracy in the South China Sea*, p. 11.
28 International Institute for Strategic Studies (IIAS), *The Military Balance 2002/2003* (London: Oxford University Press, 2002), p. 141.
29 Amitav Acharya, in *The Quest for Identity: International Relations of Southeast Asia* (Singapore: Oxford University Press, 2000), p. 5, argues the cultural differences between the typically mainland-oriented states versus the maritime/archipelagic states is a potential source of disagreement.
30 Sidharto Suryodipuro, "ASEAN: The Challenge of Integration, Cohesion, and Maritime Cooperation", *Indonesian Quarterly* 30, no. 2 (2002): 208–09.

[31] Suryodipuro, "ASEAN: The Challenge of Integration, Cohesion, and Maritime Cooperation", p. 216.

[32] For an article on the differences between Indonesian, Malaysian, and Singaporean interests in the Strait of Malacca see Lydia Lim, "Dire Straits?" *The Straits Times*, 15 May 2004.

[33] For some articles that examine the socio-economic aspects of piracy, see Eric Frécon, "Piracy and Armed Robbery at Sea along the Malacca Straits: Initial Impressions from Fieldwork in the Riau Islands", in this volume; James F. Warren, "A Tale of Two Centuries: The Globalisation of Maritime Raiding and Piracy in Southeast Asia at the end of the Eighteenth and Twentieth Centuries", *Asia Research Institute Working Paper Series No. 2*, June 2003 <http://www.ari.nus.edu.sg/docs/wps/wps03_002.pdf>; Jason Abbot and Neil Renwick, "Pirates? Maritime Piracy and Societal Security in Southeast Asia", *Pacifica Review* 11, no. 1 (1999): 7–24.

[34] For a thorough look at the economic and social impact of the crisis on the region see Gordon Betchman and Rizwanul Islam, eds., "East Asian Labor Markets and the Economic Crisis: Impacts, Responses, and Lessons", *World Bank Publication no. 21904*, February 2001, available at <http://www-wds.worldbank.org/servlet/WDS_IBank_Servlet?pcont=details&eid=000094946_01032006582817>.

[35] Dana Robert Dillon, "Piracy in Asia: A Growing Barrier to Maritime Trade", *The Heritage Foundation Backgrounder*, no. 1379 (22 June 2000) <http://www.heritage.org/Research/AsiaandthePacific/BG1379.cfm>.

[36] Dillon, "Piracy in Asia: A Growing Barrier to Maritime Trade".

[37] Sudha Ramachandran, "India Signs on as Southeast Asia Watchdog", *Asia Times*, 5 April 2002 <http://www.atimes.com/ind-pak/DD05Df01.html> (accessed 15 September 2004).

[38] "US Wants Marines to Guard Malacca Straits", *Straits Times Interactive*, 5 April 2004; "Countries Oppose US Offer to Patrol Malacca", *FT.com Financial Times*, 5 April 2004.

[39] See Adam J. Young and Mark J. Valencia, "Conflation of Piracy and Terrorism in Southeast Asia: Rectitude and Utility", *Contemporary Southeast Asia* 25, no. 2 (2003): 269–83. One example would be a recent speech by Singapore Minister for Defence Tony Tan calling a 2004 pirate attack in the Straits of Malacca using sophisticated weaponry and high-speed boats one that follows a "different pattern" from previous pirate attacks and "reminiscent of the pattern by which terrorists mount an attack". From "Terror Threat Swells at Sea", *World Net Daily*, 8 June 2004 <http://worldnetdaily.com/news/article.asp?ARTICLE_ID=38835>. Although many pirate attacks in the region have typically been low-intensity armed robbery, attacks involving small, fast craft and high-powered guns have been increasing worldwide for years.

[40] For an examination of the connection drawn between regional terrorists, piracy and maritime terrorism see Tamara Renee Shie, "Ports in a Storm? The Nexus

Between Counterterrorism, Counterproliferation, and Maritime Security in Southeast Asia", *Issues and Insights* 4, no. 4 (July 2004) <http://csis.org/pacfor/issues/v04n04.cfm>.

41 Personal communication with Ahmad Mokhtar Selat, ASEAN Secretariat Deputy Secretary-General of Corporate Affairs, 8 February 2003.

42 "Work Programme to Implement the ASEAN Plan of Action to Combat Transnational Crime", Kuala Lumpur, 17 May 2003, available at <http://www.aseansec.org/5616.htm>.

43 The Statement's text is available at <http://www.dfat.gov.au/arf/statements/10_piracy.html>.

44 The dates the SUA came into force in these countries are as follows: Myanmar — 18 December 2003, Brunei — 3 March 2004, Philippines — 5 April 2004, Singapore — 3 May 2004.

45 For more information on the *Achille Lauro* hijacking see Jeffrey D. Simon, *The Implications of the Achille Lauro Hijacking for the Maritime Community* (Santa Monica, CA: RAND Corporation, August 1986).

46 For a comprehensive discussion of this see, Beckman, "Combatting Piracy and Armed Robbery Against Ships in Southeast Asia", pp. 321–26, 329–30.

47 Article 13 of the SUA Convention requires State Parties to "cooperate in the prevention of the offences set forth in article 3, particularly by: (a) taking all practicable measures to prevent preparations in their respective territories for the commission of those offences within or outside their territories; (b) exchanging information in accordance with their national law, and coordinating administrative and other measures taken as appropriate to prevent the commission of offences set forth in article 3". The full text is available at <http://www.unodc.org/unodc/terrorism_convention_maritime_navigation.html>.

48 "ICC Report Sends Six Warships into Battle Against Pirates", 12 February 2002 <http://www.iccwbo.org/home/news_archives/2002/piracy.asp> (accessed 16 November 2002).

49 "Malaysia, RP Begin Maritime Exercises", *Jakarta Post*, 13 May 2002.

50 "RP, RI, Japan to Hold Anti-Piracy and Anti-Pollution Drills", *Jakarta Post*, 27 February 2003.

51 For information on the RMSI see the Pacific Command RMSI webpage: <http://www.pacom.mil/rmsi>.

52 "Malaysia, Indonesia Rule Out Joint Patrols in Malacca Straits", *Channel NewsAsia*, 1 July 2004 <http://www.channelnewsasia.com/stories/southeastasia/view/93163/1/.html>.

53 "Thailand May Join Patrols of Malacca Strait", *Channel NewsAsia*, 6 August 2004 <http://www.channelnewsasia.com/stories/southeastasia/view/996021/1/.html>.

54 "Vietnam Tightens Sea Border Security", *Vietnam Net Bridge*, 18 October 2004 <http://english.vietnam.net.vn/politics/2004/11/336400>.

55 "Thai-Malaysian Marine to Conduct Joint Security Operations", *Xinhua News Net*, 26 October 2004 <http://news.xinhuanet.com/english/2004-10/26/content_2139882.htm> (accessed 11 April 2005).

56 The sixteen countries are: Bangladesh, Brunei, Cambodia, China, India, Indonesia, Japan, Laos, Malaysia, Myanmar, the Philippines, Sri Lanka, Singapore, South Korea, Thailand and Vietnam. Donald Urquhart, "New 16 Nation Anti-Piracy Campaign Soon in Asia", *Business Times*, Singapore, 19 November 2004.

57 "Malaysia to boost Malacca Strait security with 24-hour radar system", *Channel NewsAsia*, 11 March 2005 <http://www.channelnewsasia.com/stories/afp_asiapacific/view/136822/1/.html>.

58 Sim Bak Heng, "Big Drop in Piracy Cases in the Straits", *New Straits Times*, 23 June 2001.

59 ICC-International Maritime Bureau, *Piracy and Armed Robbery Against Ships Annual Report 2004*.

60 Shanmugam Jayakumar, "UNCLOS — Two Decades On", *Keynote Address at 2005 Conference on Law of the Sea Issues in the East and South China Seas*, Xiamen 9–12 March 2005 <http://app.sprinter.gov.sg/data/pr/2005031201.htm>.

61 At the July 1998 ASEAN Ministerial Meeting Thailand's Foreign Minister Surin Pitsuwan suggested an amendment to the non-intervention principle, but at the time it was only supported by Thailand and the Philippines. Emmers, "The Securitization of Transnational Crime in ASEAN", p. 19.

62 For a comprehensive breakdown of the benefits of coast guards or similar paramilitary maritime law enforcement agencies over navies see Sam Bateman, "Coast Guards: New Forces for Regional Order and Security", *Asia Pacific Issues* 65 (January 2003) <http://www.eastwestcenter.org/stored/pdfs/api065.pdf>, p. 5.

63 Some of these counter-terrorism measures are the Proliferation Security Initiative (PSI), the Container Security Initiative (CSI), the International Ship and Port Facility Security Code, and the Regional Maritime Security Initiative. For more on these initiatives and the Southeast Asian response, see Shie, "Ports in a Storm?".

10

The Rhine Navigation Regime: A Model for the Straits of Malacca?

Ahmad Ghazali Bin Abu Hassan

Introduction

To a landlocked state, the issue of its accessibility to the sea can be as crucial as the right of innocent passage over the territorial water of other countries. Both kinds of issues can become a potential source of conflict if they are not handled carefully and judiciously with the other neighbouring or riparian states involved in such matters. As a close example, Iran and Iraq have actually gone to war over a dispute since 1935 over the navigation rights of the Shatt el Arab waterway that constitutes part of the Iraq-Iran border river and formed by the confluence of the Tigris and Euphrates rivers, flowing southeast towards the Persian Gulf. Full-scale war between the two countries broke out in September 1980, leading to nearly a decade of attacks upon coastal areas by both sides.[1] Typical of a landlocked state, the economic sanctions imposed upon Iraq during the Saddam regime prior to the American-led invasion of 2003 were quite effective because Iraq's access to the sea (and therefore world trade) is highly dependent upon its access of passage through Khor Abdullah waterway to the port of Basrah and the Shatt el Arab to the port of Umm Qasr which it shares with two other neighbours.

The tendency of countries to jealously guard their rights over such rivers is therefore understandable given the potential importance that the rivers hold both in terms of source of water supply and means of accessibility to the sea. In this respect, the example set by the riparian states of the Rhine can be regarded as unique and worth emulating considering the fact that these countries on the basis of common interest, were willing to regard the Rhine as a river for international navigation, and to come together with a unique arrangement that facilitates efficient and effective management of the river in terms of navigational, environmental and other related aspects. This chapter aims to look at the possibility of the navigation and management regimes that regulate the usage of the Rhine as possible models to be modified and applied for the Straits of Malacca.

The Rhine River

The Rhine flows through one of the most densely populated and industrialized part of Europe and has been an important and busy transport artery ever since the Roman era and the Middle Ages. The name was derived from the Celtic word *renos* which means "raging flow" reflecting the magnitude and the strength of the current at its source: The Rheinwaldon Glacier at the Swiss Alps. The Rhine flows northeast for approximately 1,320 kilometres, passing through or bordering on six different countries (Switzerland, Austria, Liechtenstein, Germany, France, and the Netherlands) before entering the North Sea. The navigable part of the Rhine runs for a distance of about 800 kilometres from Basel in Switzerland. However large ocean-going vessels can only travel up to Cologne in Germany before the cargoes are transferred into smaller ships or barges to be taken to their destinations to the various ports up river in France, Germany and Switzerland. For this purpose some 8,000 units of special vessels of varying purpose and capacity are employed.[2]

By virtue of various countries that it passes through, the Rhine has four names, "Rhein" in Germany, "Rhine" in France, "Rijn" in the Netherlands and the ancient name of "Rhenus". Its main tributaries are the Aare, Neckar, Main, Lahn, Ill, Mosel, Ruhr and the Lippe. Other principle rivers of Europe such as the Seine, Elbe, Ems, Rhône and the Saône are linked to it by canals. An important canal link to the Danube was completed in 1992, opening up shipping movement between the North Sea and the Black Sea passing through the Main River.[3]

The Rhine is generally navigable throughout the year due to the availability of technologically sophisticated electronic navigational charts and information services and surveillance systems for transportation safety. It is regarded as the backbone of inland waterway transport of Europe facilitating the transportation of heavy loads such as coal, iron ore, grain, potash, petroleum, iron and steel, timber and other commodities, to and from the industrial heartland of Europe. It is estimated that 300 million tonnes of cargo are transported through the Rhine every year. For Switzerland, the innermost state of the Rhine, about 15 per cent of its external trade and 40 per cent of its fuel and chemical imports were transported through the Rhine. In the nineteenth century, the river enabled the transportation of raw materials to feed the fledgling industries that scattered all over the region which eventually transformed areas such as the Ruhr, Mainz, Frankfurt, Mannheim and Karlsruhe into centres of heavy industries.[4]

Like most temperate rivers, the Rhine is physically subjected to changes in geographical and seasonal conditions. In the Netherlands, the Rhine has to pass through a delta area that is located below sea level which is kept from flooding by the dykes. In 1993 severe flood forced total disruption of shipping movements along the river and about 60,000 people living along its bank had to be evacuated, causing ten deaths and an estimated damage of about US$1 billion. A more devastating flood took place two years later in 1995 forcing around 250,000 people to flee their homes in the Netherlands and forced the river to be closed to commercial traffic for more than a week. In Cologne the depth of the river exceeded ten metres, the greatest depth recorded in over 200 years. The cost of damage as a result of this flood was estimated to be around US$2 billion.[5]

Consequently, continuous efforts have to be made to improve its physical condition in facilitating safe and efficient passage by the vessels at all times. Among the efforts that have been taken were, the removal of the sand banks in the lower part, levelling of the rocks and waterfalls in the Middle Rhine region and partial canalization in the upper section to enable navigation and generation of electric power.

Apart from meteorological disasters, the Rhine has also been confronted with environmental disasters brought about by the effect of heavy industrialization around the region. Severe pollution prompted the Netherlands, France, West Germany, Luxembourg and Switzerland to come together into signing a treaty in taking up the effort to clean up the river in 1976. The treaty however was faced with the problem of compliance.

Despite this difficulty, there was some recorded improvement in the water quality level along the river.

The most disastrous experience suffered by the Rhine in terms of pollution took place in 1986 when a massive chemical spill in Basel discharged around 30 tonnes of toxic waste including mercury and fungicides, killing about 500,000 fish and closing water systems in West Germany, France and the Netherlands. Due to the scale of its effects, it was generally regarded that the spill is the greatest non-nuclear disaster that ever hit the European continent in a decade. Other environmental consequences resulting from the pollution of the Rhine include the extinction of the River Otter in 1988, the weakening of the immune system of 70 per cent of the Wadden sea seals, and the reduction of the survival rate of the Cormorant chick in the Rhine delta to only one in six.[6]

The Rhine Commissions

There are two major commissions that regulate the activities of the Rhine. The first is the Central Commission for the Navigation of the Rhine (CCNR) and the second is the International Commission for the Protection of the Rhine against Pollution (ICPR).[7] The CCNR was established by the Congress of Vienna in 1815 and derives its authority from the Mannheim Convention concluded in 1868. The membership of this commission consists of Belgium, France, Germany, the Netherlands, and Switzerland. Each member state has one representative on the commission and the chairmanship of the commission is rotated among the member states. As the mandate of the commission is limited to issues pertaining to navigation, it can involve itself in matters related to pollution only if the problems of navigation stem from problems of such a specific nature.[8]

To tackle the critical problem of pollution, the ICPR was established by the Netherlands, West Germany, France, Luxembourg, and Switzerland in 1963. The commission is tasked with the responsibility of preparing and carrying out research to determine the nature, quantity and origin of pollution in the Rhine. The commission is also authorized to advise the European Union and national governments on pollution prevention measures and acts as a coordinating body in streamlining the efforts made by member countries in pollution prevention measures. In 1988 the member countries of the commission adopted the Rhine Action Plan which identified four goals as its main focus of action; namely, the creation of conditions conducive to the return of larger vertebrates, the safeguarding of drinking water supplies, the elimination of sediment pollution by hazardous compounds and the protection of the North Sea's ecology.[9]

Of the two commissions, the ICPR appears to be the weaker one. The ICPR has no independent power and cannot on its own consider an issue unless authorized by the signatory governments. Another factor that severely curtailed the authority of the ICPR is the fact that it is overlaid by an older and apparently more powerful commission, namely the CCNR. The entirely different mandates led to the potential clash of interests and actions between the two commissions. For example, the dredging of certain stretches of the waterway to facilitate safer flow of traffic by the CCNR, would not be viewed so positively by the ICPR as that would lead to stirring up of pollutant-containing sediments that could adversely affect the quality of water in the river. This potential conflict of interests perhaps highlights one of the weaknesses in the management of a waterway that would otherwise be regarded as one of the best managed in the world in terms of navigational facilities and regulations.[10]

The CCNR

The CCNR derives its strength and authority from the close strategic cooperation fostered by the five riparian states of the Rhine: Switzerland, Germany, France, Belgium and the Netherlands. The CCNR was created by the Congress of Vienna in 1815 at a time when multitude of restrictions, duties and privileges were hampering the movement of ships resulting in shipping on the waterway coming to almost a standstill. Imposition of tolls and taxes along the waterway was a common practice that took place since the Roman times and throughout the Middle Ages. The Treaty of Paris in 1814 required that there be freedom of navigation on Europe's major international rivers. The Congress of Vienna reasserted this agreement by stipulating that river commissions be established for major international rivers in Europe, namely the Rhine and the Danube.[11]

The CCNR was established with the view of setting up a centralized regime for navigation on the Rhine that should, as far as possible, correspond to the regime of the seas, the main principle being the principle of freedom of navigation. In 1831, the Mainz Accord was signed to eliminate tolls and taxation stations along the Rhine. In 1868, the Revised Convention Concerning the Navigation on the Rhine (commonly known as the Mannheim Convention) was concluded, setting up comprehensive rules and guidelines forming the Rhine regime to date. Despite the changes made to the convention in keeping up with development, it continues to remain in force until today making it one of the oldest active conventions in the world.[12]

Until today, the CCNR with its headquarters in Strasbourg works with a mandate from member states with the task of comprehensively and uniformly manage the waterway under the main principle of liberal and equal treatment which requires:

a. Freedom of navigation and equal treatment to all parties;
b. Exemption from duties on the act of navigation;
c. Uniform regulations for the safety of vessels, navigation and the Environment;
d. The commitment by the member states to maintain the waterway;
e. Uniform jurisdiction in navigational affairs in the form of Rhine Shipping Courts.

The Committee at its inception based on the guidelines stipulated by the Congress of Vienna was initially intended to function as permanent diplomatic conference. However with unified regime and common instruments developed over the years, coupled with the transfer of competence by the individual states to the commission, it certainly appears that CCNR has now transformed into a supranational institution, an international organization with well-defined regulatory powers yet maintaining physical organizational characteristics of a typical commission. Despite the enormous authority that it has, the commission has only fifteen permanent staff in it ranks.[13]

As a conference, the CCNR reaches its decisions through unanimous voting, in which case they would be binding on the governments. In the case where decisions are reached only through majority voting, they would be considered as recommendations where countries are encouraged to implement. The decisions at the conference are made by delegations from the member states, consisting of four commissioners from each state and presided by a president appointed for a two-year term. The incorporation of these decisions as national laws however is not automatic. Appropriate national procedures have to be taken to enable the enforcement of the decisions at respective national levels.

The CCNR functions through close cooperation among the member states where experts in various fields are grouped in working committees where they share their experience and knowledge to carry out research and studies in tackling issues pertaining to the improvement, development and well being of navigation along the waterway. Currently there are fifteen committees and working groups working on the various projects for the commission. The budget towards the running of the commission is shared equally among the member countries.[14]

Establishing a Commission for the Navigation in the Straits of Malacca: The Case For and Against

Rivers, from the perspective of international law, are regarded as internal waters and therefore are integral parts of the sovereign territory of a state. As a result, states can exercise more comprehensive legal authority over their rivers compared to their territorial waters. In the case of the Rhine, these normally jealously guarded rights have been ceded by the riparian states through which the river runs or borders on, for the sake of navigational safety, common regulations and economic and environmental interests.

The scope of the legal rights and obligations that littoral states can exercise over the Straits of Malacca as stipulated by the 1982 United Nations Law of the Sea Convention (UNCLOS II) is obviously not as comprehensive as their rights over their internal waters. One therefore might argue that getting the littoral states to adopt a regime similar to that adopted by the riparian states of the Rhine would be easier. However, this might not be the case. The status of the Straits of Malacca as a waterway for international navigation with the inherent rights and obligations were thrust upon the littoral states by UNCLOS II. The initial draft prepared by Malaysia along with seven other countries that conferred more rights to the littoral states was rejected and a compromised draft was introduced and accepted. The new draft sub-categorised straits into five different categories and the Straits of Malacca was categorized as a straits that is subjected to the regime of transit passage. Based on the above background, it might be safely concluded that getting the littoral states of the Straits of Malacca to come together and to establish a common instrument that could comprehensively manage the multitude of navigational, security, environmental, customs, sanitary, and police and other aspects might be difficult especially if it involves further erosion of what they might perceive as their already limited rights.

The nations of Europe were forced to adopt the position of accepting their rivers as international waterways because the multitude of laws, procedures, tolls and taxation imposed unilaterally and without coordination were crippling the navigational process along their rivers, a condition that could adversely affect their economies. This pressing situation however does not exist in the Straits of Malacca and therefore littoral states might argue that the establishment of a commission such as the one governing the navigation on the Rhine might not be necessary.

Another argument that might discourage the establishment of a similar commission for the Straits of Malacca is the type, scope and the magnitude of the problems that besiege the Straits are quite different from those affecting the Rhine. The problems faced by the Straits of Malacca is more numerous and appears to be more formidable. To impose the Rhine commissions as the template for the Straits of Malacca is therefore rather impractical or even unrealistic to some degree. For example, the Rhine commissions do not have to contend with the issues of armed robberies at sea, smuggling and human trafficking; at least not on the scale that plagued the Straits of Malacca. Navigational issues, which is the main (or even only) focus of the commissions' activities, is just one of the many issues that the Straits of Malacca has to deal with.

However, the above argument can also be reversed to argue that because of the scale and scope of the problems, it is all the more reason why such a commission needs to be established. Currently the management of navigation and coordination of various other related activities in the Straits of Malacca is rather fragmented. Regionally, it is divided by separate national jurisdictions of the littoral states. Further division takes place at the national level where various enforcement agencies have to perform their given tasks, sometimes without the benefit of knowing what other agencies are doing. The establishment of a commission for the Straits of Malacca may address this problem of poor coordination, not only between the relevant national agencies but also between the relevant authorities of the littoral states.

In establishing a commission to regulate navigation in the Straits of Malacca, the littoral states need not necessarily adopt the Rhine model wholesale. The organizational framework of the Rhine Commission could be effectively adopted with certain modifications to suit local regional situation. The terms of reference and the scope of authority given to the commission must be as broad as possible to cover the whole spectrum of issues affecting the navigation in the Straits of Malacca such as navigational safety, security, environment, immigration, customs and law enforcement.

On the issue of finance and the provision of the budget for the commission, the disparity of the level of income between the littoral states might pose a problem if the equal contribution formula as adopted by the Rhine Commission is adopted. Even if this formula can be exercised, the amount collected might not be enough to finance the running of the commission. To get around this problem, user states could be invited to become members of the commission with equal voting rights, thus reducing the financial burden that otherwise would be borne solely by the littoral states. The formula to determine the quantum of contribution and how they should be disbursed can be worked out by the parties concerned. Another advantage that can be derived through the participation of user states is the benefit of the availability of the latest technological know-how and technical assistance that otherwise might not be readily available to the littoral states.

Concluding Remarks

As it was mentioned earlier in this chapter, the biggest stumbling block envisaged that prevents the establishment of a special commission to regulate navigation and other related activities in the Straits of Malacca is the reluctance of the littoral states to participate in efforts which, from their point of view, might potentially erode their sovereign rights and authority particularly in their respective territorial waters. A seamless operation coordinated by a single organization to oversee all aspects of navigational safety, security, customs, immigration and environmental issues in the Straits of Malacca is perhaps the ideal solution for solving the many problems that are faced by the littoral states with regards to this strategically important waterway.

With respect to the issues of laws and regulations, it would be ideal if related laws common to all the littoral states can be legislated to enable the commission to function smoothly. In areas where this is not possible, efforts must be made to harmonize the laws so that conflicts and incompatibilities do not exist so as to allow the effective and efficient functioning of the commission. In the end, the structures of the various regulatory mechanisms adopted by the Rhine commissions can be used as a general model and its application must recognize the futility of having a uniform set of laws throughout the waterway of the Malacca Straits is impossible in light of the ambiguous boundaries between the littoral states. In the case of the Rhine, states were encouraged to harmonize their laws that govern the passage through their respective territories with other riparian states to avoid possible conflict of laws. Consequently, the ensuing laws and regulations have been placed into different categories according to whether they are applicable throughout the waterway, in certain sections of the waterway or under other exceptional circumstances. In this way, this model may be applicable to the Straits of Malacca in areas where differences in the national regulations may demand that different set of laws prevail in different sections of the waterway.

In the final analysis, in order to address the fear of the loss of rights and erosion of sovereignty by the littoral states, it must be made clear that the establishment of a commission for the comprehensive management of the Straits of Malacca should come under the principles of reciprocity and voluntary participation. The willingness of the littoral states to give up some of their rights to facilitate the establishment of the commission should also be matched by equally substantial concessions by other participating user states.

Notes

[1] In 1935, an international commission gave Iraq total control of the river, leaving Iran with control only of the approaches to its chief ports of Abadan and Khorramshahr. Having lost the ability to develop new port facilities in the delta, Iran built ports on the Persian Gulf to handle foreign trade. This helped Iran to deny the Iraqis the opportunity to exert political pressure or interfere in its oil and freight shipments flowing along the Shatt el Arab. While both countries did negotiate several territorial agreements over the Shatt el Arab waterway in 1975, by the end of the decade, skirmishes in the area became prevalent leading up to war in 1980. The Shatt el Arab used to flow through a broad, swampy delta, but the marshlands in Iraq was drained in the early 1990s in order to increase government control over the Arab Shiites (known as Marsh Arabs) who lived there. The restoration of the marshlands began in 2003, following the second invasion of Iraq by American-led forces since 1991. The river continues to supply fresh water to southern Iraq and Kuwait and is navigable for ocean-going vessels as far as Basra, Iraq's chief port. The Shatt el Arab still remains a source of conflict for countries that border it, as limited water access and unresolved maritime boundaries in the region persist.

[2] "The Rhine". *Microsoft Encarta Online Encyclopedia*, 2004 <http://encarta.msn.com/encyclopedia_761578232/Rhine.html>; and Harm Oterdoom, *The International Commission for the Protection of the Rhine*, 2002 <http://www.dse.de/ef/nile/oterdoom.htm>.

[3] Ibid.

[4] Harm Oterdoom, *The International Commission for the Protection of the Rhine*, 2002 <http://www.dse.de/ef/nile/oterdoom.htm>.

[5] Ibid.

[6] Ibid.

[7] The official website of the CPNR can be found at <http://www.ccr-zkr.org/>.

[8] Werf, Hans van der. *The Central Commission for Navigation of the Rhine*, 2002 <http://www.dse.de/ef/nile/werf.htm>; and Harm Oterdoom, *The International*

Commission for the Protection of the Rhine, 2002 <http://www.dse.de/ef/nile/oterdoom.htm>.

9 Harm Oterdoom, *The International Commission for the Protection of the Rhine*, 2002 <http://www.dse.de/ef/nile/oterdoom.htm>.

10 Hans van der Werf, *The Central Commission for Navigation of the Rhine*, 2002 <http://www.dse.de/ef/nile/werf.htm>.

11 Ibid.

12 "The Mannheim Convention", *The Central Commission for the Navigation of the Rhine*, 2004 <http://perso.wanadoo.fr/ccnr2/En/ActeMannheim.htm>; and Hans van der Werf, *The Central Commission for Navigation of the Rhine*, 2002 <http://www.dse.de/ef/nile/werf.htm>.

13 "The Mannheim Convention".

14 Ibid.

11

Whither the Malacca Straits?
The Rise of New Hub Ports in Asia

Jose L. Tongzon

Introduction

The Straits of Malacca is an important shipping lane connecting the Indian Ocean with the South China Sea and the Pacific Ocean. It is said that 50,000 or more cargo ships a year transit this lane to carry the goods traded between the Atlantic and the Far East — carrying half of the world's oil supply and a third of global trade. From the perspective of the ports of Singapore and Malaysia, this shipping lane has been an important source of their competitive advantage *vis-à-vis* other ports in Asia. Their proximity to this shipping lane has made them attractive ports of call. It is said that it would cost ships more time to transit the Atlantic and Far East corridor if they had to pass through other lanes. The threat of maritime terrorism after 9/11, rising piracy in the Malacca Straits and the rise of new hub ports in Asia have, however, raised a question about the future of Malacca Straits and therefore the future of the ports of Singapore and Malaysia as hub ports.[1]

In this light, this chapter intends to evaluate the importance of Malacca Straits to maritime trade, the possible threats to its current utility, emergence of new ports in Asia and the implications of these developments for the hub ports of Singapore and Malaysia. The chapter is organized as follows: The first section looks at the shipping traffic through the Straits and its importance to maritime trade followed by the possible threats to its current utility; the second section discusses the importance of Malacca Straits to the ports of Singapore and Malaysia, the emergence of new hub ports in Asia, and the likely implications for the hub ports of Singapore and Malaysia.

The Economic Importance of the Malacca Straits

The importance of Malacca Straits to the maritime trade is indicated by the fact that this shipping lane offers to shipping lines the shortest route between three of the world's populous countries — India, China and Indonesia. 50,000 vessels or more per year transit the Straits and oil flows (in 2003, eleven million barrels per day) to the destinations in Japan, South Korea, China and other Pacific Rim countries.[2]

In the past decades Asia's relatively high growth, industrialization and continued openness have resulted in tremendous expansion of trade and growth in containerization. These trends, supplemented by the emergence of China and other emerging Asian economies as manufacturing bases and increasing regionalization, have led to the concentration of maritime trade within Asia and the Pacific. A fundamental factor contributing to this economic dynamism has been the free passage of shipping along Asia-Pacific sea lanes, especially through the Straits of Malacca.

The future importance of the Malacca Straits to maritime trade would depend on the following key drivers: (1) the continued growth and industrialization of China, (2) the growth of trade between Asia and the rest of the world and (3) the growth of Asian economic integration.

Growth and Industrialization of China

Due to the growing industrialization and growth of China, it has become one of the leading petroleum importing countries in the world, with a status comparable to Japan. China imports petroleum *via* three shipping routes: Middle East route (from Persian Gulf *via* the Hormuz Straits, the Malacca Straits, Taiwan Straits to the mainland); the African route (from Mediterranean Sea, Cape of Good Hope to the Malacca Straits) and the Southeast Asian route, four-fifths of which geographically passes through the Malacca Straits. It is estimated that almost 60 per cent of the ships passing through the Straits are Chinese ships. Thus, the future of the Malacca Straits is closely linked with the Chinese economy and its petroleum imports. With oil imports increasing from the Middle East, the Straits is likely to grow in economic importance in coming years.

To show how oil imports by China can have an impact on the number of ships passing *via* the Malacca Straits, a regression analysis was applied to historical data on the number of tankers passing through the Straits against the value of China's imports of oil for the period of 1990 to 2002 (the latest year for which data is available).[3] As Figure 11.1 shows, a casual inspection seems to show some close correlation between China's oil imports and the number of oil tankers passing through the Straits. This is confirmed by Table 11.1 below which shows that the role of China's oil imports accounted for about 85 per cent of the variations in the number of oil tankers passing through the Straits — quite high, considering that there are other factors that could have influenced the number of oil tankers passing through the Straits.

Growth of Trade between Asia and Europe

The cross-trade between Asia and the rest of the world (and Europe-Far East trade in particular) should have a significant impact on the number of ships passing through the Straits. Two opposing forces are at play which could increase or decrease Europe-Asian trade: (1) the continued opening and sustained economic dynamism of Asia could lead to more Europe-Asian investments leading to more trade between these two regions, while (2) greater economic integration in Europe could lead to less Europe-Asia trade in the short and medium terms. The future importance of the Malacca Straits therefore would largely depend on which of these two forces will dominate. On the assumption that greater economic integration in Europe will result in greater economic growth in the long run, consequently, that region is more likely to see more trade between Asia and Europe.

Growth of Asian Economic Integration

Growth in trade between the littoral states of Southeast Asia and Northeast Asia will also determine the future importance of the Malacca Straits. The littoral states of Indonesia, Malaysia and Singapore in particular have seen tremendous growth in their trade with China and if this trend continues, we should see more cargo and thus ships passing through the Straits.

FIGURE 11.1
China's Oil Imports and Number of Oil Tankers Passing *via* Malacca Straits[4]

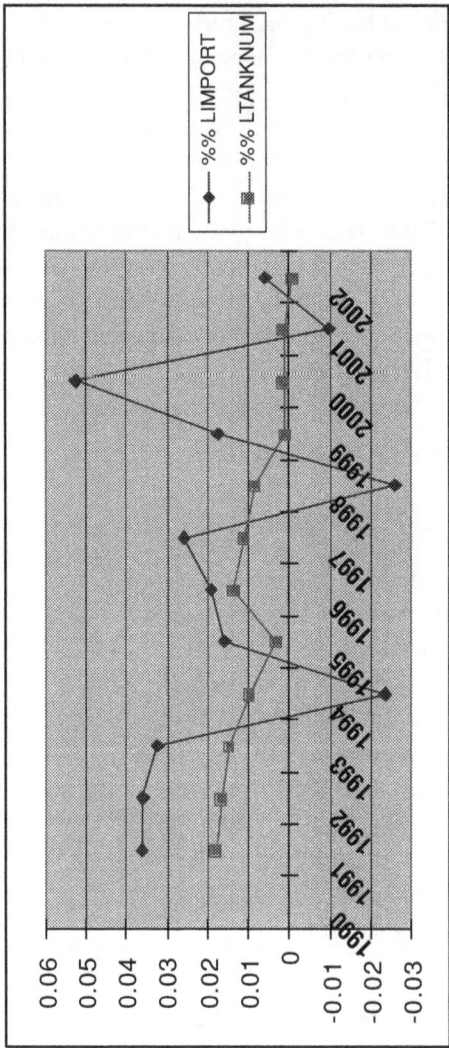

TABLE 11.1
Regression Results: China's Oil Imports and No of Tankers[5]

Dependent Variable: LTANKNUM
Method: Least Squares
Date: 09/05/04 Time: 12:29
Sample(adjusted): 1990–2001

Included observations: 12 after adjusting endpoints

Variable	Coefficient	Std. Error	t-Statistic	Prob.
C(1)	3.782392	0.687000	5.505665	0.0003
LIMPORT	0.346239	0.044007	7.867739	0.0000
R-squared	0.860920	Mean dependent variable		9.180953
Adjusted R-squared	0.847013	S.D. dependent variable		0.300048
S.E. of regression	0.117360	Akaike info criterion		−1.296134
Sum squared resid	0.137733	Schwarz criterion		−1.215316
Log likelihood	9.776802	Durbin-Watson statistic		1.409181

Possible Threats to the Malacca Straits and its Importance to Singapore and Malaysian Ports

The importance of the Malacca Straits to the littoral ports of Singapore and Malaysia is indicated by the fact that these ports are transshipment and hub ports. In the case of Singapore, for example, around 85 per cent of its cargo are transshipped. It is therefore crucial that they can attract the main liners to call at their ports. Their proximity to the Straits has made them more attractive for ships to call at. While these factors point to the future importance of the Straits and its contribution to the port business of the littoral states, there are also other factors that tend to pose a threat to its future importance and the future of the existing hub ports of Singapore and Malaysia.

China's Oil Pipeline

China wants to build an oil pipeline to a port in Myanmar to reduce its vulnerability over imported oil shipped *via* the Malacca Straits. This will ensure that supplies will continue even when passage through the narrow and already very congested waterway is disrupted for whatever reason. Compared with the current oil route *via* the Malacca Straits, this means a saving of about 2,000 kilometres. The cost of construction is about US$2 billion. This pipeline is the preferred option because it also tallies with another strategic railway that China wants to build, the Kunming-Yangon line which opens up an Indian Ocean outlet for its otherwise landlocked southwest provinces.[6]

Thailand's Strategic Landbridge

Many years ago the Kra Canal project was proposed to promote Thailand as a new regional hub. However, this project suffers from several disadvantages. First, if Thailand is cut into two parts, the whole country will be automatically separated which means that both portions can be significantly different, presenting new potential problems to the nation. Second, the concept of being "Thai" which translates into "freedom" would lose its meaning to the Thai people, especially when the traditional idea of Thai sovereignty in territorial and political terms is affected. Moreover, as a third point, a decades-old separatist struggle in the southern region of Thailand, which abated in the 1980, has flared up once again in 2004, already threatening the division between the North and South. If Thailand actually becomes physically divided by the Kra Canal, it may have an adverse effect on the political situation between the separatists and the central government in Bangkok.

However, Thailand has recently come up with another new project involving the construction of a strategic energy "landbridge", which has a function similar to the Kra Canal project with the difference being that it does not require any physical land division.[7] Like the Kra Canal, the project aims at reducing Thailand's energy dependence and to promote regional competitiveness as well as develop itself as a regional hub for mineral oil and refined products. Located at Thab Lamu in Phang Nga province at one side and at Sichon District in Nakron Srithamarath province at the other end, this landbridge links the Andaman Sea with the Gulf of Thailand, which will shorten the oil transportation distance from oil producers in the Middle East to oil consumers in Southeast Asia and the Far East; avoiding the threat of piracy that often occurs in the current routes such as the Malacca route. This can create oil stockpile and induce joint investment between oil consumers and oil producers so as to strengthen regional energy security. It may also eventually nullify the Far Eastern premium in the world's oil market trading regime.

The Rise of New Hub Ports in Asia

One of the recent significant maritime developments is the emergence of new ports in Asia, which could pose a threat to the future of the hub ports of Singapore and Malaysia. Over the years, some of these major container ports have built up a significant container cargo base mainly as a result of the surge in international trade in the region buoyed up by the remarkable trade-oriented growth of the economies they have served particularly in the latter half of the 1980s and the 1990s. As it can be gleaned from Figure 11.2 below, the ports of Tanjung Pelepas and Laem Chabang have over the years registered one of the highest growth rates in terms of container throughput. The port of Tanjung Pelepas, in particular, has surpassed the port of Singapore in terms of growth rate since it commenced operations in 2000.

Port authorities and operators in these major container ports of Southeast Asia have attempted to upgrade their ports and improve their efficiency with the aim of attracting more local and international cargo to their ports. Economic considerations and political factors have both motivated the port of Laem Chabang in Thailand, and the port of Tanjung Pelepas in the southern tip of Malaysia to aspire to be hub ports in the region. Malaysia in particular has been attempting to reduce its volume of cargo transshipped through the port of Singapore by lowering their port charges, improving their infrastructure and efficiency, and adopting punitive measures including the imposition of additional levies for cargo coming out of and entering into Singapore. An investment of S$2.6 billion on port development has been committed for the last five years,[9] while Tanjung Pelepas, a newly opened port in Johor Baru, Malaysia, has commenced operation since 2000.

The Thai Transport Ministry has also announced plans to cut its dependency on other ports for transshipments. The port of Bangkok had launched a modernization programme aimed at improving the port's operational efficiency by simplifying their wharf procedures and reducing their container handling operations in 2000.[10] One proposal being considered was for master vessels to be offered lower handling charges in return for loading their cargo directly at the port of Laem Chabang in eastern Thailand.[11] The Philippines, on the other hand, has been seriously marketing the strategic location, excellent infrastructure and natural harbours of Subic Bay (the former U.S. naval base, the biggest outside the United States) as a regional hub port since the expiry of the lease agreement

FIGURE 11.2
Comparison of Selected Ports' Container Handling from 1997–2004 (TEUs)[8]

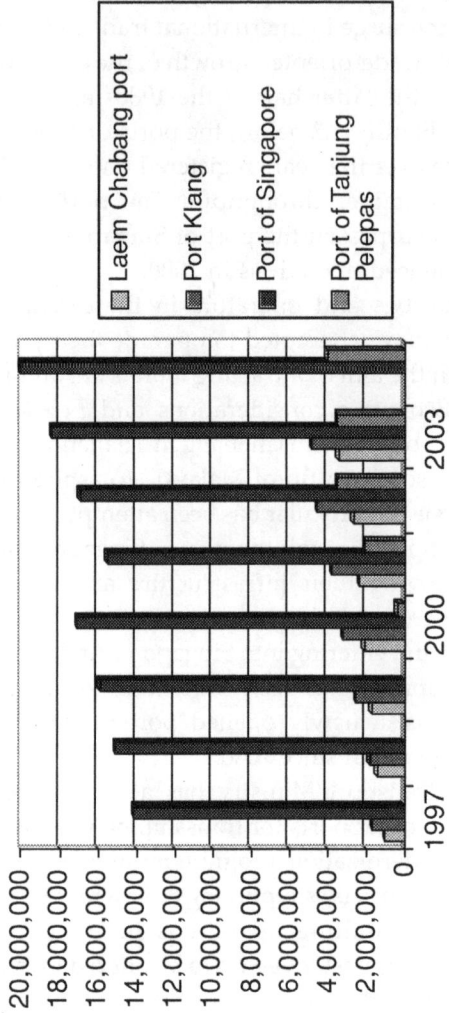

between the United States and the Philippines. Indonesia has planned to develop its port in Batam (*The Straits Times*, 10 July 1996). The Asian financial crisis has put this plan on hold due to financial difficulties, but once Indonesia is back on the road to economic recovery, it is likely that this plan will be implemented. Although these ports are relatively undeveloped in terms of throughput and infrastructure, they are, however, as well located geographically to service Asia. With adequate investments in technology and infrastructure, it may just be a matter of time before they can become a real threat to other transshipment ports.

Other considerations have been responsible for the trend towards indigenous port development and aggressive modernization plans in the region, as follows. Firstly, the inadequacy of their port infrastructure to accommodate the rapid increase in cargo flows, especially in containerized traffic, has resulted in severe port congestion. These countries have experienced trade-oriented rapid growth rates for the past decades, and this economic dynamism has stretched their port infrastructure to their limits. Another consideration is the growing deficit in their services sector particularly for Malaysia, which has traditionally been using the port of Singapore as a transshipment port for a great bulk of its inward and outward-bound cargo. Estimates have placed the amount of Malaysia's cargo going through Singapore within the range of one quarter to more than half of Malaysia's foreign trade, which totalled 374.4 billion Malaysian ringgit in 1995.[12] The use of foreign-registered ships has also contributed to the outflow of their foreign exchange. Port development has also become an integral part of their national development strategy to maintain and improve its international competitiveness. Realizing the importance of port development to its overall national development plans, the respective governments of these countries have launched an aggressive drive to promote their ports as hub ports to attract cargo and global carriers.

The Rise of the Port of Shanghai

The Shanghai Port Container Terminals consist of the Container Terminals of Zhanghuabang, Jungonglu, Baoshan, Waigaoqiao, Longwu and Yangjing. Among them, the first four terminals cater towards foreign trade while the others service domestic trade. The logistics infrastructure of these container terminals is shown in Table 11.3.

The construction of a 117-kilometre railway in Pudong may begin in 2004 and it is expected to help Shanghai develop into a shipping and

TABLE 11.2
Ten Largest Container Ports: 1995–2002[13]

Rank	1995	TEUs	1997	TEUs	1998	TEUs	2002	TEUs
1	Hong Kong	12 549 746	Hong Kong	14 567 231	Singapore	15 100 000	Hong Kong	19 140 000
2	Singapore	10 800 300	Singapore	14 135 300	Hong Kong	14 582 000	Singapore	16 800 000
3	Kaohsiung	5 232 000	Kaohsiung	5 693 339	Kaohsiung	6 271 053	Busan	9 436 307
4	Busan	4 502 596	Busan	5 233 880	Busan	5 945 614	Shanghai	8 610 000
5	Yokohama	2 756 811	Shanghai	2 520 000	Shanghai	3 066 000	Kaohsiung	8 493 000
6	Tokyo	2 177 407	Yokohama	2 347 635	Manila	2 690 000	Shengzhen	7 613 754
7	Keelung	2 169 893	Tokyo	2 322 000	Tokyo	2 168 543	Rotterdam	6 515 449
8	Manila	1 687 743	Manila	2 121 074	Tanjung Priok	2 130 979	Los Angeles	6 105 863
9	Shanghai	1 527 000	Tanjung Priok	2 091 402	Yokohama	2 091 420	Hamburg	5 373 999
10	Nagoya	1 477 359	Kobe	1 944 147	Kobe	1 900 737	Antwerp	4 533 212
11							Klang (12)	4 533 212
12							Pelepas (26)	2 660 000

TABLE 11.3
The logistics Infrastructure of Shanghai Port Container Terminals (2004)

Name of the Container Terminals Co.	Number of Berth	Space of Terminal (m²)	Max. Draft _m_	Current Capacity	
				Design Capacity (TEU/yr)	Ship Size (max. slot)
SCT*: Zhanghuabang	3	303,036	−12.5	740,000	4,000
Jungonglu	4	307,000	−10.5	760,000	3,000
Baoshan	3	218,051	−10.5	200,000	2,000
Waigaoqiao Phase 1	3	500,000	−12	750,000	5,000
Waigaoqiao Phase 2	3	1,000,000	−13.2	750,000	5,000
Waigaoqiao Phase 3	2	630,000	−13.2	650,000	5,000
Waigaoqiao Phase 4	4	1,630,000	−14.5	2,000,000	6,000
Longwu	4	260,000	− 9.5	400,000	550
Yangjing	1	90,000	−11	160,000	1,000

*Shanghai Container Terminals Co. Ltd.

aviation hub in Asia. The railway links suburban areas, such as Jinshan, Fengxian, Nanhui and Pudong will be put into use before the 2010 World Expo. The new railway will mainly transport cargo between Pudong International Airport, Yangshan Deep Water Port District, Waigaoqiao FTZ, and Caojing Chemical Industry Park.

However, the Port of Shanghai's shallow waters have made it a less than ideal shipping location, with quayside draught at Waigaoqiao twelve metres at high tide (and Yangtze River at seven metres at low tide). To address the problem, work on a US$1.9 billion dredging and dyke-construction project began in 1998. Port authorities hope that the main channel will be deepened to 12.5 metres by 2006, adding 20 per cent of cargo handling capacity.

The Chinese Government plans to implement policies to help speed up the development of infrastructure for a deepwater port, and introduce GIS geographic management system and barcode system. To maintain the port's status as an international shipping centre, the Shanghai government has invest RMB7 billion (about US$843 million) in port construction in the tenth five-year-plan starting from 2001. Over 80 per cent of the investment is supposed to build new container handling facilities and/or to expand existing facilities. Shanghai is also building the Yangshan Deep Water Port District to handle more than 25 million TEUs per year by 2020. Phase 1 is planned for completion by the end of 2005 with an investment of RMB14.31

billion (about US$1.73 billion). At present, the average distance between cranes at Shanghai Port container terminals is about 100 to 110 metres. The Port of Shanghai is planning to make full use of the waterfront by shortening this distance and employing more cranes. This measure would increase the port's capacity by about 30 to 40 per cent.

The Shanghai Port Container Terminal is negotiating with a number of small terminal owners in Shanghai to lease terminals to accommodate small vessels traversing the inland waterways. Currently the port uses international container berths to accommodate these vessels. It is also presently developing a value-added logistics service. For example, a logistics centre, with a total investment of RMB600 million (about US$73 million), is under construction in Pudong.

The functions of the terminals along Huangpu River will be adjusted properly. The environment-friendly devices on the cargo berths for commodities such as coal and ore will be built up to meet the requirements of international metropolitan Shanghai. The functions of the terminals in the city centre are transformed according to the city development plan. The central business district (CBD) and the sightseeing zones along Huangpu River will also be expanded to meet the requirements of the World Exhibition 2010 to be held in Shanghai. The terminals for ore in the city centre will be moved out from Huangpu River. The facilities for passenger ships in the city centre will be improved accordingly to meet the developing trend of the passenger traffic. After the restructuring in 2002, the Shanghai Port Authority (SPA) was split into an administrative institution (retaining the name of SPA), and an operator and independent controller of almost all port assets located in Shanghai, called the Shanghai International Port Group (SIPG).

The rise of Shanghai Port does not necessarily reduce the importance of the Malacca Straits particularly in the case of China-Europe trade, but could have a negative implication for the littoral ports of Singapore and Malaysia. The building up of a cargo base at the Shanghai port has already resulted in many mainliners being almost fully loaded before sailing for its European destination with little shipping space left for cargo transshipped at the ports of Singapore and Malaysia, leading to some congestion. If the mainliners are fully loaded and most of the cargo is destined for Europe, it may not be cost effective for the mainliners to call at hub ports in Southeast Asia anymore and thus bypassing the ports of Singapore and Malaysia. The trend towards increasing ship size and direct sailings have also reduced the importance of hubbing and thus affecting the positions of these littoral ports. The same could also apply to the China-U.S. east coast trade to a lesser extent.

The Rise of the Port of Tanjung Pelepas

Another significant port development in the region is the construction of a new port on the southwestern tip of Peninsular Malaysia, adjacent to the Second Link connecting Malaysia and Singapore across the Johor Straits. It has been in operation since January 2000. Since then, the volume of its throughput has doubled from 2 million TEUs in 2001 to 4 million TEUs in 2004. The construction of this port began after the signing of the Build Operate Transfer (BOT) privatization agreement between the Malaysian Government and Seaport Terminal (Johore), which relegated its rights and obligations to its wholly subsidiary, Pelabuhan Tanjung Pelepas. The concession period for the BOT project is for sixty years.

The development of this port consists of five phases running up to 2020, and is worth 10 billion Malaysian ringgit. The first phase, which was completed in June 2001, provides six berths along 2.16 kilometres of linear container berth with a capacity to handle 3.8 million TEUs. The first two berths opened in late 1999, the next two in 2000 and the remaining ones in June 2001. The port is now equipped with 18 Super Post and Post Panamax quay cranes with a lifting capacity of 40 tonnes and an outreach of 53 metres, capable of serving the biggest containership, and 58 rubber-tyred gantry (yard) cranes. The port of Tanjung Pelepas is now linked to national road and rail grids that has put the entire Peninsular Malaysia and Thailand within reach. Currently, 30 daily domestic scheduled block train services and 10 weekly international block train services are moving up and down between various destinations in Malaysia. More upgrading of these rail links is being undertaken to provide more seamless transportation of cargoes between major seaports and inland ports in Malaysia.[14]

The port of Tanjung Pelepas possesses some characteristics which could make it an alternative port of call for mainline operators. First, it is rather strategically located. In this regard, it is less than an hour from the region's international shipping lanes *via* the Straits of Malacca, and thus offers ships a low deviation from the trading lanes they are normally used to. Although it is not as close to the main shipping routes as the port of Singapore is, the port of Tanjung Pelepas is certainly close enough to them to be considered as a viable stop. Like Singapore, it also has a naturally deep harbour with a draught of 15 metres supported by a 12.6-kilometre channel of approach 250 metres in width with a 600-metre turning basin which allows for a two-way passage of vessels and a quick turnaround in a vessel's transit time. In addition, it has a sheltered bay, which makes it protected from any possible natural disturbances.

The port of Tanjung Pelepas is also close to the physical vicinity of local markets, which can provide an added base and potential hedge in the event that market forces and other factors compel significant shifts in transshipment patterns. Unlike a hub port entirely dependent on the discretionary transshipment cargo, the port of Tanjung Pelepas would have sufficient internal cargo as a result of its proximity to the domestic market. It has a wide back-up area and covers a spacious area of 1,935-acres (784 hectares) solely for port-related industries. The area around the port has been earmarked for maritime and port-related activities. An area of 903 acres (365 hectares) has been identified for commercial and industrial activities of which a distribution centre or "distripark" covering an area of 290 acres (117 hectares) would be developed for warehousing and distribution, while the remaining 613 acres (248 hectares) are available for port-related industrial activities. There is also a large land reserve covering an area of more than 5,000 acres (2,025 hectares) for subsequent development projects that may arise. In addition, the cost of using the port of Tanjung Pelepas' services and facilities is much lower than that of major hub ports such as the one in Singapore, Hong Kong and even other emerging hub ports in Asia, as Table 11.4 shows.

Significantly, the port of Tanjung Pelepas uses start-of-the-art information technology and equipment, which gives every port user instant access to the port's Integrated Terminal and Port Management Information

TABLE 11.4
Container Handling Charges (Per Container) for Selected Ports[15]

	Port Klang		Port of Singapore		Laem Chabang		PTP	
	20ft	40ft	20ft	40ft	20ft	40ft	20ft	40ft
FCL	190	285	270	382	972	1462	189	267
	(US$50)	(US$75)	(US$155)	(US$220)	(US$23)	(US$34)	(US$109)	(US$154)
LCL	330	490	565	786	2500	3995	395	550
	(US$87)	(US$129)	(US$325)	(US$452)	(US$58)	(US$93)	(US$227)	(US$316)
Trans-shipment	160	240	174	252	462	697	121	176
	(US$42)	(US$63)	(US$100)	(US$145)	(US$11)	(US$16)	(US$70)	(US$101)

System (ITPMIS). By synergizing all the port's operations and communication centres, the ITPMIS facilitates a free flow of updated information and provides near paperless transactions between port personnel, shipping lines, various marine services and freight forwarders. An automated gate system, berth allocation, ship planning and yard planning have also been fully computerized to facilitate the smooth flow of containers and other commodities with a reduction in waiting time. The computerization of this port also allows users to inquire and track the status of their containers through an on-line system.

This young port is reportedly moving aggressively to achieve its goal of securing a position as Southeast Asia's premier transshipment hub. Like the port of Singapore, transshipments make up the bulk of its business, with transshipped containers accounting for 85 per cent of its total throughput for the year 2000. To achieve this goal, the management has focused on securing mainliners as well as feeder operators to call at the port by offering incentives: Dedicated berths to certain customers, the same level of service and efficiency as PSA but at a cost which is 30 per cent lower.[16] As compared to Singapore, Malaysia can offer lower rates due to her cheaper labour costs, availability of land and government incentives. As a result, it has already gained some two million TEUs a year from Maersk-SeaLand and a growing number of feeder operators have expressed their keen interest. Since its operation in 2000, it has already attracted four main shipping lines, including Maersk-Sealand, APL-NOL, K-Line and Mitsui OSK Lines, to call at its port. The recent relocation of Maersk-Sealand, the word's biggest container shipping line, and Taiwan-based Evergreen from the port of Singapore to this port has provided a big boost to the port's transshipment status.

The Malaysian Ministry of Finance in a bid to increase the port throughput has lifted a levy on container trucks ferrying goods from Singapore to Tanjung Pelepas, as well as on trucks transporting goods that arrive at Tanjung Pelepas bound for Singapore. Raising the levy on trucks ferrying containers to Singapore is currently under consideration. It is estimated that more than 2,000 trucks move goods from Johore to Singapore daily, carrying almost one million TEUs a year to Singapore. Malaysia hopes to plug this leak.[17]

The Malaysian Government has also made it easier for cargo to be channelled from Pasir Gudang port to that in Tanjung Pelepas by doing away with detailed customs procedure and other documentations, when the cargo is transported from Pasir Gudang in eastern Johore to the port of Tanjung Pelepas in the west for subsequent export.[18]

Although the port of Tanjung Pelepas has much lower container-handling charges than the port of Singapore (while its container handling efficiency is catching up with that of Singapore), the port of Singapore still enjoys an edge over its counterpart at Tanjung Pelepas in terms of connectivity and frequency which could be more important to shippers. From the viewpoint of commercial shipping lines, Singapore tends to be a prime choice as a cargo base, which is an important factor influencing their choice in calling at a hub port. Although the port of Tanjung Pelepas does not pose any threat to Singapore's hub port position in the short and medium term, this possibility cannot be ruled out in the long run if the expansion of the cargo base at the port of Tanjung Pelepas continues. However, changes in the allocation of cargo between the ports of Singapore and Tanjung Pelepas do not diminish the importance of the Malacca Straits as long as there is an overall increase in cargo throughputs at these ports.

Rise of the Port of Laem Chabang

Located at the eastern shore of the upper Gulf of Thailand, approximately 110 kilometres south of Bangkok, the port of Laem Chabang was constructed to relieve the port of Bangkok of cargo and thus alleviate the traffic conditions in the city. By putting a cap at one million TEUs for the Bangkok port, it implies that any growth in container volume will have to be absorbed by the port of Laem Chabang. Unlike the port of Bangkok, the port of Laem Chabang is managed and operated under a public-private partnership. It operates eleven terminals to accommodate various types of vessels. Five of the terminals are container terminals; the other three comprise a coastal terminal, bulk terminal and general cargo terminal. The rest are under design and construction. More than 80 per cent of sea-borne cargo handled by LCP is containerized.

Although this port is expected to generate only about 2 million TEUs — a small figure compared to the more established ports in the region — it has a good prospect of becoming a transshipment hub for Indochina. The geographical proximity of the port of Laem Chabang to the neighbouring countries of Vietnam, Laos and Cambodia — and other factors such as the former's well-sheltered site, deep draught and spacious hinterland with improved standards of operating efficiency — have already attracted the networks of five world leading ocean liners offering regular post-Panamax and Panamax vessel services for the purposes of commercial freight.

With the expectations of an increase in container throughput exceeding the total capacity of the existing terminals in Phase 1 of the project, the Port Authority of Thailand (PAT) has already started its second phase of the development project. This phase calls for an expansion of the port through the construction of a third pier enclosing a second mooring basin located immediately south of the existing port. The new 500-metre by 1,750-metre mooring basin will be oriented along the 73-253 bearing, which is shifted by 14 degrees relative to the existing orientation established by Phase 1. The new basin and the port fairway will be dredged to a depth of 16 metres at Mean Sea Level (MSL) to accommodate fully loaded Panamax vessels. Container terminals C1-C3 and D1-D3 are sited on the north and south sides of the new mooring basin, respectively. The existing breakwater will be extended southward to provide protection to the new mooring basin and the extended fairway. This increased capacity will enable the port to handle large container vessels with the draft of as much as 80,000 DWT (Dead Weight Tonnage) or of over 4,000 TEUs in capacity. This second phase is expected to be completed by 2009. Upon completion of Phase 2 development, the annual capacity at the port of Laem Chabang will be increased to 5 million TEUs. The execution of Phase 3 of development will be considered in the decade after Phase 2 has been completed.

In addition to the above expansion, the port of Laem Chabang has developed inter-modal transport. For example, there are plans for an efficient inter-modal transport systems like a double-track railway and highway network as this will give them the ability to facilitate faster and more efficient cargo consolidation or deconsolidation, storage and regional redistribution of cargo. It also offers a comprehensive attraction to the direct call of shipping lines. As part of the Thai Government's development programme plans are also in the pipeline to improve the port service roads — including the construction of flyover bridge at the crossing points between highway or railway — in order to fully utilize the existing main road network capacity.

Though the port of Laem Chabang has undergone a wave of upgrading projects to its port facilities — including the simplification of its custom procedures — there is still room for further improvement, especially with respect to the issue of inland traffic. The famous Bangkok traffic congestion may delay the transportation of containerized cargo, and can act as a deterrent to potential clients from using the port of Laem Chabang. Even though the port of Laem Chabang is not directly affected by this traffic congestion because it is located near the highways which lead to northern part of Thailand bypassing Bangkok), port-related services such as banking and insurance, which are core commercial businesses, are mostly located in Bangkok. Thus, solving this problem of traffic congestion should be one of the immediate priorities for Laem Chabang's port planners to tackle.

The rise of Laem Chabang can reduce the importance of the Malacca Straits and the hub position of the littoral ports particularly in relation to the Far East-North America trade. With more mainliner ships calling at the port of Laem Chabang, more transshipped cargo could be diverted from the ports of Singapore and Malaysia. The geographical proximity of Laem Chabang to the Indochinese states makes Laem Chabang an attractive transshipment port for Indochinese cargo.

Conclusion

It is not possible to come up at this point in time with a categorical prognosis of the future of Malacca Straits and the littoral ports of Singapore and Malaysia. As the analysis above shows, there are certain developments that seem to work in favour of the Straits. The growing demand for oil by China, increasing trade between Europe and Asia and the intensification of Asian economic integration would result in the use of the Malacca Straits for supporting these developments. On the other hand, there are also developments that seem to work against the Straits. The rise of Shanghai and Laem Chabang and the building of China's pipeline and Thailand's landbridge could lead to the diminishing importance of the Straits and thus the littoral ports of Singapore and Malaysia. Whether the positive factors would prevail largely depends on a number of factors including the success or failure of maintaining maritime security in the Malacca Straits, government policies and future shipping trends.

Notes

[1]   The waters around Singapore may be among the most dangerous in the world. In the first six months of 2004, pirate attacks in the Malacca and Singapore Straits almost doubled from 15 to 27 — in sharp contrast to waters elsewhere in the world where such attacks dwindled. Given the importance of these waters to Singapore and international trade, these figures are worrying. See "Pirate Attacks in Region's Waters Double", *Straits Times*, 26 July 2004, p. A16. Quite recently, Singapore, Malaysia and Indonesia agreed to work closer to enhance maritime security and fight terrorism: "KL, Singapore Focus on Straits Safety", *Straits Times*, 28 July 2004, p. 1.

2   Taken from *Asia Times* (online), "Malacca Strait: Target for Terror", 11 August 2004 <www.atimes.com/atimes/Southeast_Asia/FH11Ae02.html> accessed on 11 June 2005.
3   These data were obtained from China's *Customs Statistical Yearbook 1990–2002* and the Singapore Maritime Port Authority's website, <www.mpa.gov.sg>.
4   Ibid.
5   Adjusted R-squared statistic indicates the goodness of fit and thus tells to what extent the independent variable (in this case, China's oil imports) explains the dependent variable — the number of oil tankers passing through the Malacca Strait. Durbin-Watson statistic indicates whether the estimates are subject to serial correlation while the t-statistic measures the statistical significance of the variables used. As a rule of thumb, these t-statistics should have a value of at least 2 for the variable to be statistically significant.
6   "China Pipeline Plan to Secure Oil Supplies", *Straits Times*, 31 July 2004, p. A1.
7   It is reported that the main features of the landbridge include (1) a pipeline that links the Andaman Sea and Gulf of Thailand at 240 kilometres in length; and (2) a new oil depôt on the Andaman side. Tankers from the Middle East will dock and unload their crude oil. Nearby countries could load crude oil at this point without having to sail through the Malacca Straits and go to Singapore. There would also be a new petrochemical complex along the Gulf of Thailand. The refinery complex would have a capacity of one million barrels per day. The landbridge would serve as a refinery product provider to Thailand itself, as well as China, Japan, Hong Kong, Malaysia and other countries that would benefit from a shorter travelling distance, compared to a journey made to Singapore. The investment cost is reported to be about US$719 million. From a draft analysis performed by the Thailand Ministry of Energy, this project is estimated to cut oil prices significantly by about US$1.50–$2.00 per barrel.
8   Computed from figures taken from <http://www.mpa.gov.sg>, <http://portfocus.com/Malaysia and http://www.lcit.com>, *Container International Yearbook 2005 and Fairplay Portguide 1999/2000*.
9   Taken from *Straits Times*, 26 June 1996.
10 Taken from *Straits Times*, 5 September 1998.
11 Taken from *Lloyd's List Maritime Asia*, January 1996.
12 "Battle on the High Seas", *Far Eastern Economic Review*, 6 June 1996, pp. 56–58.
13 Collated from the *Containerisation International Yearbook*, various issues.
14 A. Nesathurai, "Key Players in the Logistics Chain", 24 March 2003, <http://www.mima.gov.my>.
15 The exchange rates used at the time of writing are US$1=S$1.74, US$1=RM3.8 and US$1=THB42.8. Though not shown in Table 11.4, the currency unit is the Malaysian ringgit (RM) for Port Klang; the Singapore dollar (S$) for the Port of Singapore; the Thai baht (BHT) for Laem Chabang and the Singapore dollar (S$) for the Port of Tanjung Pelepas (PTP). According to *Fairplay Port Guide*,

PTP's rates are calculated at an estimated 70 per cent of Singapore's rates, according to industry estimates.

[16] "PTP Shifts Focus to Securing more Common Feeder Operators", *Shipping Times Online*, 13 November 2000.

[17] "New Malaysian Port Moves to Gain Singapore Business", *Journal of Commerce*, 24 January 2001.

[18] "KL Gives Further Boost to Tanjung Pelepas Port", *Shipping Times*, 13 February 2001.

12

Piracy, Seaborne Trade and the Rivalries of Foreign Sea Powers in East and Southeast Asia, 1511 to 1839: A Chinese Perspective

Xu Ke

Introduction

Maritime piracy[1] in East and Southeast Asia is as old as the seaborne trade, which it preys upon. Before the advent of European colonizers in early sixteenth century, the relation between piracy and seaborne trade was simple: The pirates were the predators and the merchant ships were their prey. As such, the pirates robbed merchant ships on the trade routes and captured goods and people as their booty. In 1511, the Portuguese captured Malacca, and started the history of European colonial sea power penetration in Southeast Asia. The European colonizers — the Portuguese, the Spaniards, the Dutch and the British — successively seized the main entrepôts, plundered the wealth of indigenous and Chinese traders and eventually set up their colonial domains in East and Southeast Asia. The link between piracy and seaborne trade relations became complex, since piracy was used by

European colonizers as means to control seaborne trade and to expand their influence and domains. The colonial powers also attempted to establish trade relations with China. Consequently, the Chinese Empire was plagued by Japanese piratical attacks (*Wo Kou*), leading to the banning of overseas trade (*Haijin*) in order to increase the security of the Middle Kingdom against foreign influence. Interestingly, during the *Haijin* period, illegal private seaborne trade with Nanyang actually boomed. In fact, the illegal private traders were characterized as "merchant pirates" who possessed paradoxical dual identities of being both merchants and pirates at the same time. In general, they became active in trading first with Nanyang and, later, with the colonial powers. The rivalries of foreign sea powers in East and Southeast Asia can be divided into two layers or forms of rivalries, first, among the state actors in the form of European sea powers and the Chinese Empire; second, among state actors and non-state actors in the form of European colonizer and Chinese merchant pirates.

This chapter focuses on the interplay between historical piracy, seaborne trade and the rivalries of the foreign sea powers in the early modern history of Southeast Asia between 1511 to 1839. It argues that the diverse perception and policies among Chinese Empire and colonial powers (who were also sea powers) resulted in the reconfiguration of the balance of maritime power in East and Southeast Asia. The chapter unfolds in three parts. First, it reviews the history of piracy and the seaborne trade in East and Southeast Asia in the pre-colonial period. Second, it surveys piracy and seaborne trade relations within the colonial era and specifically, the turbulent period, which saw clashes between the colonial powers and the Chinese Empire. The third part discusses the relations between the European colonialists and Chinese merchant pirates.

Piracy and Seaborne Trade before the Advent of European Colonialism

Nanhai Trade and the Chinese Tributary System

In the age of sail, seaborne trade was highly dependent on the monsoon seasons.[2] Through the dictates of geography and weather conditions, many entrepôts and kingdoms arose in East and Southeast Asia where traders could best exploit the change of monsoon or the arrival of trading partners.

For example, these entrepôts and kingdoms were located at the intersection area of the monsoons' coverage, along the Andaman Sea, the Gulf of Thailand, and the Java Sea; especially the Straits of Malacca, Funan, Champa, and Sri Vijaya in the first millennium.[3]

As early as three centuries before the advent of Christianity, the Chinese had traded with Southeast Asia in what was termed the Nanhai trade. Historical records show that the trade route extended from China's southern ports to west Borneo, Palembang, the Indian Ocean and eventually the Roman Empire, though the detail of the trade was not clear.[4] From the fifth to the ninth centuries, Chinese Buddhist pilgrims began to use this trade route to India. They came also to the Indonesian empire of Srivijaya to learn Buddhist teachings, sutras and languages before they headed for India.[5]

It was not until the Song Dynasty (960–1279) that the Chinese historical records make any mention of Chinese merchants going to Nanyang in significant numbers, and generating significant profits from their trading activities.[6] The following Yuan Dynasty adopted the Song policy of promoting the Nanhai trade after their conquest of China. The Yuan government also provided loans to Chinese traders, and extracted seventy per cent of the trade profits. Wang Dayuan (*Wang Tayuan*), the famous traveller who visited Nanyang at that time, recorded that Chinese traders had begun to turn their efforts towards local trade instead.[7]

In 1368, the Yuan Dynasty was overthrown by the Ming Dynasty. The founder of the Ming Dynasty, Emperor Hongwu, suspected that the seaborne trade might be a threat to the new empire. It compelled him to impose severe restrictions on the trade with Nanyang. Consequently, private trading was banned, and the official tributary system of such trading — trading through the nominal diplomatic missions — was revived and even enhanced.[8]

When the Emperor Yongle ascended to the Ming throne in 1402, he dispatched Admiral Zheng He to Southeast Asia and the Indian Ocean. The maiden voyage of Zheng He's naval expeditions led him to Malacca where he met with Prince Paramesvara's imprimatur in July 1405. The armada consisted of sixty-two "treasure ships" some of which were nine-masted with four decks, nearly 440 feet (135 metres) in length and 180 feet (55 metres) in width. Some other 255 smaller vessels were used. In total, the first expedition consisted of almost 28,000 persons, including diplomats, sailors, pilot, soldiers and other experts. From 1405 to 1433, Zheng conducted seven legendary voyages of diplomacy, commerce and scientific exploration.

The main purpose of these voyages was to enhance the Middle Kingdom's suzerainty over Southeast Asian kingdoms as well as to expand its tributary system. Under this system, all the overseas kingdoms wishing to trade with China had to pay tribute to the Chinese Empire. In general, tributary states had to accept Chinese customs and practices as well, including the use of the Chinese lunar calendar as well as to consent in their formal investiture of their rulers through the Chinese authorities, thereby legitimizing the Chinese Empire's suzerainty.[9] In return, the Chinese emperors returned favours and privileges that were more than the real value of the tributes. It was a huge expense for the Ming governments, which was one of the reasons that no more similar voyages continued after Zheng He's seven voyages to Southeast Asia.

Piracy in the Early History of East and Southeast Asia

Maritime piracy in East and Southeast Asia is as old as the seaborne trade which it preys upon. The trade among these entrepôts and kingdoms inevitably caused the piracy. The earliest historical record on piracy in the Nanyang trade dates back to the first century. A famous Chinese historian, Ban Gu (32 A.D. to 92 A.D.) recorded the existence of piracy in the trade route from China *via* Singapore (*Duyuan Guo*) to Sir Lanka (*Yichengbu Guo*).[10] Shi Fan Xian, a well-known Chinese Buddhist pilgrim, who travelled to India and returned to China by sea in 412 A.D., documented the existence of piracy in the Straits of Malacca in his famous travel note, *Fa Xian Zhuan*: "The sea is infested with pirates, the passengers who encounter them will lose everything".[11]

In the late seventh to the twelfth centuries, Srivijaya — the famously powerful Buddhist kingdom in South Sumatra whose trade links spanned from Arabia to China — also experienced the pilferage of sea marauders, which preyed upon the passing merchant ships. Srivijaya's monarchs were unable to suppress these pirates, and eventually had to surrender a portion of the port revenues to some of the pirates in return for not raiding their ships at sea.[12]

At the end of the thirteenth century, Srivijaya was eventually conquered by the rise of a new and powerful Javanese Hindu empire called Majapahit centred in East Java. Piratical attacks in its waters were recorded in the *Zhu Pan Zhi*, written in 1225:

The foreign ships were often attacked by pirates. The captives were the favourite of pirates, one captive can sell for 2 *liang*[13] or 3 *liang* gold, the piracy prevents the merchants from visiting the ports.[14]

As the seaborne trade increased, the southern end of the Straits of Malacca became a piracy-prone area. Wang Dayuan described piracy activities near Temasek — the name for current Singapore before it was founded by Sir Stamford Raffles in 1819 — in 1349 in the following terms:

> The Dragon-teeth Strait (*Longyamen*)[15] is between the two hills of Temasek barbarians, which look like 'dragon's teeth'. Through the centre runs a waterway. The fields are barren and rice harvest is poor. The climate is hot with heavy rain in April and May. The inhabitants are addicted to piracy...When junks sail to the European Ocean (Indian Ocean), the local barbarians allow them to pass unmolested, but when the junks reach the Auspicious Strait (*Jilimen*) on their return voyages, some 200–300 pirate *prahus* [boats] will put out to attack the junks for several days, the crew of junks have to fight with their arms and setting up cloth screen as a protection against arrows. Sometimes, the junks are fortunate enough to escape with a favouring wind; otherwise, the crews are butchered and the merchandise becomes pirates' booty.[16]

In the first decade of the fifteenth century (the early Ming Dynasty), an infamous Cantonese pirate Chen Zuyi fled to Palembang in Sumatra, which had a large Chinese population. The pirate fleet robbed the ships that passed the Straits of Malacca. The Ming Dynasty became concerned about the security in the Malacca Straits. In 1405, the Ming emperor sent Admiral Zheng to suppress the pirates. The pirate chief, Chen Zuyi and his associates feigned surrender but secretly plotted to attack the imperial navy. Zheng found out about this plot and quickly marshalled his troops. When Chen's forces finally attacked, Zheng troops were ready. Consequently, Chen suffered a great defeat. Over 5,000 of his bandits were killed, ten of his bandit ships were burnt and seven were captured. Chen was eventually captured and beheaded in the capital of the Chinese Empire.[17]

The Rivalry among Foreign Sea Powers in East and Southeast Asia, 1511–1839

The rivalry of foreign sea powers in East and Southeast Asia began in 1511 when the Portuguese captured Malacca. The rivalry had two levels: The rivalries among the state actors, and the rivalry between the state actors and non-state actors. On one level, the rivalries were within the European colonial sea powers, and among the European colonial sea powers and the Chinese Empire. On another level, were the rivalry between the European colonizers and Chinese merchant pirates, which will be elaborated later in the third part of this chapter.

Rivalries among the European Colonial Sea Powers

The Portuguese

A major impetus for Portuguese overseas expansion was the lucrative spice trade — which included pepper, cinnamon, and the highly desired trinity of clove, nutmeg, and mace. In the second half of the fifteenth century, Turkish control of the Levant forced the traditional spice routes to move away from the Persian Gulf to the Red Sea. In order to escape this dependence on the Turkish monopoly and participate directly in the highly lucrative spice trade, the Portuguese kept searching for a new sea route to Asia. The Prince Henry the Navigator strongly supported for a campaign of discovery and expansion overseas. It culminated in Vasco da Gama's successful voyage to the west coast of India in 1498, hence breaking the impasse. In 1511, the Portuguese captured Malacca, the lynchpin of seaborne trade, in 1511, and began its plan for the monopoly of the spice trade.

The Spaniards

The earliest Spanish contact with Asia was in March 1521 when Magellan's expedition reached the Philippines. However, in comparison to their Portuguese predecessors, Spain's enterprise in Asia was a modest affair, confined almost exclusively to the Philippines. It was in the shadow of the Spanish Empire in the Americas, being under the direct jurisdiction of the Viceroyalty of *Nueva Espana* (New Spain, present-day Mexico). However, the economic prospects of the Philippines as the prospects of establishing a colony appeared to be bleak. The only marketable spice was cinnamon, which grew in the hostile Muslim dominated island of Mindanao in the Southern Philippines. In addition, the quantity of cinnamon available was not sufficient to sustain a Pacific trade with the Americas, while gold as the main commodity for trade was becoming scarce. Furthermore, the natives were too poor to provide a ready market for manufactured products. In this light, the governor Miguel Lopez de Legazpi realized that there was greater potential for Spain's alternative participation in the thriving seaborne trade between the Philippines and China.[18]

The Spanish colonial government moved from Cebu to Manila in 1571 to promote direct trade ties between the Spanish and the Chinese traders. By 1576 the Chinese traders frequently visited the port of Manila as they had done in pre-Hispanic times, but this time dealing with the Spaniards rather than with their former local trading partners. Legazpi suggested that a trade in Chinese silk could perhaps replace the loss of the trade in spices to the Portuguese. Thus began the galleon trade, where merchants from Macao brought Canton silk, cotton cloths, and other wares to waiting merchants from Acapulco, who offered their silver from the American colonies in exchange.

The best years of the galleon trade were the last decades of the sixteenth century and the first decades of the seventeenth century. In the peak year of 1597, the amount of bullion sent from Acapulco to Manila reached a total of twelve million pesos, a figure exceeding the total value of the official trans-Atlantic trade, although the normal value of the trade was still an impressive three to five million pesos. Despite the later restriction of a single galleon leaving annually from each of the two ports, the galleon trade remained a dominant force in the Spanish Philippine economy until the late eighteenth century and was abandoned only in 1815.[19]

After Spain established its main colony in Manila, other European powers tried to gain a foothold there. In the early seventeenth century, the Dutch raided the islands, capturing not only Spanish ships but also Chinese, Japanese and Portuguese traders visiting the archipelago. The Dutch did not lose interest in the Philippines until the more lucrative spice islands came under their control.

The Dutch

After the Netherlands declared independence from Spain in the late sixteenth century, the Dutch made a dramatic entrance into international trade and politics. Portuguese Far Eastern colonies were the most inviting targets, so the Dutch sent traders to compete with the Portuguese in the spice islands. Unlike the Portuguese and Spanish expeditions, which were paid for by the crown, the Dutch merchants collectively raised enough money for their voyages.

In 1602, the Dutch formed the *Vereenigde Ost-Indische Compagnie* (Chartered East India Company), also known as the VOC. The VOC was a complete success, and within a decade the Portuguese were out of the spice trade. In 1619, the VOC seized the port of Jakarta, renamed it Batavia, and made it the company's headquarters. The Dutch took Taiwan from China in 1624 and captured Malacca from the Portuguese in 1641. The Dutch also besieged Manila, but failed to defeat the Spaniards. When fighting ceased, Spain remained in control of the Philippines while the Portuguese held onto Macao, Goa, and East Timor, while the remaining commerce in the Far East was under VOC control.[20]

However, in 1661, the Dutch lost Taiwan to a Chinese pirate named Zheng Chenggong, known to Europeans as Coxinga. Because of a combination of bad business practices, corruption among company employees, and a profitless war the company was brought down in the late eighteenth century.

The VOC's fate was sealed in 1780 when the Netherlands declared its support for the American Revolution. England sank more Dutch ships than it could replace, and in the treaty ending the war in 1783, the Dutch were forced to give up all monopoly trading claims. Indonesian ports were open to foreign shipping, and the VOC found it could no longer compete with the other traders. The company declared bankruptcy in 1791; seven years later its holdings were taken over by the Dutch Government.[21]

The British

While the Dutch were forcing their way into East and Southeast Asia, the British was starting its own East India Company (EIC). The EIC was organized in 1600, two years before the formation of the VOC. It embodied the spirit of mercantilism in its manipulation of political power and privileges for commercial goals. After several voyages to Southeast Asia from 1604 to 1606, the English realized that the English goods would not be profitable in the Malay-Indonesian archipelago, and what was needed were a greater variety of products from Europe. They also learned through their contact with Portuguese traders that Southeast Asian goods were vital for trade with China.

In 1615, the EIC founded factories at Masulipatnam at Ayutthaya and at Pattani. In eastern Indonesia, the EIC had successfully opened a factory in the kingdom of Makassar and gained control of the islands of Run and Nailaka in the Banda islands. The EIC's presence on these sites obtained access to the cloves, nutmeg, and mace, thereby imperilling the monopoly of these valued spices by the VOC. In 1622, the chief factor of the EIC and others at the English factory in Ambon were killed by the Dutch, ending England's century-long involvement in the spice islands.[22]

In 1786, the English leased Penang island in Malaya from the local sultan and seized the port of Malacca from the Dutch in 1795, which was recognized by the Dutch in the Anglo-Dutch treaty signed in 1824. In 1819, the British commander, Thomas Stamford Raffles, set up Singapore as a colony and gave Britain a dominant role in Far Eastern commerce. Raffles turned Singapore's harbour into a free port which made Singapore a more attractive port than Dutch Batavia.[23]

It was the adventures of another British army officer, James Brooke that gave Britain a foothold in Borneo. In the early nineteenth century the sultan (prince) of Brunei claimed the whole island and the nearby islands for himself. However, when Brooke arrived on his personal yacht in 1839, he found the sultan in trouble by a rebellion in the southwest corner of his realm, Sarawak. Brooke called in the British Navy to suppress the local pirates, who were supported by the Sarawak rebels. The grateful sultan rewarded Brooke by crowning him prince of Sarawak, and gave Britain the small offshore island of Labuan for use as a coaling station. Queen Victoria knighted Brooke, and he became known locally as "the White Rajah". Sarawak was governed by the Brooke family until 1946, when it was bequeathed to the British Government.[24]

'Legitimate' Pirates and 'Indigenous' Pirates

The nineteenth century was the "golden" century of piracy in East and Southeast Asia. After the European colonizers seized the main entrepôts in the Southeast Asia, the local sultans' control on trade networks were cut off and their revenues from the trade were deprived; the indigenous people had to fend for themselves by becoming pirates. Tarling comments, "The old empires decayed, but were not replaced, and with their boundaries marauding communities appeared, led by the adventurous Sharifs, or deprived aristocracies, or hungry chiefs."[25]

Tarling also discusses the different types of indigenous pirates in this period: the Malays of Johore and Riau-Lingga; the Bugis, the Brunei Malays and the Dayak; the Iranuns and the Balangingi. In particular, the Iranun and Balangingi of the Southern Philippines who were sponsored by the local sultans were the most feared of all pirates. Iranun and Balangingi squadrons plundered the shores of the

Philippines, and sailed around Borneo, the Celebes and the Moluccas,
Java, the east coast of the Malay Peninsula, the Gulf of Siam, Riau and
up the Straits of Malacca to the Mergui Archipelago of Burma for the
capture of booty and slaves.

At the beginning of the nineteenth century, the EIC also supported
the Iranun and Balangingi as its privateer[26] against its Dutch counterpart,
the VOC, in the "Malay world".[27] However, the privateers were too
powerful to be controlled. European colonizers eventually realized that
the piracy in the Malay world was their common threat. In 1824, five
years after the British founded Singapore, the former signed a treaty
with the Dutch. The treaty led to the reconfiguration of their respective
domains in the Malay world. The British withdrew from Java and
Sumatra, and undertook to make no settlements or political connections
there. In return, the Dutch recognized the British capture of Malacca. The
Straits of Malacca became the boundary of the Dutch and British colonies.
The Dutch and British also agreed to cooperate to suppress the Malay
pirates in the treaty which stated in part:

> Their Britannic and Netherlands Majesties in like manner engage to concur
> effectually in repressing piracy in those seas: they will not grant either
> asylum or protection to vessels engaged in piracy, and they will in no case
> permit the ships or merchandise captured by such vessels to be introduced,
> deposited, or sold in any of their possessions.[28]

After the signing of the Anglo-Dutch Treaty, there were many attempts
by the British to suppress piracy. Between 1845 and 1848, the British
attacked the principal Iranun base in Marudu in north-eastern Borneo
and other Iranun bases in Tempasuk, Pandasan and Tanku. By around
1843, white Rajah Brooke and Henry Keppel destroyed the following
strongholds: Saribas at Padu, Paku, Rembas as well as Sekrang, Patusan
and Undap. In 1848, the Spanish, with the aid of steamboats, destroyed
the Balangingi's stronghold at Sipac and deported hundreds of
Balanginigi people to the distant mountain valleys of north central Luzon
to become tobacco and corn farmers. The Balangingi pirates were
eradicated in the process.[29]

Another dimension of this anti-piracy campaign was the elimination
of slavery to destroy the markets of the maritime marauders. In 1836, the
British destroyed the slave marts at Galang and Endau. With the founding
of a naval base and commercial port in Labuan in 1846, the maritime
marauders could no longer sell their booty there.[30]

Rivalries among European colonizers and the Chinese Empire

The Portuguese and the Chinese Empire

After the Portuguese seized Malacca in 1511, the King of Portugal sent his ambassador to China in order to establish direct trade links with China. Meanwhile, the king of Malacca appealed to his suzerain, the Chinese Empire for help. Tuan Mohammed, a son of the fugitive king of Malacca, was sent to Peking (now Beijing) to report the Portuguese outrage toward Malacca:

> The Franges (Portuguese) robbers audaciously came to Malacca with many men, took the land and destroyed it, killed many people, plundered them, took others prisoner. The people that remain are under the jurisdiction of the Franges. For this reason, the king of Malacca had a sad heart oppressed with great fear. He took the seal of the King of China and fled to Bentao where he now is. My brothers and relatives fled to other countries. The ambassador of the King of Portugal who is now in the land of China is [a] sham. He does not come in earnest, but to deceive the country of China. In order that the King of China may show grace to the King of Malacca whose heart is oppressed, he sends a present, and begs for succour and men so that his may be restored to him.[31]

The Chinese emperor was unwilling to help the king of Malacca, since the priority of the Ming Dynasty at that time was to expel the Mongol raiders from Northern China and to protect its coastal provinces from Japanese piratical attacks. Nevertheless, orders were issued to the high officials in Canton to hold members of the Portuguese Embassy in custody, to discontinue foreign trade, and to liberate the Portuguese only after the Portuguese authorities in Malacca in India had promised to restore the former place to its legitimate king.

The Portuguese were also reported to have committed other outrages in Canton. The Portuguese were recorded to have pillaged and extorted money from all the ships bound from or to the ports of China. They carried off young girls from the coast, seized upon the Chinese, and made slaves of them:

> The Portuguese committed the most licentious acts of piracy, and the most shameful dissoluteness…They regard trade and piracy as almost identical: a conception which was certainly not shared by most of the Asiatic and European peoples.[32]

The Dutch and the Chinese Empire

In 1601, Dutch sailed to Macao with the attempt to establish direct trade links with the Canton and Ming governments. However, the Portuguese prevented the Dutch from contacting Chinese officials. Thus, the Dutch failed to accomplish their aims. The governor, Jan Pieterszoon Coen, planned to drive the Portuguese out of Macao and defeat the Spanish fleets in Manila, so that the Dutch could monopolize the trade between China and Japan. In 1622, Dutch fleets attacked Macao, but were defeated by the Portuguese.[33]

However, the Dutch were able to seize the Pescadores (Penghu) from China and robbed the coastal cities of Fujian. Dutch Captain Willem Bonteko, recorded the raids in his travel notes, *Memorable Description of the East Indian Voyage 1618–25*:

> [In 18th October 1622] We, namely eight sail, three ships and five sloops, were ordered to go to the river Chinchu and the coast of China to see if through fear of our enmity and force we could move them to traffic with us, we came about ten miles too low. Three of our ships were parted from us; we were then five, and cast anchor in a bay where by our sloops we set afire as much as sixty or seventy junks great and small.[34]

> [1st May 1623] On our way we met with another Chinese junk, richly laden to a value of thousands that was bound for the Manilas [Manila]. We took it, it had in as much as 250 souls. Took in most of the men save about twenty or twenty-five and put with them fifteen or sixteen of our own men; we tied the junk to our ship and towed it...We brought them all the Pescadores; there, with the other Chinese we had brought in other ships and sloops, we tied them together in pairs. We used them to carry earth to the fort, yea, when the fort was built, they were as much as much as 1,400 in number, who were afterwards taken to Batavia and there sold.[35]

However, the full horror of these captives does not appear in Bontekoe's account of them, not many of the 1,400 captives mentioned by him as working on the Pescadores ever reached Batavia, whether to be sold or indentured. One hundred and eighty captives, transferred to the *Haerlem* from the *Groningen*, seem to have arrived at Batavia. More than half of the remaining 1,150 died on Pescadores in 1623. Only 571 were left to be shipped to Batavia, and no more than thirty-three disembarked alive.

The commander of the expedition, Dr. Sonck, wrote to the Governor-General De Carpentier, "Our proceedings on the coast of China have so embittered the whole of China against us that we are looked upon as no better than murderers, tyrants and pirates. Our dealings with the Chinese have indeed been very hard and cruel, and in my opinion such that the desired trade could never be obtained by them."[36]

The British Opium Trade and the Chinese Empire

After several direct frustrated diplomatic contacts with the Chinese Empire, the British also began to face several commercial problems with the latter. Since the 1720s, the rapidly increasing tea consumption of the Europeans, especially the British public, drove tea into a primary export from China through booming demand. In order to restrain European commercial expansion, the Qing government set up the Canton System to administer China's trade with the Europeans. The result of the international tea trade was the amount of silver flowing into China because there was virtually no market for European products in China and the Europeans had therefore to import silver bullion into China in exchange for tea. Once the source of silver was exhausted and the traditional Sino-European trade structure was broken, the British smuggled opium into China with which to purchase tea. Based on opium for tea, they were able to redress the imbalance of Sino-European trade. When this balance was threatened by the firm attitude of the Qing government against opium smuggling, the British did not hesitate to abandon their commercial effort and resort to military force to maintain the *status quo*. Hence, the Opium War in 1840 marks the process of the European expansion to China changing from commercial effort to military conquest.[37]

The European Colonizers and Chinese Merchant Pirates

State Actors versus Non-state Actors

From the sixteenth to the nineteenth centuries (from the Ming Dynasty to Qing Dynasty), private trade with Nanyang was prohibited by law, the main reason being that the Chinese Empire wanted to monopolize trade with Nanyang. It is important to note that the official trade was done under the tributary system. The Chinese emperors considered the European colonial sea powers as the tribute states. If they did not follow the tribute system, their requests to establish regular seaborne trade relations were declined.

However, the European colonial powers gradually established their colonies in Southeast Asia, and controlled the trade routes in Southeast

Asia. Their main aim was to establish direct links with the Chinese Empire as it was clear that the Chinese Empire had no interest in trading with its European counterpart. Since the Chinese courts banned overseas seaborne trade (or limited it to a small scale), the European colonizers had to conduct their business with Chinese illegal private traders, hence rivalling Chinese merchant pirates.

As mentioned earlier, the Chinese Nanhai trade existed for over thousands of years. The lucrative Nanhai trade was the best means of survival for the coastal people for it was an efficient and lucrative way of making a living. During the time of the ban on seaborne trade, the Chinese private traders had to turn to illicit trading activities with Nanyang. Attacked by the Chinese Government and the European colonizers, the Chinese private traders had to arm themselves. Thus in the late Ming and early Qing Dynasty, there emerged a special kind of pirate, the "merchant-pirate" in the Nanhai trading system. These merchant pirates had paradoxical dual identities of being merchant and pirate at the same time. If opportunities presented themselves, they robbed the goods, and subsequently used the goods to trade with Nanyang.

In the Ming Dynasty, there were many merchant pirate groups who had direct trade links with Southeast Asia: Zheng Zhilong and his son Zheng Chenggong (Coxinga), Lin Feng and Lin Daoqian. During the Qing Dynasty, Zhengyi and his pirate confederation were the most notorious pirates. The rest of this chapter focuses on two typical merchant pirate groups, led by Zheng Zhilong and Zhengyi, and summarizes the description of the other groups.

Zheng's Merchant Pirate Group

Zheng Zhilong's merchant pirate group was the most famous and powerful pirate group in the history of Chinese private seaborne trade.[38] Zheng Zhilong's life started in Macao where he worked under the Dutch in Taiwan before heading to Japan. In Japan, Cheng came into contact with several wealthy oversea Chinese merchants, such as Li Dan and Yuan Siqi. Cheng's knowledge of commerce and creative entrepreneurship made him popular among the Chinese merchants. After the death of Yan Siqi in 1625, Cheng took over all of Yan's commercial fleets, which traded between Cochin China and Japan. Cheng sold some of the vessels and turned to the trappings of piracy. In the chaos that constituted the interim period of 1640–46, of the Ming Dynasty and Qing Dynasty,

Zheng Zhilong controlled maritime trade with Indian, the Portuguese, the Spanish and the Dutch.

Zheng's main profits came from the trade with Nanyang. In 1628, for example, Zheng signed a silk purchase contract with Dutch VOC. According to the contract, Zheng supplied silk worth 3,000 *dan*, sugar valued at 6,000 *dan* and 5,000 pieces other the silk products to the Dutch who paid out 3,000 *dan* worth of pepper as well as cash.[39]

In 1646, Zheng Zhilong was lured to Beijing by the Manchus who later killed him. Subsequently, his son, Zheng Chenggong, took over the powerful fleet. The young Zheng then evicted the Dutch from Taiwan in 1661, and occupied other coastal provinces of China. However, the Dutch continued its trade with Zheng, for they depended on Zheng for Chinese merchandise.

Over time, young Zheng's group acted as the "semi-government" in the coastal provinces. They imposed taxes on the private seaborne traders by issuing the Guoxin Pass. The cost of procuring the Guoxin Pass was subject to the tonnage of the ships, usually between 2,000 to 3,000 *ling* worth of silver.[40] If the private traders refused to pay, their ships would be robbed and destroyed. The young Zheng also supported the declining Ming Dynasty, and fought against the southward Manchus. After the last member of the Ming family passed away, and the Manchu's Qing Dynasty gained control of the mainland, young Zheng retreated to Taiwan, and established his own kingdom. However, in 1683, the grandson of Zheng Chenggong surrendered Taiwan to the Manchus.[41]

Lin Feng (Limahong)

Lin Feng (alias Limahong as he was know to the Spanish) was a pirate chief from Canton. He participated in the illicit trade with Nanyang at the age of nineteen. In 1574, Lin Feng attacked Huilai in Guangdong province. The Imperial Coast Guard defeated the Lin Feng fleet. As a result, Lin Feng was no longer able to find a safe refuge along the Chinese coast. He then attempted to move his base to Luzon and set himself up as sovereign of the Philippine archipelago. Lin Feng armed 72 junks, loaded with 2,000 soldiers and experts in various fields, and 1,500 women in the attempt to set up a colony in Manila. In November 1574, Lin Feng's fleet attacked Luzon. Subsequently, they attacked Manila, but they encountered strong resistance from the Spaniards and the residing natives. Lin's Japanese Admiral Sioco was killed and the pirates retreated to the Cavite. Lin abandoned his plans to use Manila as his capital and proceeded back up the coast to Lingayen, Pangasinan. At the end of March 1575, the Spaniards besieged Lin Feng's pirate fleet. After several months of fighting, Lin Feng made a daring escape using small craft under the cover of darkness in August 1575. The Chinese Navy at Fujian tried to pursue him but failed. The Chinese viceroy at Fujian was annoyed at the Spaniards for the narrow escape of Lin Feng. As a result, the Spaniards failed to receive the permission to establish a trading post in Amoy (Xiamen) as they had been initially promised in exchange for the capture of Lin Feng.[42]

Lin Daoqian

Like Lin Feng, Lin Daoqian was also a pirate chief from Guangdong. In 1566, Lin's fleet attacked and robbed Zhaoan, Fujian, before burning down hundreds of houses and killing thousands of people. The imperial governor Yu Dayou and his army fought back, forcing Lin and his pirates to flee to Beigang, Taiwan, where they buried their treasure in the nearby Mount Dagu. In 1567, Lin unpacked his treasure in order to recruit more followers for his trading exploits with Cambodia, and Siam (Thailand) and Annam (Vietnam), robbing ships from time to time when the opportunity arose. The Chinese Government never succeeded in catching Lin who later died at Patani, Thailand.[43]

Zheng Yi

Zheng Yi was a leader of a pirate confederation consisting of four pirate groups numbering a total of between 50,000 to 70,000 pirates residing along the coast of Guangdong province by 1805. The pirate confederation controlled trade and fishing along the coast of Vietnam and Guangdong province. The Chinese junks had to pay the pirates protection money when they left the port. From the coast, the pirates moved into the waterways of the interior, where they extorted considerable sums in the form of semi-annual payments from the villages and towns, burning with impunity those that refused to pay. The confederation also captured European seafarers for ransom, with the Portuguese on the brigs from India and Philippines being the most vulnerable. Englishmen, Dutchmen and Armenian were also taken from time to time. For example, J.L. Turner, chief mate of ship *Tay*, together with six sailors were captured in December 1806. A series of negotiations followed, after five-month long discussions. The pirates were able to negotiate a ransom valued at 7,150 Spanish dollars.[44] Nevertheless, on 20 April 1810, the Qing government brought the pirates to terms through a policy of pardon and pacification.

Concluding Remarks

The perception and policies toward piracy and seaborne trade of the foreign sea powers in Southeast Asia affected the outcome of their rivalries in the region. The European colonial sea powers resorted to piratical activities to set up their colonial domains, and labelled the indigenous people who fought for their own homelands as pirates in order to justify their military activities. In a series of linkages, the colonizers accrued wealth gained in part through their piratical activities, which in turn supported their naval enterprises which were encouraged to step up the training of its seamen and the development of its arms amidst the context of burgeoning seaborne trade.

In his famous monograph, *The Influence of Sea Power upon History, 1660–1783*, A.T. Mahan, listed six principal conditions affecting the sea power of nations: Geographical position; physical conformation, including as connected therewith, natural productions and climate; extent of territory; number of population; the character of the people; the character of the governments.[45] Compared with the European sea powers, in terms of geographical position, physical conformation, extent of territory and number of population, the Chinese Empire had advantages over the Western colonizers. Referring to the social "character" of the people, the Chinese were just as economically motivated as the Western colonizers were. However, the point of departure between the two civilizations was the "character" of their governments which perceived piracy and approached seaborne trade in different ways.

The "agrarian dominance" policy was well entrenched during the Chinese Empires. The importance of sea power was ignored, thus the policy of Ming courts toward seaborne trade was negative. The Chinese Empire attempted to monopolize the seaborne trade with Nanyang *via* the tributary system while private seaborne trade was banned or restricted. In fact, the Chinese Empire was destroying itself economically in the rivalries in Nanyang by its prohibition of seaborne trade policy.

Due to the prohibition on seaborne trade, many private traders had to partake in illicit trading. Accordingly, they were faced with a two-fronted attack: One from the Chinese Government and the other from the colonizers. Thus, they had to arm themselves and inadvertently became merchant pirates. In the eyes of the Chinese mandarins, trade and piracy were closely intertwined. Whenever security was at risk, their first recourse was to advocate the prohibition of trade as an expedient means of restoring the *status quo*. Ironically, the prohibition of seaborne trade fuelled the rise in piracy. The Chinese Government took pains to suppress these merchant pirates, thus reducing the incentive of such trading activities. However, this was done at the cost of losing its opportunity of enhancing its sea power relative to its European counterparts, causing China's influence upon Southeast Asia to eventually fade.

Turning to present times, since the last decade, piracy incidents in the region have dramatically increased and received increasing amount of media and political attention. After the event of the 9/11 terrorist attacks, piracy in Southeast Asian waters have become a greater concern through the possibility of the conflation between this activity and "maritime terrorism" reflected in various analyses in the mass media and academic journals. When we cast a glance at contemporary piracy in East and Southeast Asia, we will find out that the fundamental problem of piracy finds its roots in the colonial era. For example, in the 1824 Anglo-Dutch Treaty, the Straits of Malacca became a boundary of the British and Dutch colonies. Today, the Straits of Malacca belongs to Indonesia, Malaysia and Singapore. Thus the sovereign concern always is one of the main problems hindering the efficiency of anti-piracy measures.

However, compared to the piracy in the colonial era, most of contemporary piratical attacks in the region are mundane crimes committed at sea, just as in the advent of European colonization. To a large degree, whether there is a nexus between piracy and terrorism or not may not be as important if we account for the fact that terror was widely used by pirates to frighten their prey throughout history. The intriguing part is that beyond the debate on the supposed "nexus" between piracy and terrorism, a "New-Age" set of rivalries between foreign and regional sea powers in modern Southeast Asia have begun amidst the attempt to secure the Malacca Straits. The question is, will history repeat itself? Further study is in order in our quest to draw lessons from history as we attempt to congeal the factors that can help us understand the dynamics of a phenomenon in modern times.

Notes

1   In this chapter, the definition of piracy is close to the Chinese term *Haikou*, literally meaning "sea-thieves" or "bandits at sea", and it implies persons arriving by the sea from elsewhere to prey upon a place or ship.
2   From April to August, the monsoon winds blows northwards towards the Asian land mass; from December to March it blows southward from the Asian continent into the Indian Ocean and South China Sea. The traders made their

long journeys at times of good following winds and returned on the opposite monsoon. Chinese ships sailing south to Southeast Asia, or Nanyang, followed the northern monsoon in January or February and returned home in June, July or August with the southern monsoon. South Indian ships sailed eastward between April and August under the southwest monsoon of the Indian Ocean. They stayed to trade and returned in December with the monsoon blowing southward.

3   Anthony Reid, *Southeast Asia in the Age of Commerce, 1450–1680* (New Haven: Yale University Press, 1988), pp. 64–65.

4   Wang Gungwu, *The Nanhai Trade: Early Chinese Trade in the South China Sea* (Singapore: Eastern Universities Press, 2003).

5   Jing Yi, *Nanhai Ji Gui Nei Fa Zhuan Jiazhu* (Beijing: Zhonghua Shuju, 1995).

6   Zhao Rushi, *Zhu Pan Zhi* [Description of the Barbarians] (Beijing: Zhong Hua Shu Ju, 2000).

7   Wang Dayuan, *Dao Yi Zhi Lue Jiao Shi, Zhong Wei Jiao Tong Shi Ji Cong Shu* (Beijing: Zhong Hua Shu Ju, 1981).

8   Wang Gungwu, ed., *Community and Nation, Essays on Southeast Asia and the Chinese*. Southeast Asia Publications Series no. 6 (Singapore: Published for the Asian Studies Association of Australia by Heinemann Educational Books Asia, 1981), p. 14.

9   Chang Pin-Tsun, "The Global Opportunity", in Felipe Fernandez-Armesto, ed., *An Expanding World: The European Impact on World History 1450–1800*, Vol. 1 (Aldershot; Brookfield, 1995), p. 114.

10 Ban Gu, "Dilizhi", in *Han Shu* (Beijing: Zhonghua Shuju, 1983).

11 Faxian Shi, *Fa Xian Zhuan Jiao Zhu* (Shanghai: Shanghai Guji Chuban She, 1985), p. 167.

12 Nicholas Tarling, *The Cambridge History of Southeast Asia*, Vol. 1 (Cambridge: Cambridge University Press, 1992), p. 202.

13 A Chinese weight unit for gold.

14 Zhao, *Zhu Pan Zhi* [Description of the Barbarians], p. 61.

15 The Dragon Teeth Strait was the present-day Keppel Harbour passage between the South coast of Singapore island. The dragon teeth were the twin rocks overlooking the European entrance to Keppel Harbour. One of rocks, known as *Batu Belayar* was demolished in 1848 during the widening of the Strait.

16 Wang, *Dao Yi Zhi Lue Jiao Shi*, pp. 213–14.

17 *Ming Shi Lu*, Vol. 11 (Taiwan: Zhongyang Lishi Yanjusuo, 1966), p. 987.

18 Tarling, *The Cambridge History of Southeast Asia*.

19 Ibid., p. 357.

20 Nicholas Tarling, *The Cambridge History of Southeast Asia*, Vol. 2 (Cambridge: Cambridge University Press, 1992), pp. 144–60.

21 Ibid.

22 Ibid., p. 358.

[23] Nicholas Tarling, *Piracy and Politics in the Malay World: A Study of British Imperialism in Nineteenth-Century South-East Asia* (Singapore: D. Moore, 1963), p. 13.

[24] Steven Runciman, *The White Rajahs: A History of Sarawak from 1841 to 1946* (Cambridge: Cambridge University Press, 1960).

[25] Tarling, *Piracy and Politics in the Malay World*, p. 8.

[26] "Privateers" referred to men who were issued letters of commission to captain private vessels giving them the "right" to plunder enemy ships in wartime. Privateers were used to expand a government's resources at the expense of its enemies.

[27] "Malay world" refers to the present-day Malaysia, Indonesia and the Philippines.

[28] Henry Keppel and James Brooke, *The Expedition to Borneo of H.M.S. Dido for the Suppression of Piracy; with Extracts from the Journal of James Brooke*, 3rd ed. (London: Cass, 1968), p. 272.

[29] Owen Rutter, *The Pirate Wind: Tales of the Sea-Robbers of Malaya* (New York: Oxford University Press, 1986), pp. 99–126.

[30] Tarling, *Piracy and Politics in the Malay World: A Study of British Imperialism in Nineteenth-Century South-East Asia* (Singapore: D. Moore, 1963).

[31] Tien Tse Chang, *Sino-Portuguese Trade from 1514 to 1644: A Synthesis of Portuguese and Chinese Sources* (Leiden: E.J. Brill, 1969), p. 52.

[32] Ibid., p. 66.

[33] Kristof Glamann, *Dutch Asiatic Trade, 1620–1740* (Copenhagen: Danish Science Press, 1958), pp. 230–31.

[34] Willem Ysbrantsz Bontekoe, *Memorable Description of the East Indian Voyage, 1618–25* (London: G. Routledge, 1929), p. 92.

[35] Ibid., pp. 112–13.

[36] Ibid., p. 15.

[37] Zhuang Guotu, *Tea, Silver, Opium and War: The International Tea Trade and Western Commerical Expansion into China in 1740–1840* (Xiamen: Xiamen University Press, 1993), pp. 1–2.

[38] Zheng Guangnan, *Zhong Guo Hai Dao Shi* [A History of Chinese Piracy] (Shanghai: Huadong Ligong Daxue Chubanshe, 1998), p. 260.

[39] Van J.C. Leur ed., *Indonesian Trade and Society, 1967* (Hague: 1955), p. 399.

[40] Nie Dening, *Mingmo Qingchu Haikou Shangren* (Taibei: Yang Jing Quan, 1990), p. 175.

[41] Zheng, *Zhong Guo Hai Dao Shi* (A History of Chinese Piracy), p. 268.

[42] Emma Helen Blair, James Alexander Robertson, and Edward Gaylord Bourne, *The Philippine Islands, 1493–1898* (Mandaluyong, Rizal: Cachos Hermanos, 1973), Vol. 4, pp. 21–48.

[43] Zheng, *Zhong Guo Hai Dao Shi* [A History of Chinese Piracy], pp. 226–27.

[44] Dian H. Murray, *Pirates of the South China Coast, 1790–1810* (Stanford: Stanford University Press, 1987), p. 85.

[45] A.T. Mahan, *The Influence of Sea Power upon History, 1660–1783* (New York: Dover Publications, 1987), p. 29.

CONCLUSION
Building Upon the Research Agenda

Graham Gerard Ong-Webb

The insights generated in this volume can be clustered around the issues of regional piracy, the threat of maritime terrorism and the security of the Malacca Straits. First, it is clear that piracy is a multi-faceted phenomenon that has evolved in form and interpretation throughout history, as chiefly exemplified by Xu Ke's analysis of Chinese and regional piracy in the sixteenth to the nineteenth centuries. Today, piracy is now perceived in its modern manifestation as a menace to state and societal security, and the ensuing threat perception is informed by the following three factors:

1. The direct and indirect threat of piracy upon the efficient flow of shipping through the Straits and the impact upon regional economy and the world at large;
2. The exacerbation of this threat through rising levels of violence of attacks when they occur; and
3. Southeast Asia's continuing hold on its quarterly share of the world's reported attacks annually, despite their overall decline in numbers in any one year.

When framed as a security problem, the general consensus by the authors of this volume is that the pirates continue have all the advantages despite headway in cooperation and the technical advances in current counter-measures.

Besides the short-term goal of tackling the symptoms of piracy — such as eradicating their bases of operations for example — medium to longer-term solutions geared towards nullifying the root causes of piracy would have to be found within socio-economic endeavours that go beyond the purview of hard security. As Mark Valencia and Tamara Renee Shie have argued, these include empowering marginalized societies, groups and individuals with better education, and access to employment and the dividends of economic growth. The quest to accomplish the medium to long-term goals would also involve coming to grips with the socio-cultural and historical underpinnings of piracy and other criminally related activities that have existed in the region. This is crucial in piercing the veil of piracy (and even terrorism for that matter) as Eric Frécon's chapter sought to do. This is a crucial project underpinning any development policy since any related problem-solving will require framing pirates as social actors responding to circumstances that are amendable (the premise being that modifying environmental factors will lead to the modification of the perceptions and behaviour of actors), rather than utilizing the analytical methodology within mainstream security studies that necessarily refers to pirates in terms of a criminal and violent archetype indisposed to redemption, which can only either be suppressed through law enforcement or negated through military force.

Second, the verdict upon the threat of maritime terrorism is still not entirely clear. Abhyankar and Valencia argue that a "nexus" between piracy and maritime terrorism (and with terrorism in general) remains generally unfounded. In the Philippine case, as Eduardo Ma R. Santos and Stefan Eklöf Amirell separately show, the link is either tenuous or one that could fester into a significant relationship. However, they may still be some conceptual dividends for maintaining a link between piracy and maritime terrorism — no matter how hypothetical — not least because terrorism has helped to ratchet an unprecedented interest in tackling piracy at the levels of intelligence gathering and security policy-making. Brian Fort argues that while all international crime does not always lead to piracy and (maritime) terrorism, following the trails of international crime can provide related leads to these activities because of the common financial motive cutting across most criminal operations.

Third, though the challenge of securing the Malacca Straits is generating certain positive results, many current endeavours remain either limited or flawed. Valencia questions the efficacy of naval patrols on legal and operational grounds. Carolin Liss also offers a note of caution on the current effectiveness of Private Military Companies (PMCs) and Private Security Companies (PSCs) against piracy and maritime terrorism, although she does herald their significant role once a better system of conduct and practices is established. J. N. Mak argues that attempts towards fostering cooperation between the littoral states of Malaysia, Indonesia and Singapore especially in the "third battle" over the approaches to safeguarding the Malacca Straits against pirates and terrorists will continue to be fraught by a clash of interests between the coastal states of Malaysia and Indonesia possessing relatively insular interests, and maritime nations such as Singapore tending to have global interests. Unfortunately, this will help to defend the paltry record of maritime cooperation in the ASEAN region which has been marked by significant levels of contention, dissension and contestation on such matters.

Shie, on the other hand, stresses the need to acknowledge the efforts by ASEAN in the new millennium instead of writing it off as critics have in the past. Denunciation only serves to: (1) overlook the value of studying the factors steering regional responses towards piracy within an evolving international system, especially since 1967 when the organization was formed; (2) relieve the organization's members from their collective responsibilities towards action in this regard; and (3) diminish their current support towards addressing the problem. If the internal and external pressures motivating collective action can actually compel regional state actors into overcoming the barriers of sovereignty and conflicting interests that stem from them, normative suggestions such as Ahmad Ghazali bin Abu Hassan's idea of a management regime in the Malacca Straits approximating the Central Commission for the Navigation of the Rhine (CCNR) and the International Commission for the Protection of the Rhine against Pollution (ICPR) could very well become a possible end-state within the future regional political landscape.

However, as Jose L. Tongzon warns, the prescriptive and normative discussions about securing the Straits will also become moot if the waterway loses it strategic and economic value. In truth, while the geography of the Straits is fixed, dynamic factors such as technology, the economic competitiveness of the littoral states and their national ports, and the employment of creative economic strategies to bypass geographical constraints, can serve to strengthen or wither its importance. On the one hand, certain developments that seems to work in favour of the Straits. The growing demand for oil by China, the intensification of trade links between Europe and Asia, and growing Asian economic integration would result in the use of the Malacca Straits for supporting these related economic developments. On the other hand, the rise new ports and pipelines in the Asia-Pacific region could lead to the diminishing importance of the Straits and the littoral ports of Singapore and Malaysia by extension. In the final analysis, the prevailing value of the Straits would have to be defended by securing its waters in the short term, and by the implementation of prudent government economic strategies for the long term. This means that the debate about piracy and other transnational maritime threats such as maritime terrorism and the imperative of securing the Malacca Straits is not a foreclosed one despite the apparent flurry of positive developments in the declining numbers of attacks, the absence of a maritime terrorist attack, and the implementation of unprecedented regional patrolling arrangements until the time of press. Ultimately, the actors (pirates and terrorists against shippers, states and regions), the stage (the international and regional environment as well as the Straits itself) and the script (history, national interests and policy goals) are variables subject to change and the future is left contingent.

Building Upon the Research Agenda:
A Reflexive Assessment of the Second Volume

The remaining section is a reflexive assessment of this volume drawn from the feedback of the various paper presenters — most of whom are the contributors to this volume — at an authors' roundtable at the IIAS and ISEAS joint workshop in Singapore on "Maritime Security, Maritime Terrorism and Piracy in Asia: Issues and Perspectives" in September 2004.[1] The various points serve to shore up the inherent limitations of this volume and the criticisms that will help clarify the form and substance of a burgeoning research agenda crystallized through the first and second volumes in the IIAS-ISEAS Series on Maritime Issues and Piracy in Asia.

To recapitulate, the suggested research agenda comprises two functions. The first function is to provide an overview of the current knowledge and key themes in piracy studies *vis-à-vis* Southeast Asia, in order to provide a reference resource for those working on the topic. These themes cluster around two broad categories which were (1) the characteristics of piracy in Southeast Asia — in terms of definitions (including whether or not maritime terrorism fits into the description); the magnitude and nature of the incidences; and the forms of piracy; and (2) the measures to suppress this activity (when framed as a security threat) in the region. The second function of is actually multi-faceted one consisting of three epistemological components: (1) as a platform to bridge existing efforts within piracy studies; (2) as a means of establishing both the agenda and the "building blocks" or key research questions for research that will underpin the second volume and the rest of the series; and (3) as a preliminary indication of new and important avenues for research.

The first function was taken to task mainly through the demand for a multi-thematic approach that extends from the inherent complexity of piracy and the equally multi-layered temperament that obtains from counter-piracy measures generated as a function of law enforcement operations, state and regional security, national and regional policy-making, and political bargaining. At the operational level, a post-9/11 maritime environment has led to the collapse of the classical distinction between maritime safety and maritime security, such that it has become impossible to make separate commercial and social claims from security, military and policing ones. However, the post-9/11 environment has also led to the issues to being coloured heavily in security terms to the point where seemingly mundane matters such as the plight of underdeveloped maritime communities and their cultures — and the sociological and anthropological endeavours needed to inform policy and the media — have become largely silenced.

At the same time, the weight of certain themes related to piracy explored as independent units must also be further amplified in their undertaking. Specifically, the debates in international law on the questions of piracy and armed robbery at sea should be better emphasized. It could also be made to include the role of legal institutions beyond UNCLOS II, including the response of the International Criminal Court. Next, the fundamental question of state and territorial sovereignty needs to be more deeply addressed as researchers and policy-makers will not be able to move forward on the issues of regional and international cooperation until political actors understand their inherent limitations, as well as to identify the conceptual pockets that allow the injection of nominal compromises and even the creation of new models for collective action.

New themes may also need to be added. First, the role of technology as a driver for both modern piracy and counter-piracy may need to be further explored; possibly to a technical extent. With better access to information, modern pirates have a stronger handle on technology and the acumen to detect the technological developments in counter-piracy during and after their encounters with naval and law enforcement patrols. This situation can and may already lead to an action-reaction cycle where pirates and their adversaries seek to technologically outmanoeuvre each others capabilities and skill competencies. On the state side of the equation, the theme on technology would look at developments in defence science, especially radar tracking and surveillance technology, and to understand the perceptions of scientists that inform their understanding of piracy and which features translate into the kind of tangible signals that allow their detection and interception.

Second, while the discussions of piracy and security have overlapped extensively, the issue of naval security has only been obliquely addressed. There may be a need to push the role of navies and the consequence of their operations against piracy into the foreground. Among other things, it can help answer the question as to whether maritime forces are a viable option in making waters safe from piracy and maritime terrorism. Two burgeoning hypotheses follow from this question The first posits that the "maritime presence" — a term used by navies as the presence of naval vessels operating in a specific area — of a state's navy or conglomerate of separate naval forces can be a sign that safe passage is guaranteed and even deter piracy in effect. The second proposes that maritime presence can actually act as a "lightning rod" for maritime terrorism since terrorists have been shown to prize explicit military targets given their significant symbolic value.

In terms of the epistemology of the research programme, future discussions could be better structured in several ways. As several presenters had noted, the key challenge of any research programme on piracy remains to be how the intersecting set of disciplines of anthropology, criminology, development studies, economics, international relations, law, sociology and security studies could be brought to bear on maritime issues such as piracy in a manner that is coherent and systematic. The answer to this grand challenge remains a difficult and elusive one that cuts through a host of other fields of enquiry that demand multi-disciplinary rigour, but it deserves to be overcome along the way.

Second, there is a strong consensus that the research into the nature of piracy in its relation to state control and law, could be better served by using a criminological lens as a focal point. This would include paying stronger attention piracy that is linked to organized crime at the national and transnational levels. It would also include taking into serious account of the conjecture that piracy belongs to a myriad of unlawful activities at sea — such as (1) illegal fishing, (2) the smuggling/trafficking of narcotics, arms, people and contraband, (3) maritime fraud, and (4) terrorism — that criminals undertake in the maritime realm today. At a definitional level, such an approach may include expanding the scope of activities in the maritime realm where violence is a common feature; hence the use of the term "maritime violence" by some scholars and analysts in order to keep the conceptual doors for discussion open as opposed to the narrower scope that is carved out through legal and policy-based approaches. There is also a strong connection between criminality and threats to security here, and there appears to be a need to embroider the "tapestry of threats" that exist in the maritime realm and to establish the linkages and overlaps between them.

Third, if the research agenda is to take the framing of piracy as a security problem seriously, then it should also be conducted through the lens of human security. This would mean shifting away from state-centric analyses towards the welfare of individuals, groups and societies as the main referents of inquiry. Questions should also be asked as to whether state-sponsored counter-piracy policies and initiatives have the effect of fuelling piracy rather than suppressing it, such that state-driven endeavours compromise the security of their people rather than strengthen it. A robust approach towards human security analyses would entail the adoption of a value neutral position that allows questions to be raised about the role of the state in marginalizing communities and people that may consequently turn to crime including piracy for their socio-economic survival. In other words, a human security approach could help make room for policy-makers to investigate the root causes of piracy (including why individuals choose to become pirates) and to create the appropriate social and governmental measures to address them. Lastly, it also serves to allow researchers to re-occupy the position of asking critical questions about piracy including those that run against the immediate priorities and interests of regional governments such as poverty and under-development.

Fourth, the policy-driven demands of a piracy research programme may be better met if the epistemology incorporates the utility of scenario planning — both rudimentary and complex — on how the threats can play out and how states may choose to respond against both the threats and against other states with conflicting policy initiatives for problem-solving. For example, possible threat scenarios can better inform political and strategic analyses about the kinds of conditions required for states such as the littorals of Indonesia, Malaysia and Singapore to make compromises on their individual national interests towards fostering closer cooperation and greater action. In its simplest form, scenario planning would mean asking basic questions geared towards understanding how the interests of state actors drive their behaviour, which is often overlooked amidst the apparent complexity of the threat of piracy and the politics that come with it. Thus for example, with regard to the role of "user states" employing the Malacca Straits as one of their vital SLOCs, fundamental questions must be asked about what players such as China, India, Japan and the United States stand to gain from participating in the politics and security surrounding the waterway, and what these states are willing to accept or reject from the barter. At the complex end of scenario planning, such kinds of analyses would be useful in reminding policy-makers that the costs incurred by a piracy or maritime terrorist attack are not quantitatively clear especially when human, environmental, and physical costs are taken into account.

Therefore, any immediate and concrete claims by littoral and user states of the Malacca Straits as to how the impact of piracy and maritime terrorism stands to affect them must also be further investigated, against the natural tendency to lend haughty weight to arguments from authority. This would be detrimental to a robust research agenda on piracy whose building blocks elicit little compromise on the value of critical enquiry.

Note

[1]   A copy of the minutes for this roundtable can be obtained from the editor of this volume by contacting him at <grahamgerard.ongwebb@gmail.com>, with the subject of the e-mail entitled as "ISEAS-IIAS 2004 Workshop: Request for Minutes for the Paper Presenters' Roundtable".

Index

www.ingramcontent.com/pod-product-compliance
Lightning Source LLC
Chambersburg PA
CBHW020811100426
42814CB00001B/18